Calling the Circle

Also by Christina Baldwin

Life's Companion:
Journal Writing as a Spiritual Quest

One to One:
Self-Understanding Through
Journal Writing

CHRISTINA BALDWIN

Calling the Circle

The First and Future Culture

ILLUSTRATIONS BY COLLEEN KELLEY

BANTAM BOOKS
NEW YORK   TORONTO   LONDON
SYDNEY   AUCKLAND

CALLING THE CIRCLE

A Bantam Book / published by arrangement with the author

Publishing History
Swan Raven and Company edition published 1994
Bantam trade paperback edition / March 1998

See page 240 for permissions.

BOOK DESIGN BY KATHRYN PARISE.

LIBRARY OF CONGRESS CATALOGING-IN-PUBLICATION DATA
Baldwin, Christina.
Calling the circle : the first and future culture / Christina Baldwin.
p.   cm.
Includes bibliographical references (p. 229).
ISBN 0-553-37900-3
1. Ritual—Psychology.   2. Circle—Religious aspects.   3. Communication in small
groups.   4. Decision-making, Group—Religious aspects.   I. Title.
BF1623.R6B35   1998
302.3′4—dc21   97-26911
CIP

Published simultaneously in the United States and Canada

Bantam Books are published by Bantam Books, a division of Random House, Inc. Its
trademark, consisting of the words "Bantam Books" and the portrayal of a rooster, is
Registered in U.S. Patent and Trademark Office and in other countries. Marca Registrada.
Bantam Books, 1540 Broadway, New York, New York 10036.

PRINTED IN THE UNITED STATES OF AMERICA
BVG   10 9 8

CONTENTS

YOU HAVE SEEN HOW IT IS
    that we are a Strong People—
        one who has walked out
            from a thundering Earth
            and an Ocean that became sky.

YOU HAVE SEEN HOW IT IS
    that we are a Wise People—
        one who learns survival quickly
            against a changing circumstance.

YOU HAVE SEEN HOW IT IS
    that we are an Enduring People—
        one who continues in the Chosen Purpose
        against great difficulties.

YET YOU HAVE SEEN HOW IT IS

    —and she traced in the air
    the closing of the circle of her thought—

    that we are a Young People—
        like small ones
            whose teachers go away
                before they have learned enough
            who quarrel over the resolution of this and that.

SO
    LET US NOW LEARN HOW TO BE A PEOPLE
        WHO SEEK THE WISDOM OF ORDERED COUNCIL.

    LET US REMEMBER
        HOW QUICKLY ONE WHO LEADS
        MAY BE TAKEN FROM US.

    LET US UNDERSTAND
        THAT WHAT MAY BE IMPOSSIBLE FOR ONE
        MAY BE POSSIBLE FOR MANY.

    AND IF ALL THIS ESCAPES YOUR MEMORY
        REMEMBER ONLY THIS:
            SEEK THE WISDOM OF ORDERED COUNCIL—

    HOWEVER MANY
        HOWEVER FEW
            HOWEVER OLD
                HOWEVER YOUNG

    SEEK THE WISDOM OF ORDERED COUNCIL.

PAULA UNDERWOOD,
The Walking People

PREFACE TO THE NEW EDITION

Between 1992 and 1994 I wrote a book titled *Calling the Circle: The First and Future Culture.* It was published by a small press, Swan Raven and Co., an imprint of Blue Water Publishing, both then located in Hillsboro, Oregon, just outside Portland. The people who owned this press, David Kyle, Patt Lind-Kyle, Pamela Meyer, and Brian Crissey, were fellow seekers intrigued by the model of the circle I was presenting.

The first version of the book was an intense, visionary statement of belief that gathering in peer-led, spirit-centered circles could help us successfully face the challenges of our times.

I was writing during a time of tremendous personal upheaval. I didn't understand why this idea had chosen me to be its voice. I just kept writing. When the book came out, the small press struggled valiantly to keep it in distribution—as all small presses struggle. The book developed a following in independent bookstores. Letters of response began trickling into my office; people were excited and resonating with this vision.

They said things like, "I've been in a circle for five years. Now I understand why it worked for us, and why it didn't." "This is the first book on group process that made me want to slow down and pay attention to group process." "First the circle saved my business, and now it's saving my marriage." They said, "Thank you."

In the next year and a half, over fifteen thousand people found their way to *Calling the Circle*. By the late 1990s other books began coming out. Articles on the influence of circle, council, and tribal learning systems were appearing in periodicals from *The New Age Journal* to *The Wall Street Journal*. Several leading organizational development models began incorporating learning circles and study circles. It wasn't such a strange idea anymore. David, Pam, and I agreed the book needed a big publisher to give it full exposure, and my agent contacted Toni Burbank, at Bantam, who has supported my work for years. We negotiated for rerelease of the book, with whatever revisions I wanted to make.

Between editions, I spent three years teaching, consulting, living with the circle, and deeply learning from it. This new version of the book has been almost entirely rewritten—whole chapters have been deleted and new ones inserted. What you have here is a new book, still titled *Calling the Circle: The First and Future Culture*.

It is now an intense, visionary statement *from experience* that gathering in peer-led, spirit-centered circles does help us successfully face the challenges of our times.

It's been quite a journey to claim this work and begin to share it with the world. I know this journey is just beginning. May it begin, or continue, for you also—somewhere in the great circle of life.

Christina Baldwin
Summer 1997

WHAT IS A CIRCLE?

The teenage son of a friend asks, "Mom, why do you always light a candle when you want to talk seriously with me?"

The mother says, "The candle sets the tone. I want you to notice that this is going to be an important conversation and to pay attention to me in a different way from when we're just passing each other in the house."

"Okay, cool," he says, and they are in circle.

A minister is meeting with two parishioners who have been involved in a long-standing argument. She joins them in the library, where three comfortable chairs have been pulled around a coffee table. There is a Bible opened to one of her favorite passages for conflict resolution. There is a candle. She lights it, looks in the faces of the two men. "Are you ready to begin?" she asks. She waits for them to nod. She reads the scripture. She puts a palm-sized rock on the table. "There will be no casting of stones in this conversation, but whoever

wishes to may hold the stone while he speaks, and we will listen."
They are in circle.

A man is called into personnel, given notice of immediate termination, and told to clean out his desk. Humiliated and in shock, he carries an empty box back to his cubicle. His coworkers help him pack up his personal belongings. Spontaneously, they begin to recite everything they appreciate about him. "Stop, stop, please," the man says. "I don't want to lose it in front of you guys. . . ."

"We want you to know we'll miss you," another man says. They decide to meet for supper so they can talk about approaching management as a unified group, to see if management will let them influence how these layoffs are handled, to see if they can become part of the decision-making process, not its victims. They are in circle.

A woman visits her elderly parents to tell them she is getting divorced. This will be hard news for them. She spends two days bringing little things to their kitchen table: a feather, a piece of bark, photos of her husband and children taken the previous Christmas. Her mother adds a small vase of flowers. There is no language between them to acknowledge what they're doing, but the actions of the mother and daughter are natural rituals of centering. When the woman feels centered, she invites her parents to sit down with her and begins the conversation. They are in circle.

A community takes up the challenge of dealing with vandalism in a rural area where adolescents are being accused of defacing bridges with graffiti, knocking over mailboxes, stealing street signs, and other destructive mischief. A group of retired businessmen volunteers to meet with the teenagers. They begin a tentative process of getting to know each other, talking on the roadside and at hangout spots, the older men careful not to accuse. Then they take a group of boys fishing for a day, ending with a beach picnic and campfire. One of the men simply suggests, "What if we pass this beach stone around and anyone who wants to can share a story—something you wish you could tell your own grandfather, or something you wish you could tell your own grandson. Let's see what happens. . . . And if you don't feel like talking when it's your turn, just pass the stone on." In the gathering dusk, they enter the circle.

The director of a nursing home that has operated for years on Catholic spiritual values suspects that certain conflicts within the staff are personifications of the tensions in the health care industry itself. She wants to help people be able to talk about these changes and their accompanying tensions, rather than acting them out in anger on the nursing teams. She sets up a Listening Council that meets every other Tuesday at the end of each shift. The council serves as a place to air grievances and garner innovative ideas. Within months, conflicts have diminished, morale is improving, and religious and nonreligious staff are beginning to understand each other's values. They are in circle.

A group of women have been to Baja California, kayaking among gray whales in the waters of their calving grounds. Every night they sat in circle to help each other make holy stories of the day's events. Los Angeles International Airport was the meeting and departure point for the group. When they return to LAX at the end of the trip they have several hours of leave-taking, as one by one the women peel off from the group to fly home to cities across the continent. They find some space at the side of a corridor and spontaneously sit down in a circle. Speakers are blaring flight announcements, babies are crying, people are whizzing by on either side of this seated circle of fourteen strong, tanned women and their piles of luggage. Because they have listened attentively to one another all week, they can listen attentively now to one another's farewell statements. One at a time, each woman holds a shell and speaks of her learning. The chaos around them melds into one sound: All they can hear is one woman's voice and the ocean's roar.

A church calls a circle to discuss the homeless people in their downtown parish, and how the church might respond. The homeless people hear of the meeting and join it. "We know what our needs are," they tell the parishioners. "Do you want to listen?" The group holds a council in which every person's voice is heard. The church moves out of its traditional position of "providing for the poor" into a position of participating with the homeless people to empower change. They expand the circle.

In a neighborhood elementary school, the children form a council to provide creative, nonviolent solutions to their everyday conflicts. The council members—fourth-, fifth-, and sixth-graders—wear badges on the playground and intervene when trouble occurs. They call a circle when one is needed, so that each child gets heard and a solution is reached. One teacher sits with them as a witness, but she doesn't interfere unless the children's process gets stuck and they call on her for assistance. They are learning circle.

One evening at Christmastime, a multigenerational gathering of family decide to honor their mother/grandmother with a "coming of age" ceremony. On the rec room carpet, they lay out two large circles of yarn: red to signify the blood ties, green to signify the marriage alliances. The four grown children all light candles representing their births and offer an appreciation to their mother. Each of the dozen grandchildren brings a carnation; they make a bouquet in the center, and tell Grandma stories. And so they call the circle.

It is through such ordinary acts that the circle reenters the world. It is through these ordinary acts that the world is changed. The most important step we can take with the circle is to use it—now, today. We can set the circle simply in place in our lives, in our work, in our neighborhoods, in our civic centers, in our religious or spiritual communities, in our families and friendship groups.

Where might you call the circle?

There is no one but us.
There is no one to send,
nor a clean hand nor a pure heart
on the face of the earth, nor in the earth,
but only us,
a generation comforting ourselves
with the notion that we have come at an awkward time,
that our innocent fathers are all dead
—as if innocence had ever been—
and our children busy and troubled,
and we ourselves unfit, not yet ready,
having each of us chosen wrongly,
made a false start, failed,
yielded to impulse and the tangled comfort of pleasures,
and grown exhausted, unable to seek the thread, weak, and involved.
But there is no one but us.
There never has been.

ANNIE DILLARD, *Holy the Firm*

CHAPTER 1

Awakening—
Where We Are Now

I come from the middle. I grew up in Indiana and Minnesota, in the matrix of two families: descended from my mother's line of Scandinavian farmers and my father's line of Scotch-Irish-English tinkers, beekeepers, and preachers. I spent the first twenty years of my adult life living in the middle of the country, in the middle of the middle class. This sense of personal placement is important because it is the rootedness of middle ground I bring to my own awakening—and to the work of the circle I present in this book.

On the suburban edge of Minneapolis, where I lived most of four decades, the air is still breathable, trees grow, and children cluster brightly on street corners to wait for the school bus. From this center place, throughout the 1980s and early 1990s, I ventured out across the continent to teach but always returned to rest in the lake-studded city with its drastic seasons. Here I was surrounded by the moderate people who collectively represent the "American dream" of a decent and comfortable life. It teaches us much, this life in the middle, whether in Missouri, Minnesota, or Manitoba; downtown Chicago, London, Frankfurt, Cape Town, or Sydney; farms in Kansas or Sweden, vineyards in Spain or Israel. While taking on the cultural flavors of a thousand different surroundings, the stability of middle-class existence has become the dominant model of modern life worldwide. This is the vision we have been taught to aspire to, the scene that shows up in countless variations on television, in movies, and in books to reinforce the collective fantasy about what is desirable and achievable. It is this fantasy that is falling apart.

As we grapple with the awareness that our personal lives cannot be separated from the life of our times, we are forced to reconsider the assumptions, expectations, and values that have guided our lives thus far. One by one by one by one, something happens that shakes us into awareness.

When one vision falls, another vision rises. This is not usually a sudden switch, but a long process of the old paradigm fading away—struggling with itself to let go, subverting new forces, becoming reactionary and rigid exactly *because* the inevitable is obvious. We are losing our way of life; and we *need* to lose it, in order not to lose life itself.

Our awakenings come in many guises—some surprise life has up its sleeve—and *bang*, we are shifted out of personal or cultural sleep. Trying to describe this phenomenon once to a friend, I remember saying, "I've been lifted up, given a brisk shaking by huge unseen hands, and set firmly down again. Everything around me looks the same, but everything inside me will never be the same again. And then somebody casually asks, 'Hi, how are you?' and I don't know what to say."

And so the fading of what-is-established gives rise to what-is-possible. The new vision starts to come into focus—struggling with itself to shift from dream to reality, tangential, experiential, a vulnerable and determined seed. We are claiming a more aware way of life; we need our awareness in order to save life itself.

Questions flood us: How will we live through this much change? How will our children and grandchildren live? From what sources will we draw our values? What will have meaning? What will offer stability? How will we take care of ourselves, our loved ones, and all the world's strangers? How will we care for the planet that sustains us? Is everything all right?

As our vision of what constitutes successful living shifts from acquisition to accountability, we seek social and spiritual forms that help us address these questions. It is the premise—and the promise—of this book that gathering in peer-led, spirit-centered circles provides such a community forum.

The Experiment

We are living in the middle of an experiment in how to be human. Since around 1970, with the rise of popular psychology, millions of people have gone through some form of awakening to consciousness. Tumbled along with everything else that is happening in the culture and in our personal lives, there is this added ingredient: consciousness. Throughout human history there have always been lone visionaries, but never before has the call to awaken been heeded by so many ordinary people.

In a decade-long series of studies, Paul H. Ray, a research sociologist, has identified three main worldviews that act as dynamic subcultures in the United States: three different worlds of meaning and valuing.[1] The first worldview is held by Traditionalists, or Heartlanders, who believe we can correct the ills of the modern age by returning to small-town, religious America, corresponding to the period 1890–1930. The second worldview, held by 47 percent of Americans, is that of Modernists, who idealize capitalism, technology, materialism, and science. The third worldview is held by Transmodernists, also called Cultural Creatives, who push the edge of social-psychological-spiritual movements.

While I personally identify with the Transmodernists, the circle as it will be presented throughout this book can be applied within all three worldviews. The central example concerns a group that is certainly Modernist in its view, and many short examples show the circle in Traditionalist settings, being used to uphold the values of the middle ground from which I come.

Though Ray's study was conducted in the United States, the roots of these subcultures arise from European history and can be seen in

---

[1] Paul H. Ray, "The Rise of Integral Culture," *Noetic Sciences Review* (Spring 1996), pp. 4–15.

other Western nations as well. The amazing statistic in this study is that 24 percent of the American population identifies itself as Transmodernist. We're talking about forty-four million mostly middle-class, highly educated people, about 60 percent women, 40 percent men. Cultural Creatives tend to be savvy idealists who consume in an ecologically sound manner, support diversity and self-actualization, and are determined to integrate their personal experience with an optimistic view of the future. As Ray points out, the basic question Transmodernists ask is, "Having reinvented ourselves, how can we reinvent society?"

Forty-four million people contemplating the connection between personal growth and social change sets loose an amazing force in the United States, and the impact of these numbers keeps multiplying, country by country, throughout Western culture. This is a force way beyond the "hundredth monkey." We are a global subculture based on consciousness. We do not know what long-term influence our consciousness will have on the species—but it is certainly shaking things up, speeding up the rate of change, and generating tremendous social and spiritual tensions. It is my greatest hope for the circle that it can provide a forum for bringing these tensions into dialogue.

A basic definition of consciousness is the mind's capacity to observe the self in reality and to be thoughtful about our actions. I remember the day I really "got" consciousness. I remember it because I was twenty-four years old.

It was early spring of 1970, the year Ray cites for the inception of Transmodernism, and I was living in England, working part time and actively seeking something for which I had no words. I wandered around London, especially the Soho district, the focal point of the counterculture. There was a head shop I hung around, soaking up the atmosphere, the incense, and many cups of jasmine tea. I was still a not-very-worldly, drug-free onlooker to most of the hippie scene. One day in the midst of a small group conversation, a man leaned toward me and said, "I have a message for you. What you seek you will find in the Chalice Gardens at Glastonbury." Before I could question him, he was gone.

Two days later I took the train to Bath and the autobus over to

Glastonbury. I visited the abbey where Guinevere and Arthur are buried and wandered around the town looking for gardens, growing increasingly frantic. Here I was at the beginning of my quest, and whatever I was looking for, I couldn't find it. Missing the signals I was sure were all around me, I felt stupid, alone, and misled. "What am I doing here?" I kept asking. "Who is trying to guide me? What do you want?" No insight or answers came.

The Chalice Gardens turned out to be a large cemetery outside town. In early April, the green hillsides were spotted with gravestones and daffodils. I came upon a small, empty chapel. Thumbing through a Bible on the altar, I closed my eyes, let the book fall open wherever it willed. My finger came to rest on Isaiah 55:12: "Ye shall go out with joy and be led forth in peace; the mountains and the hills before you shall burst into singing, and all the trees of the field shall clap their hands."

Suddenly I was crying. I lay down on a long cart at the back of the chapel (only later did I realize it was a casket cart) and tried to calm myself as best I could. Taking long, slow breaths, I recited the phrase over and over: "I shall go out with joy . . . I shall go out with joy."

I must have napped briefly. When I woke, the sun, which had been obscured by clouds all day, was flooding through the chapel window, the beam of light moving up my body in the waning of the afternoon. Warmth. I lay there accepting the caress. When the light reached my head, something changed: The light seemed to enter my mind—to turn my whole being to light. I was, literally and metaphorically, illumined. A capacity opened in my mind that allowed me to observe myself as I never had before.

Many people can tell stories about coming awake—a click in the mind that enables us to witness ourselves in the midst of our own actions. In consciousness, the larger Self and the smaller self become aware that they are accompanying each other. The ego has a consultant, an inner voice of guidance: the Soul's voice joins the journey.

Consciousness is not a steady state for most of us, not an uninterrupted ascent of growth. We awaken, fall back, awaken more fully; go through periods of intense insight; plead for a little status quo to rest within. As Mary Catherine Bateson says, "Any place we stop to rest must also serve as the platform from which we leave."[2] Yet, with all the erratic uncertainties of growth, we continue to experience an arousal of collective mind.

Thirty years down the line, we discover we're a quarter of the population of our countries. Though many of us aren't quite sure how to direct this force beyond our personal lives, we hang on the precipice of awareness, unable to fall back, unsure how to go forward.

Over and over again I hear people express their longing to know what to do, how to apply personal consciousness to the world in some helpful way. I believe we can apply consciousness to heal the world— and we already are. Great power lies within us. What has been missing is the mechanism for organizing this power. I believe this mechanism of empowerment and action is *the circle*.

The kind of circle this book addresses is a council of ordinary people who convene to create a sacred space and from that space accomplish a specific task, supporting each other in the process. Because it has a sense of containment, the circle has a beginning, middle, and end that are framed through simple rituals appropriate to the group and setting. The circle has a shared, verbalized intention so that everyone knows why they are gathered. The circle self-governs and corrects its course through the adoption of commonsense agreements of behavior. And when confusion arises, or the way is momentarily lost, everyone agrees to fall into reflective silence, refocus on the group's highest purpose, and follow protocols for problem solving that reestablish trust and cohesion. In such a circle leadership rotates, responsibility is shared, and the group comes to rely deeply on spirit.

Calling the Circle

Calling the circle is a simple idea—any one of us can do it. The circle emerges wherever it is invited. Calling a circle doesn't have to be a huge risk or lengthy experiment. We can start small, start with one evening.

---

[2] Mary Catherine Bateson, *Composing a Life* (New York: Atlantic Monthly Press, 1989).

In the early 1990s, when circling was still a fairly new concept in the Midwest, I called a circle as part of my twenty-fifth college reunion. I wanted to see if the readiness to try this form was present among women who had largely grown up in the traditionalism of the American middle. One early evening in St. Paul, Minnesota, in June of 1993, we closed the doors to the girls' dorm, and twenty women from Macalester College, class of '68, looked at each other anew.

On a coffee table, I laid out a scarf and several candles. Each woman contributed an object that symbolically represented her current life: photos of family, a favorite book, an identification badge from work, a running shoe, a rock from Lake Superior. We lit the candles and looked at each other in the flickering light, seeing remembered twenty-year-old faces in our forty-seven-year-old eyes. It had been a quarter of a century since we came of age: now what? As we went around the group, each woman held her object, said what she had come to say. It took three hours of close attention.

The specific issues brought forward may be different, but in circle after circle, our personal life stories are laced with comprehension of the immensity of the challenges we face. In this circle, we acknowledged that these challenges are real and unavoidable, that they will consume the rest of our lives and our children's lives, whether we want them to or not.

We teetered on despair, but kept asking: "What can we do? How can we imagine responding?" After the first round of listening to each other's stories, we opened discussion and began thinking together. By midnight, we had come up with "A Manifesto of the Heart" for activating values in our own lives. I enclose it here because it is the sort of collective wisdom that arises when the circle is called. It is a reminder of the position women find themselves in at the end of the twentieth century.

We believe that the level of sharing and intimacy among midlife women is unprecedented in human history. We are committed to figuring out what this means and what gifts it brings us. We know our children are watching; our mothers are watching; our husbands and brothers are watching. We must explore our own power because ultimately all politicians and systems disappoint. The 1960s demonstrated, through charismatic leadership, what it is now possible for the ordinary individual to do. Yet, with all our freedoms, we seem to have lost our outrage and our willingness to limit other people's behavior when it infringes on our values. To solve the problems facing us, we need to become a vocal majority. We need, above all else, to be consistent with our children, to not lie, to utilize stability and unconditional love wherever we find it. We make the following commitment: We will practice making decisions based on their impact for the next seven generations. We will keep in mind that our lifetime goals and dreams are bigger than we are and cannot really be finished. So we will trust spirit, and put our lives into a larger context. We will cleave to joy. We will keep praying: It is positive energy going out into the world. We will keep opening our hearts to loving-kindness. We will create circles among those who pray with us and for us.

Years have passed, yet I am confident that circle has become part of our consciousness as we've traveled on. The invitation to council has become part of the reunion tradition at Macalester, and it is spreading among other small colleges. These circles are able to happen because the circle itself is being reintroduced into our culture in profound ways.

Circles of Recovery and Healing: The Bridge

At a lecture in the mid-1980s, a participant asked psychologist and author M. Scott Peck what he considered to be the most significant source of social change in the twentieth century. He replied, without hesitation, "Alcoholics Anonymous, because it introduced the idea that people could help themselves." His surety of comment fascinated me, and I began to study the origins of the Twelve Step movement. What I found was the circle.

From the onset, AA's founders assumed that a circle of peers was the only form of counsel that could really help them abstain. Dr. Smith and Bill W., both alcoholics, had tried many times to relieve their compulsive drinking through willpower or by submitting to various promises of cure. It was only when they decided to place themselves in a circle and place Spirit, invoked as Higher Power, at the center of the circle that they were able to stop drinking. Something in them knew what to do. These two white men, one a struggling businessman, the other a small-town doctor, reintroduced the circle as a form of social and spiritual power, and their discovery set off immense changes in Western culture.

Twelve Step groups usually meet in a circle, with the facilitator changing from meeting to meeting. People introduce themselves with a first name and a statement of self-disclosure: "Hello, my name is Jack and I'm an alcoholic." Everyone is present for a similar purpose. The meetings open with a recitation of the Twelve Steps, which provide the focus of the group. Usually, one Step is discussed and meditated upon at each meeting, with people sharing their stories and talking about what that Step means to them. They listen without interrupting each other. There are strict guidelines for confidentiality, safe social structure, and support or guidance. The more experienced members volunteer to act as sponsors for new members, and so they mentor each other without developing a hierarchy. *The Big Book* and other materials provide each group with a sense of history and format. The Twelve Step program has its own vocabulary, slogans, and affirmations. Meetings close with ritual—usually the Serenity Prayer and the invitation "Keep coming back!" It is a system that throughout its sixty-year history has kept a clear sense of peer leadership and peer support.

Looking back twenty-five years, to the inception of her own sobriety, a dear friend recalls her entrance into AA:

Because I insisted, they avoided the word *God* and gently taught me the simple rituals that became my lifeline. We sat in a circle. Our leaders rotated. Responsibility was shared. (I loved the willingness of the men to empty the ashtrays and make the coffee.) And ultimate reliance was placed on something greater than ourselves. As we joined hands, became silent, and said the Serenity Prayer at the end of the meeting, I could feel something stirring at the center of our circle. It was clear then that one plus one equals more than two. And even in my spiritual denial, I was willing to admit that this "something" was considerably more powerful than any one of us. I felt, for those few minutes each day, like I used to feel at five o'clock, when I had poured my first drink—that I had come home.

The imprint held—and K.W., like millions of others, drew upon the strength of the circle to help her maintain her own recovery.

A few pages earlier, I said I believe we can apply consciousness to heal the world, and that what has been missing is the mechanism for organizing our power. A few decades ago, people with addictions had no mechanism for healing; Alcoholics Anonymous brought in the prototype. Studying its success and worldwide impact, we can see the power unleashed when personal need is held within a form that meets that need.

Now, our personal need is to use individual recovery, healing, and awareness as the source for making spirit-based cultural change. And here is the circle, waiting for us to apply it broadly and boldly.

In 1990, when I finished writing my book *Life's Companion*, I had the distinct impression that I had "finished" my life to date, healed myself as much as I knew how. *Life's Companion* was the forum through which I shared that healing and the spiritual journey that came to lead me back into the heart of the world. The evidence of the end of my old life was everywhere around me. It was exhilarating and disorienting: I was traveling without a road map, teaching at retreat centers, discovering an international community of seekers, looking for the next step.

Part of the next step was an association with a group called Women's Alliance. Over a twelve-year period, from 1982 to 1994, in California and then in Washington, Women's Alliance brought together a faculty of women authors, artists, and musicians and designed a week of lectures, electives, ritual, and fun known as the Women's Alliance Summer Camp. Depending on the size of the rented facility, between 150 and 250 women showed up for this event, many of them returning year after year. In 1992 I was asked to join the faculty to teach journal writing. Around a small lake in western Washington, we took over a Girl Scout camp, set up an elaborate altar in the meadow behind the dining hall, and called ourselves into community.

I came to camp from the Midwest, from my life in the middle. Under the warm August sun and full harvest moon, ten facilitators and five Alliance staff members gathered a few days early to set the vision of the camp. We wandered the rim of the lake and selected teaching sites. We sat on the dock with our feet dangling in the water and mapped out the week's schedule. We sang prayers to bless the space, laid out registration packets, and put up signs.

Like many people teaching in the 1980s, I had used the circle with varying degrees of formality. It was common to put chairs in a ring and for the teacher or group leader to lecture and facilitate discussion from this vantage point. By that time, I had been teaching journal writing in such informal circles for twenty years, but Women's Camp was my first experience applying the circle as a form of community governance. Accustomed to groups of journal writers, where I was the only teacher, I'd never been in a council of facilitating peers before. It was the first time someone handed me a talking stick to hold the floor. Round and round the circle the talking stick was passed as we shared experiences from our work. I wasn't even sure what to call what we were doing. "Maybe this is feminist process," I thought, "maybe this is what I've been reading about in books by California authors." I contributed my own stories, watched, and learned. In my mind I kept asking, "Where have I been? Why haven't I known how to do this? How come I haven't met any of these women before?" I got angry at Minnesota for its stolid middleness. I endured alternating waves of insecurity and confidence.

Saturday afternoon, the camp filled with the energy and expectations of 150 women. Having had two days to adjust to the new social norms, I assumed we would close the gates of the compound and enter a strange and marvelous world without men or television or outside concerns, where community would spontaneously arise. By Saturday evening I was giddy with the sense of new adventure.

When we held the first convocation, the staff made announcements but didn't ask for agreements of respect and confidentiality such as those I'd been using in writing circles for a decade. We paraded into the meadow and were asked to put something we'd brought onto the altar. No one explained the meaning of this large draped construction at the edge of the forest or talked about how we might show reverence for what we were doing. I traveled along with the crowd, trying to fit in. I assumed I was the only one surprised; after all, I was from Minnesota.

By Sunday night, the unaddressed issues between us, in an eclectic "village" of diverse women, were beginning to surface chaotically. As members of the faculty, we were under tremendous pressure to keep following the structure; we had services to provide, meals to prepare, electives to teach, rituals to organize. The staff met at lunch in harried councils, trying to help each other handle problems and run the camp.

"We're missing pieces, we're missing pieces" ran like a chant in my mind all the days of that week, "but what?" I had to stop trying to act as though I knew what I was doing. I tried instead to look at camp as though I knew nothing, assumed nothing. "If I'd just landed here from Venus, what would I see?" I asked myself.

"Lack of context" was the phrase that came to mind. We were a community of refugees, retreating from competition, gender bias, violence, and other abuses of power. We had washed up on the shores of our willingness to learn, but though the use of circles—as circle groups, listening council, staff council—permeated the camp, we didn't know how to apply the form deeply enough to really govern ourselves. We weren't sure we could trust the form to carry us through our differences. We were trying to put the circle into place without first creating a commonly understood context so that the circle could actually function.

Living in Context

Context is the social, political, cultural, and spiritual force that shapes the life of a person. Every person lives within society's context—whether we live comfortably in the middle of this collective force or straining at the edge. In every society there are seekers whose role is to push the borders of accepted experience and whose thoughts and actions expand the cultural context. Ideas and social forms pass through a culture, coming first from the edge and, as they are accepted, moving to center and becoming the "norm." Eventually many of these once innovative concepts become outdated and fall out of use.

At the interactive edge between the self and society, context is constantly shifting, absorbing new information, ideas, and technology, making room for new experiences that have proven possible. *Context is the collective atmosphere inside which something is seen and understood.* Before a human went to the moon, the context for space travel was laid in place by scientists proclaiming it was possible, by political leaders bringing the "conquest of space" into their speeches, by science fiction novels and movies, and by the development of well-publicized technology—from short rocket flights and monkeys whirling overhead to ticker-tape parades for astronauts. And one day in July 1969, while millions watched on television, Neil Armstrong went hopping around in slow motion and moon dust, and we were prepared to absorb this reality and place it into context.

Context is amazingly important. *Pushing the context is how a culture changes, both in expansion and in reaction against expansion.* As groups of ethnic and racial minorities, women, homosexuals, the physically challenged, and others have struggled for social rights, each group has expanded the contextual edge, insisting that the culture make room, rewrite laws, and get used to living with these changes. When Martin Luther King, Jr., said, "Nothing can stop an idea whose time has come," he understood the power of contextual opening—and the need to seize the moment. The cultural acceptance of civil rights may be temporarily stalled, may be reacted against, but it cannot be wiped away, because it is now included in the social context: The visionary's dream has become part of collective consciousness. It is there, part of the bedrock.

The tension between expansion and contraction as context changes is enormous and complicated. If 24 percent of the culture is pushing the opening, at least that percentage is trying to slam it shut, and another huge percentage is just trying to stay out of the controversy. And this has *always* been so.

Nevertheless, this is a moment when the circle is coming back into cultural context and we may place the power of the circle into the bedrock of the culture. We cannot have this conversation about circling without the help of context—context creates the understood "we" who travel these pages together. *Context prepares us to consider new ideas*. The collective mind has expanded to make room for the idea of circling, and while this openness exists we may move forward quickly.

Riding context is like riding the surf: We are swept up and moved along by forces that we ourselves have not called but which set the pace and support us on the journey. Context is a very important aspect of what we do now, what we do next, for we need cultural context to carry the circle forward.

To really function as a "village" that week in Women's Camp, we needed a context, much like the context that supports Alcoholics Anonymous: We needed agreements on structure, behavior, and philosophy, one-on-one mentoring, and shared purpose. In camp, the circle was spoken of and used as a ceremonial form, but we only partially understood the requirements of actually living in circle-based community. The immensity of our experiment stunned me: The camp was a threshold of context between the way things were and the way things might be. I crossed this threshold and said yes to a deeper experience of circle than I had ever before contemplated. Said "Yes, I will be your student."

We need a revolution in the West: not violent overthrow, but a willingness to take responsibility for the course of history being set forth in our names. We need a revolution determined to activate broad, inclusive social change. We need to insist that our homes, schools, neighborhoods, places of work, cities, states, and nations dialogue with us about the values set in place for this next millennium. As I stood in the meadow at camp, I knew the revolution had begun for me. And I set out to learn how to call the circle—how to create the context the circle needs in order to reenter the mainstream of our culture.

I returned home to the middle, carrying the circle like a mustard seed and asking, "What might a circle do?"

I believe this is a question that a vast community of people is ready to ask.

They say we have been here for 60,000 years, but it is much longer.
We have been here since the time before time began.
We have come directly out of the Dreamtime
of the great creative Ancestors.
We have lived and kept the earth
as it was on the First Day.
All other peoples
of the world
come from
us.

ABORIGINE ELDER, AUSTRALIA

CHAPTER 2

The Circle:
Past, Present, and Future

I came home from Women's Alliance Summer Camp ready to study and apply the circle, and my life began a cycle of great change. For weeks, images of circle—past, present, and future—filled my dreams. I went about my daily business as normally as I could, but by night I entered an apprenticeship to this ancient and modern form. I had invited revolution, and I was in it! Soon the world began giving me opportunities to practice what I was thinking about.

My friend Carol called.[1] Teachers in her school district were threatening to strike. She was nearly frantic. "I feel helpless," she said over the phone. "I have to go to work, so does John, and if the kids suddenly need watching every day, I don't know what we'll do. John's company is downsizing. He's afraid to ask for any special adjustments to handle child care for fear they'll use it as a reason to let him go. And I can't quit—we need the income. . . ."

"Well, have you talked to anybody?" I asked. "Teachers? Other parents? The school board?"

"I was up at school the other day. I've never seen Jenny's teacher so

---

[1] The names used in this example are pseudonyms.

tense. I got an earful about how the teachers think the board is stone-walling. She says the board's concerned about budget cuts and not about quality of education. At the last PTA meeting, the school board asked us to choose which extracurricular activities to cut. I think they want somebody else to take the flak. The whole situation seems near panic. Brandon says he's quitting soccer because his coach told him it's going to be cut anyway.

"Arlene, next door, is the only parent on the block who's home days. We were watching some of the kids playing hide-and-seek last Saturday when she turned to me and said, 'Well, if the strike comes, don't expect me to become den mother.' There are so many aspects to this—everything from my overall concern about what's happening to education to what I'm going to do with the kids if I have to go to work—I don't want Jenny and Brandon home alone all afternoon with the TV! What can I do?"

"You could call a circle," I suggested.

"We tried that. Last week the PTA officers hosted a community meeting so teachers, parents, and board members could hear each other out on neutral ground. It turned into a shouting match."

"No, I mean really call a circle."

By now I knew: A circle is not just a meeting with the chairs rearranged. A circle is a way of doing things differently than we have become accustomed to. The circle is a return to our original form of community as well as a leap forward to create a new form of community. As I coached Carol through the process of calling the circle, I found myself tapped into a deep well of knowing. I wasn't inventing the circle; I was rediscovering an ancient process of consultation and communion that, for tens of thousands of years, had held the human community together and shaped its course.

Remembering the First Culture

In ancestral times, the circle flourished as the primary social structure in richly diverse pockets of human community. We see the remnants of circle-based culture in archeological discoveries and among remaining indigenous peoples around the globe. The Inuits of the Arctic lands still meet in council and build round dwellings. The Aborigines of Australia paint sacred spirals on cave walls and on their bodies and still follow the songlines of the earth across vast expanses of the outback. Some African peoples build circular villages. Traditionally, the native tribes of the American plains construct teepees and set them in circles. In all these variations of human culture, the circle is the common element, the common source. And so I began calling the circle our First Culture.

First Culture was the flowering of human community based on the circle as the web of life. For tens of thousands of years, in kinship-based social groups across the globe, our ancestors in the human tribe adapted to variations of climate, terrain, and natural resources. They developed social structures that helped sustain them on the land, and spiritual myths that helped them explain the mysteries of life. These structures, and their spiritual base, are evident in paintings, carvings, petroglyphs, runes, crafts, and later in architecture. What seems to have been intact in all these settings were the concentric circles of interconnection—the campfire, the extended family, the larger society, humanity, nature, and the mystery of Spirit. *And deep in our cells, we may remember. . . .*

Many, many thousands of years ago, when we captured the spark of fire and began to carry the embers of warmth and cooking and light along with us from site to site, fire brought a new experience into being. Coming in from the plains where we had been wandering in small breeding groups, we found shelter in caves and crevasses and brought the safety of the light with us. The fire warded off predators, roasted the roots and nuts that were the staples of our diet, and cooked our meats. With the flame, we could provide more food and sustain more people.

We came into circle because the fire led us there. Struggling to keep warm, struggling to keep safe, it made sense to put fire in the center. A circle allowed space for each person to face the flame, and as a member of a fire circle, we each could claim a place of warmth and a piece of food. Out of this instinctive taking of place, community developed.

Socialization is not always a smooth process. In dreams we may still hear the snarls of males vying for control, the fierce protective grunts of the females guarding their young, the squeals of little ones cuffed aside, the sighs of the old and vulnerable.

The circle provided a format for working things out. As we refined social skills, the circle grew with us. With our faces animated by the flicker of flames, we began to recognize each other as "like kind." Surrounded by familiar kin, with bodies fed and sheltered, the rules and taboos of social conduct could be established.

When we see someone again and again in firelight, the fire becomes symbolic of our connection. Perhaps as we first faced each other across the shimmering circle of light, we were able to envision the spark of the Sacred in each other's eyes. Around the campfire, a mythology arose about our creation and our reasons for being. The fire was a sacred symbol, the source that provided a cohesive center. And when we fell asleep around the fire's coals, we dreamed.

How small and vulnerable we must have felt on the great natural skin of the planet. So many things were unexplainable. How could we be so hungry and when we cried out, one among us would find a berry bush, or a flock of birds would come within range of our slingshots? How could a woman's body swell and swell, and then, in the midst of crying and blood, push out another human being? Why did death come, and sometimes healing? Full of wonder, we developed rituals of thankfulness. Out of spontaneous gratitude, we believed ourselves to be in relationship with some Spirit Being who helped safeguard our lives.

We experienced a radical dependence upon all of nature. We were her daughters and sons, and so we named her Mother. We carved images of the goddess Mother, crawled into womblike caves, made offerings to the land, threw gifts of incense into the fire, built cairn stone altars, notched the trunks of trees to mark our passage, danced and drummed and sang, and held council in the sacred shape of the circle. Lascaux. Stonehenge. Easter Island. Çatal Hüyük. Knossos. I remember. And so do you. Our cells recall another way to lead our lives.

And now, when we stand on asphalt, lost in a forest of skyscrapers, barraged with distractions and harried by the pace of modern life, our cells lead us in a process of reclamation. The circle is calling. Listen.

The visionary Swiss psychiatrist Carl Jung noted that all human beings share a number of images that seem to spring from a common source deep within the psyche. He called this source "the collective unconscious"—consistently recurring "mythic motifs." "The brain," Jung said, "has been built up in the course of millions of years and represents a history of which it is the result. Naturally it carries with it the traces of that history, exactly like the body, and if you grope down into the basic structure of the mind you naturally find traces of the archaic mind. . . . The deepest we can reach into our exploration of the unconscious mind is the layer where man is no longer a distinct individual, but where his mind widens out and merges into the mind of mankind—where we are all one."[2]

One of the symbols that led Jung to contemplate this point of oneness was the recurring imagery of the circle. The circle, often in the form of the Sun Wheel (a pie cut in eight equal pieces), is represented in different cultures as the Medicine Wheel, the Wheel of Law and Life, the Wheel of the Year, and the Catherine Wheel. Jung traced the image of the circle back to the Paleolithic and Mesolithic periods, when wheels were carved and painted as a sacred symbol, thousands of years before the wheel was invented as an actual tool. Based on this research, Jung saw the wheel as a primary symbol, one of the mythic motifs springing from the collective unconscious.

So it seems the circle has resided within us since the dawn of time, and is a form familiar to us at a deeply resonant level. Over and over again, when this mythic resonance is activated, people experience a sense of "having been here before" as they enter the circle. Sometimes we are buoyed up by this familiarity and proceed with confidence: "I know how to do this . . . I know how to behave here." Sometimes we are shaken by how even a vestige of circle carries profound impact. When Carol and John took up the challenge to offer the circle as a way to resolve their school district's problems, they ran into resistance and confusion, not unlike my camp experience, but they were able to draw upon the motif of the circle in their own minds and in the minds of those who came to participate.

The Power of One Circle

It is dusk on a Saturday evening. Carol and John's house is quieted from its usual daily busyness. Soft music is playing as a group of teachers and parents gather. Lights are low. Carol has spread a cloth on the coffee table in the center of the living room and laid out objects depicting school life—a bowl of apples and cookies, pencils and small pads of paper, the Crestview Eagles emblem, school photos

---

[2] C. G. Jung, *The Symbolic Life* (Princeton: Princeton University Press, 1976), vol. 18, pp. 41–42.

of the children whose parents have come to circle. The objects seem to shimmer in the light of several candles.

She has called the circle with intention. It took Carol one whole evening to draft a paragraph statement asking people to participate. "I am calling another meeting," she wrote,

> to hold council about the issues facing us regarding the impending strike between the teachers of District 269 and the school board. The purpose of the meeting is to provide a forum in which teachers and parents together can develop a plan to approach the board and advocate for resolutions that will serve everyone. This meeting will be at our home and will be held as an intentional circle. We will use the structure of council to hear each other out, gather information, develop understanding, and plan considered action. Circling may be new to us, but it is an ancient form. We will literally sit in a circle, open and close formally, pass a talking piece around to share the floor (Jenny's Day-Glo pink ruler ought to work well). We will discover the outcome of the evening as we go. If you are willing to take this risk and explore a form that may really help us here, please let me know by Friday. I know this is short notice, but it's all the time we have.

In the entranceway, people introduce themselves and get a cup of tea or coffee before entering the living room. Even though it has not been articulated, there is a sense that the space has been consecrated for the evening. People settle in, expectant and a little nervous about how to behave around the centerpiece and candles. Arlene has come; so has Jenny's teacher, Bev Ebble, and several of her close colleagues. Ted Johnson, president of the Parent-Teacher Association, is here, along with John and three other fathers, as well as five mothers of Jenny and Brandon's friends.

Carol and John live on a block where people hardly know each other except for the visiting that occurs between their children. John works for a company where everyone spends the day in cubicles doing highly isolated tasks. Carol works at a software firm. Year after year, their children are educated by people they scarcely know. They go to church, where they sit in rows and listen politely while someone else talks to them of God. The closest they get to governing council is the voting booth, and most of the time they vote without much sense of what the issues really are, or what this or that candidate can really do. We know this routine; we live it, too. It's life in the middle.

John says, "Many of us are only bare acquaintances. If the circle works as Carol has explained it to me, we're going to get to know each other much better tonight. I'd like to suggest we start with a minute of silence. Whatever you want to do during that time is fine. Pray or meditate, breathe deeply, or do multiplication tables—it's all about focusing. It's helpful if we draw a line between the rest of the day and the circle so we can hear each other more accurately than we usually do and find a way to speak from our own perspective."

In ordinary settings, silence in a group usually signals discomfort rather than contemplation. We fidget. Our minds race around, looking for something to say. Silence between partners or friends may indicate anger or sullenness. Since silence has become a sign of social disapproval, we may need to retrain ourselves in order to feel comfortable with it. Breath helps. By concentrating on gentle, rhythmic breathing, we may slip into stillness, rest there, and then gently let our mental energy rise again.

John sets the example by falling silent and taking long, slow breaths. When he feels his own mental energy quieted, and senses that others in the room are also ready, he signals the end of silence by ringing a small brass bell. People open their eyes, look around, wait for leadership. The silence has lasted about ninety seconds.

Opening a circle with ritual is essential to help people drop their expectations that the circle is just another name for a committee meeting, task force, or project team. People are often surprised to find themselves in a setting that includes ritual. And yet they are also intrigued. Lighting a candle, creating even a small focal point in the center, following a time of silence by reciting a quote—whether it's a poem or a mission statement—all help us remember our roots in the circle.

After the silence Carol begins. "As convener this evening, I welcome you to circle. I appreciate your coming and your willingness to try a new form of meeting in order to resolve our problem. I've called this meeting, but it's not mine to run—the circle belongs to all of us."

In holding a circle, leadership rotates, responsibility is shared, and the center is imbued with collective wisdom. Group agreements help people feel secure and able to focus on the purpose of the circle. The purpose of this circle is to generate ideas to break the stalemate and to show support for the teachers, the children, and the school system itself. Carol suggests the group observe four basic agreements: confidentiality around personal stories, listening without interrupting, making statements that have to do with problem solving, and calling for time-out if people need to regroup and think through an issue. Carol and John are introducing this circle carefully; they want to invite people without scaring them.

After getting a nod of heads that everyone is willing to abide by the agreements, Carol introduces the talking piece. "This pink ruler grants the floor to whoever is holding it. That means we will speak one at a time—no interrupting. We'll go around once to let everyone speak their point of view. If you're not ready to talk when the ruler comes to you, it's always okay to pass. When it gets back to me, I'll hold it out for anyone who didn't speak to have a turn. At the end of the round, we can decide to keep using the talking piece, or open up conversation. Since we want to hear from everyone, let's limit our comments to about three minutes each. That's longer than you think when talking. And John's got the kitchen timer if we need to keep closer track of our contributions. Any questions?"

"Yeah," said one of the dads. "Why don't we just start with discussion? And what if I have a question?"

Carol takes a deep breath. "The reason for a talking piece council is to slow us down—so we listen without just planning our own speech, and so we hear from everyone, not just those who like to leap into open discussion. Once we've heard from everyone, conversation often works better. As for questions, take notes if you want—that's why we put out the paper—but keep on listening; it's amazing how the questions get answered." The man agrees to participate. Carol and John breathe a sigh of relief—circle form is new to them, too.

Beverly Ebble starts. "My biggest problem is isolation. I'm so busy coping with the twenty-four little bodies right in front of me, I don't feel connected to the larger picture. I want my kids to pass their grade equivalencies, but I also want to help them grow up, ready for the world. You can't imagine the level of need some of these youngsters have. Did you know it's now in the curriculum that we must teach children to wash their hands, brush their teeth, set the table, say please and thank you? I get the sense nobody is raising kids anymore, and most of us are just passing them on in the system. I get into such gloom sometimes about where they're going. And then when the school board says it's cutting the budget again—even my own salary—it makes me so mad. Let *them* come and do my job for a week!"

When the pink ruler is passed to her, Arlene says sharply, "Well, I'm raising my kids! I'm the only mother here who's home when they get home." There is an intake of breath and jerking of body postures among others in the circle, but they respect the talking piece and let Arlene finish. "Okay, okay, just listen to me. I don't mean to say you're doing it wrong and I'm doing it right. I'm saying times have changed from how it was when we were kids. I'd like to suggest some kind of coalition between parents and teachers—like getting more parent volunteers in the classroom, or coaching, or tutoring; that would save money. But if we ask parents to do something, will they take an interest? Will they tell us they have to work and don't have time? Oh, I don't know. . . ." With a deep sigh, she passes on the ruler.

This is a complex conversation about a complex problem. People need to express their overall concerns and then break the problem down into pieces small enough to let them see how they can effect change. Of course there's tension, but it's creative tension. The circle is not always a group of like-minded souls who agree with each other about everything. There is room in the circle for many opinions, voices, views. Listening to Arlene, several parents feel themselves shift into guilt and defensiveness, but because they don't interrupt her, they hear the rest of her statement and relax again.

A father named Tom takes his turn. "At work we're using quality control circles in several divisions. I'm wondering if we could adapt this concept to what's happening here. I don't think we should give up the idea of using volunteers to cut costs so there's more money for salaries. Maybe we could design teams that would take responsibility for different extracurricular activities."

John says, "There's enough of us here to do some brainstorming. Maybe after this round we should break into three smaller groups and each tackle an aspect of this, and come back to the large circle at the end of the evening and see what we've got." He passes on the ruler.

Carol and John have done it: They've brought the circle forward, and set it down in their living room. Opening with a moment of silence and passing a talking piece may be different from the last meeting you or I attended, but the format helps. Certainly the tone of this gathering is more constructive than that of the community forum hosted by the PTA officers. Meetings such as the community forum become a microcosm of what's happened to our culture as a whole. Our understanding of how to sit in council has been replaced with the drive to maintain and control access to power.

Second Culture: The Modern World

The triangle is also an archetypal and universal symbol. The Trinity, the Star of David, the pyramid, and, earlier still, the pubic triangle of the Great Mother evidence how deeply this shape is embedded in the human mind. The triangle applied to a system of social organization becomes a hierarchy. Hierarchy is a triangular structure that locates leadership at the top and grants those leaders the authority to "rule" those ranked beneath them.

The triangle does not negate the circle; in fact, in both Christian- and pre-Christian-era symbolism, they are often found together. The triangle within the circle appears on the back of a U.S. dollar bill and the front of the AA medallion. Both symbols live within us: We carry the circle *and* the triangle.

Hierarchy offers an efficient means for organizing huge systems and for carrying out specific and repetitive tasks. Hierarchy is useful for parenting, teaching, passing on information, organizing data, and mass-producing goods.

This book is not against hierarchy. In my experience, circle and triangle work naturally and spontaneously in combination. A council may be called in which every person has a voice, and then a group of elders takes all these voices into consideration and makes a decision, which they bring back to the group for a vote or consensus. Employee groups may be consulted about setting the long-range goals for a company. A church committee may sit down and set out the criteria for hiring a new pastor, and then open discussion in the congregation. A family may sit down and discuss expectations for their teenagers, with certain choices open to the children's input and other rules that the parents hold firm. Or, as with Carol and John's group, a coalition of parents and teachers (working as a peer group) may approach the school board (working as a hierarchy) with a plan for resolving budget deficits and other conflicts.

What is wrong with the modern world is not the triangle but the aggression behind it. The triangle has been turned into a spearhead aimed at systematically destroying preexisting social and spiritual structures. A Second Culture has been imposed over the First, and the circle has been negated as a model for governance, worship, and social interaction.

Sociologist Jerry Mander asserts that technological culture has, as one of its underlying aims, the desire to obliterate or enculturate native peoples so that indigenous cultures are lost and forgotten as alternative ways to live.[3] At the end of his book, Mander cites the situation of the Indians in the Amazon basin of South America as an example of how international corporate, political, and economic interests move in and take over regions that house the last First Culture societies.

The Amazon has been designated as one of the most promising areas on earth for economic development, and multinational corporations have been given sanction to pave, cut, develop, and flood the region. "At present," says Mander, writing in 1991, "the largest issue concerning rainforest Indians is Brazil's Plan 2010. Backed by the World Bank and many international aid organizations, Plan 2010 calls for development of virtually all of the Amazon's water resources, a vast supply that represents one-fifth of the whole world's developable water. Plan 2010 envisions 136 high dams in Brazil alone, 22 of which will flood a rainforest area the size of the United Kingdom and home to several nations of Indians."[4] If their homelands are submerged, and their way of life displaced, the native peoples of the region will become economically dependent on the corporation; instead of living on the land, they will have to live off the company. This is not an uncommon scenario in the world today.

In Second Culture, the circle and the triangle have been separated

---

[3] Jerry Mander, *In the Absence of the Sacred: The Failure of Technology and the Survival of the Indian Nations* (San Francisco: Sierra Club Books, 1991).

[4] Ibid., p. 375.

and the innate power and organization each of them carries have been perverted; their ability to check and balance and reflect each other has been destroyed. Hierarchy, misapplied, becomes what David Kyle terms "the Machine World."[5] The Machine World is so out of balance, it functions without soul or conscience, blindly willing to destroy the planetary ecosystem on which it depends. Every morning, nearly every person in the Western world wakes up and sets about living in ways that contribute to this destruction. Our livelihoods often depend on it. And even though we know what we are doing, we are stymied about what to do instead.

We try to stop this progression toward our own destruction, but it is very hard to think our way clear while still standing inside the Machine. "Hierarchical structure," says Kyle, "inhibits the democratic and chaotic way in which innovation, creativity and change work. What often passes for creativity and innovation in a company is problem-solving. Companies like problems solved because it makes them more efficient and saves money. . . . But to get people in an organization to be truly creative and innovative, or even eccentric, is to disrupt procedures, policies and cut across functional boundaries, as well as to raise ethical, moral and spiritual questions about what they are doing."[6]

There is no time. There is no space. There is no context for thinking our way through these dilemmas from inside the Machine. But—if we bring in the nearly forgotten power and presence of the circle, we create an oasis of time and space that is not controlled by the Machine. The circle is outside. The circle is perhaps the only way for most of us to get far enough outside our usual ways of acting and perceiving so that we can have a real experience of each other and discover alternatives for the way things are.

When we admit the pervasive influences of Second Culture, spread through the functioning of the Machine World, it's easy to see why an event, even one as simple as a community meeting, cannot easily arrive at consensus and creative outcome. Like any one of us, these ordinary citizens, unprepared to tackle what they are tackling, unedu-

---

[5] David Kyle, *Human Robots and Holy Mechanics* (Hillsboro, OR: Swan Raven and Co., 1993).

[6] Ibid., pp. 43–44.

cated in the ways of council, but sensing, sensing, that *something* could be different, cross the threshold into a vague sense of Third Culture and begin to re-create the world.

This is a tremendous challenge. Unless he is able to hold on to the rudiments of an alternative model and is able to teach it to Second Culture citizens, the president of the PTA—no matter how well intentioned—is caught up in reinforcing the model of power that is causing the problem. He may call for Robert's Rules of Order and try to provide benevolent leadership, but other people will wrest control away from him in order to establish their own point of view. Everyone is trapped, reinforcing the belief that the meeting is a contest to see whose idea "wins" the most attention, and in the ensuing power plays the whole situation blows up. Ted Johnson can bang the gavel all he wants and it isn't going to stop Joe Domingo from getting his two cents in, and it isn't going to prevent the fourth-grade teachers from walking out en masse, nor will it keep Pam O'Connell from bursting into tears of frustration and vowing that she will never again get involved in these kinds of meetings.

By hosting a meeting in a circle, Carol and John are challenging five thousand years of enculturation by saying: "Here is another way. Here power will be shared, opened up, dealt with differently, so that we may find a new way of being together."

When Carol lights a candle in the middle of a meeting and John calls for a minute of silence, when Bev Ebble articulates her frustration, when Arlene finishes her thoughts, when Tom sees the correlation between what's happening at work and what's going on at his children's school, consciousness shifts and liberation begins. When we call the circle into the midst of Second Culture, we create a new amalgam of the past and present—a Third Culture.

Third Culture: The Circle and the Triangle

To be living at the time when a thousand-year cycle turns over creates tremendous speculation in the human psyche. All of us feel the impact of this speculation, of the impulses of our own consciousness, and of the real-world needs that fuel our awakening. As we see the status quo of the world falling apart, no one needs to tell us that the paradigm is shifting again.

What I hope we see emerging as the new paradigm is a Third Culture that reinstates the circle to a place of honor and employs this adaptable and empowering form in all the settings where it will flourish.

The circle is an organizational structure that locates leadership around the rim and provides an inclusive means for consulting, delegating tasks, acknowledging the importance of people, and honoring the spiritual. Circle is a useful structure for learning, governing, creating community, providing services, envisioning, and stating long-range goals.

I use the term "Third Culture" to suggest a context for bringing the circle back into the world as more than a ceremonial experience. Through the process of revalidating the circle, we make thirty thousand years of council wisdom available to ourselves. That's quite a data bank. And making this wisdom available is exactly my intent: to practice living in circle so that we may reconnect with the circle's knowledge of human potential.

As Second Culture approaches cataclysm, we tend to feel more and more helpless. It gets bigger; we get smaller. We lose sight, if we ever had it, of our personal power and of our collective potential for coming through the paradigm shift.

As much as we may think we know about the nature of being human, the circle knows more. The circle is a form that has been able to withstand the imperfections of human interaction and survive tremendous social shifts. I believe this on both experience and faith: experience, because I have been in circles at moments of searing vulnerability and high confrontation and the circles have held me; faith, because the circle once held human society together for over thirty thousand years. This is a period six times longer than the rise and fall of Second Culture. During the Age of the Circle, we evolved from Paleolithic cave dwellers to citizens in societies as sophisticated as Minoan Crete.[7] The circle was able to help us encompass that much change.

---

[7] Many scholars and sources document this period. See any of the writings of Marija Gimbutas, and begin exploring from there.

This Third Culture is not a country we visit, or a formula already devised. You and I will choose what Third Culture is. We will set the context. One circle at a time, we will decide what Third Culture looks like and how it acts toward its citizens.

Third Culture is an interpersonal practice. It is the practice of learning how to behave with respect toward each other, toward our earthly resources, and toward Spirit. When we change how we interpret and interact with the circumstances and people right around us, we create Third Culture. Want to be in Third Culture? Then let us begin by radically changing how we behave. Don't blame me; talk with me. Don't withdraw from me; step toward me. Don't shun me; embrace me. Don't sue me; mediate with me. Don't assume; question. Don't let our difference blind us to our commonality. Who knows what risks we will take if we are asked, if the task is explained clearly, if our contribution is valued, if we can count on each other. Even the smallest child responds to the challenge of contribution when s/he is relied upon. Even the most outcast member of society has something of value to offer the whole.

Culture has always been created by taking new social risks. It has always been scary to step out of our isolated journeys into the circle of firelight, to show up in the company of strangers, to stand there and ask for entrance, or to offer it. Our hearts race with adrenaline: "Will we have the courage to see each other? Will we have the courage to see the world?" The risks we have the opportunity to take in the twenty-first century are based on the risks human beings took thirty thousand years ago in First Culture. We are not different from our ancestors; they are still here, coded inside us. They are—I thoroughly believe—cheering us on.

If there was something in the air
If there was something in the wind
If there was something in the trees or bushes
That could be pronounced
and once was overheard by animals
Let this Sacred Knowledge
be returned to us again.

ATHARVA-VEDA

CHAPTER 3

The Sacred as Center
in Everyday Life

For the circle to hold steady, there needs to be an understood authority that resides within the circle, a source that all members petition for counsel. If this authority is retained and personified by any person, the circle turns into a triangle: Someone becomes the chief, the leader, the guru, the boss, while others become the followers, the workers, the compliant or rebellious subservients. On the other hand, if authority is held as a spiritual concept, the circle can remain intact, operating as a peer group of people who choose to imbue the center with their vision of the whole and pay careful attention to how this shared vision guides the course of their interactions, determines their tasks, and watches over the life of the group.

Imagine a circle where the entire group has committed itself to problem solving and accomplishment, rather than positioning for power. The group works together to define what the problem really is, or what really needs to be accomplished, and puts this challenge out for all to work on in a setting where each person alternately assumes moments of leadership and acquiesces to group wisdom.

When authority in the circle is shared in this manner, it provides a way for us to make decisions and take action based on personal consciousness and responsiveness to Higher Knowing. In such a circle, we combine traditional form and ritual with practical problem-solving skills and organizational models that create a new amalgam.

Imagine a circle with a clearly defined intention and agreements that keep people focused on the task at hand. When a circle meets with clear guidelines for group respect, a sense of social, emotional, and spiritual health is set in place. Imagine an available process of mediation and negotiation. Imagine not being shamed or blamed. Imagine being supported in the actions we take.

The tradition of the circle maintains a respectful structure for relating to each member that can greatly increase the productivity of meetings, draw out full participation, and fulfill the group's need for bonding.

Imagine a circle where someone calls for a moment of silence, or a stretch break, or reminds people to realign with the purpose of the meeting by focusing on the symbols that have been placed in the center. Imagine being listened to with respect because the entire group believes that any one of its members may bring forth the needed wisdom.

For the interpersonal structure of the circle to be successfully maintained by participants, the center of the circle must serve as a symbol of common ground where the highest intention of the group is represented. And this center must be imbued with authority. Each of us on the rim in some way gestures our willingness to petition the center for guidance, and to wait for guidance to become clear.

The Authentic Gesture

The symbolism of the center can be simple and still be profoundly significant. I have seen staff groups put copies of their company goals into the center. I have seen couples put their wedding rings in the center. I have seen impromptu circles where each person puts one thing from their pockets in the center. What is essential, for the center to hold, is that you and I understand how to make an authentic spiritual gesture. In our mechanized Western culture, this is not something we are taught how to do.

Most of us are taught a "religion," which contains many gestures that have arisen from a particular tradition: kneeling, bowing, or standing to pray; wearing special garments and adornments; making signs—from the sign of the cross to the gentle bow that accompanies the Hindu greeting *namasté.* Religion incorporates the spiritual gesture, but if your religious training was anything like mine, what is not taught is the internal spiritual connection between oneself and the Sacred that gives the gesture its significance. In other words, an authentic spiritual gesture cannot be offered unless we have an authentic relationship with Spirit.[1] We cannot imbue the center of the circle with the strength to hold us unless we know how to shift our perception of where power lies, and how power is to be utilized between ourselves.

Several years ago I was in a circle of women and men when highly charged feelings erupted and disturbed our planned task. It became obvious that the group could not continue until we had found a respectful way to acknowledge these feelings and hear each other out. Stuck in anger and confusion, and not knowing what else to do, we took a break and met again after supper. The circle had fractured earlier in the day as people had gotten into the excitement and momentum of our task and the inherent differences between us began to emerge as conflict. Even though we had started the meeting by creating a visual center representing the gift each of us brought to the group, we had become caught in the pace of discussion and decision making and unconsciously disendowed the center of its potency. When we began to struggle, there was no place to go but into our usual ego stance.

This was our agreement that evening: We would sit in near dark-

---

[1] In this text, I use the word *Sacred* or *Spirit* to mean the Divine—which may be interpreted in whatever way is comfortable to the reader. I use the word *spirit* or *spiritual* to mean the energy that flows from the Divine and rises up within us from this source. The phrase "sacred center" refers to the consecrated space where each person can put trust in the presence of Spirit and draw on spiritual energy to sustain him/herself in the process of the circle. There is no particular religious or spiritual point of view implied. The purpose of this language is to offer the broadest possible inclusivity. The nature of the circle's center will reflect the nature of the group; the vocabulary in which the center is invoked will reflect the vocabulary of the group. This usage becomes obvious in various examples presented throughout the book.

ness by the light of one candle. We would sit with eyes closed, in silence. We would place a feather in the center, and when someone felt moved to offer a story from his/her own experience, she/he could reach for the feather and speak. We sat a long time. No one broke the silence. Finally, someone began to sing the old camp song that goes, "Peace I ask of thee, O River . . . ," and we all joined in.

We sang until our voices were steady and harmonies began to emerge. The song restored the sacred center to our circle, and once the center was restored we were able to drop our defenses and speak our vulnerable stories into the receptive half darkness of listening peers.

When we sit in circle and hold both the integrity of our self on the rim and attentiveness to spiritual purpose in the middle, we will be assisted in understanding what we need to do next. Perhaps the biggest surprise to people coming into circle for the first time is the necessity to shift into a slower pace, so that our carefulness has time to be present.

In this circle of women and men, silence and the song allowed each of us to make our spiritual gesture: to surrender a piece of our autonomy to the circle itself so that the circle, in turn, could contain the integrity of our individual feelings.

There is a "wobble" that always occurs in human relationships.[2] With this wobble our sense of direction and our purpose are lost, the communion of coming together is broken, and we face the differences each of us has carried into the group. One real gift of circle is its tenacious ability to hold us in a container of combined social and spiritual contract while we work through the wobbles to genuine community. Most of the rest of this book illustrates and explains how a methodology of circle that will be introduced in the next chapter as PeerSpirit circling can help us manage these wobbles differently. But in order to learn how to take our place at the rim of the circle, we need first to understand how to honor center.

The psychologist Alfred Adler used to say, "To live well is to cooperate." Circle takes this one step further: *To live well is to cooperate and to heed the impulses of spiritual altruism as they become clear.* To call in the

---

[2] Thank you to Rachel Bagby for introducing me to the word *wobble* and the concept behind it.

potency of the circle challenges everything we have been taught about power. To move self-assuredly within the circle, we need to have a way of personally turning to spiritual guidance. We need to be able to hold our own authority and to acknowledge that our authority springs from a spiritual, rather than egotistical, source.

Over time, calling on a spiritual source changes how we perceive events and how we react to them. As soon as we stop to ask what Spirit wants in any situation, we create a receptivity for spiritual guidance. In circles, such as the one I wrote of on page 43, getting into conflict and confusion is commonplace; what was uncommon was how we got out. Because we could agree to maintain silence until we felt spiritually directed to speak, we were able to find our way back to center and collectively ask: "What does Spirit want to have happen here, and how may I/we help?"

To ask such a question and sit in waiting readiness for the answer is a form of spiritual ritual. And for us to even notice the need for spiritual intervention, we have to be moving at a slow enough pace so that we can listen, and respond. This is the pace of ritual.

The Loss and Reclaiming of Ritual

African spiritual teacher Malidoma Somé challenges Westerners to see the speed of modern life as a form of spiritual abandonment, and blames the pace at which we live for the loss of the sacred. "When you slow down," Somé writes, "you begin to discover . . . a silent awareness of what it is you do not want to look at: the anger of nature within us, the anger of the gods, the anger of the ancestors or the spirit world. . . . Thus speed is a way to prevent ourselves from having to deal with something we do not want to face. . . . To be able to face our fears we must remember how to perform ritual. To remember how to perform ritual, we must slow down."[3]

Somé's prayer for us in the industrialized world is that we slow down enough to find the indigenous person within, to go in search of this archetypal figure residing in our collective unconscious and draw

---

[3] Malidoma Somé, *Ritual, Power, Healing and Community* (New York: Penguin, 1998).

out his/her forgotten, but retrievable, wisdom. If we are going to arc the circle forward from First Culture to create a Third, we also need to arc forward our abilities to connect directly to the Sacred. It is not "going to church" that Somé is talking about, though formal religion may be an extremely important foundation for how a number of people in the mainstream of the Western world frame the Sacred in the everyday.

When we look at indigenous life, instead of institutionalized religion we find that the Sacred comes into the everyday through commonly practiced rituals. When indigenous women rise and prepare food, their actions are often accompanied by prescribed chants and prayers that thank the grain for growing and ask for this bounty to continue. They are taught to set out spirit plates, and feed the unseen presences that are also part of the family and tribe. The men may purify themselves before a hunt, to be worthy of taking life, and thank an animal for its willingness to sacrifice its life for the lives of the people. The children are draped in amulets that contain powerful medicine to guard their well-being, and as they come of age they are initiated through time-honored, often elaborate rites of passage.

In an intact indigenous community every member is taught essential spiritual gestures upon which the survival of the group depends. Each person is expected to take responsibility for performing the spiritual gestures that maintain the connection to the Sacred in their personal and communal lives. In Somé's West African Dagara tradition, as in many other indigenous traditions, individual and group responsibility is seen as one web. If an individual fails to perform his or her ritual role in maintaining the cosmic order that holds the life of the tribe together, the whole order suffers. This sense of responsibility for collective spiritual integrity is a nearly incomprehensible thought to the Western mind. "Do I know if my neighbors are performing the rituals that help sustain my life? Do they know if I am performing mine?"

Human beings everywhere make ritual spontaneously and continuously. Even when we have forgotten its original purpose, ritual rises to fill some deeply felt void. Several years ago, while I was preparing to move from Minnesota, the lease ran out on my apartment and my brother and his family offered to take me in for several months. And so we did something that is seldom done anymore in middle America: We shared a household and melded two very different family routines. As I was working on developing practices of the circle at the time, I kept looking at the rituals of our everyday lives and the potential connection to the Sacred hidden within them.

Every weekday, my brother, Carl, like millions of other hardworking men, rises early and lets out the dog, makes a cup of coffee, lights a cigarette, and leaves for work. In a sacred context, he would do the same things with intention. Letting out the dog would grant him the opportunity to greet the day in a ritualized manner. From his first cup of liquid he would offer a libation, a drop spilled on the earth in thankfulness, then swallow the rest as a sign that he accepts the gift of the day. His drive to work would be a time of reflection, to make holy smoke and set his course for the day's activities. He could call upon spiritual power to help him make good decisions, listen wisely, and practice fair business based on spiritual principles.

As Carl leaves the house, my sister-in-law, Colleen, like millions of other busy women, rises and showers, and brings in the newspaper to read at the kitchen table, providing herself with a half hour of quiet before her day of work and mothering begins. In a sacred context, she would bathe as a rite of cleansing, washing off the old life, taking up the life of the new day. Her morning reading would offer spiritual insight for the work awaiting her. She would feel herself in a lineage of women, reciting the blessings and following rituals learned from her mother and grandmothers.

At seven-thirty, my niece, Erin, like millions of other schoolchildren, is wakened by her dog clambering over the covers, exuberantly licking her face. In a sacred context, the dog might be seen as a messenger of the day's possibilities. We elders of the extended family—for it would not be so strange to have an extra aunt in residence—would gather around to help her recall dreams and teach her to treat these stories and images as important. Before sending her off to school, we would recite prayers of protection, and help her see the studies of even a fourth-grader as relevant preparation for taking her place in the community.

Buried deep beneath our Second Culture conditioning, many of us sense the potential sacredness of ritual encoded in what we do, but there is no context for mentioning it, and so we muddle through. We are busy people, living at too fast a speed. In the evenings we ask each other, "Did you have a good day?" but what do we mean by this question? We have forgotten.

In group after group, individual by individual, you tell me you catch yourself in the middle of the day staring out the window wondering what you have been doing all these years. You tell me you hate your job, but you need the money. You tell me you are lonely. You tell me you aren't sure you're really a grown-up because there is no rite of passage that helps you feel that way. Maybe you'll get married. Maybe you'll get divorced. You tell me your husband is in the den watching war videos, looking for something he cannot name. Or you tell me your wife's side of the bedroom looks like a library of the occult, stocked with books on angels and goddesses, Tarot cards, drums and rattles, and candles. You are not privy to each other's thoughts, and have forgotten how to talk intimately somewhere along the line. You tell me that it is midnight when you get the paperwork done, or the laundry folded, and you still have dishes to wash before bed so that you can get up early and get everyone out the door for another day. You tell me you don't know what kind of relationship you want, that all the rules have shifted and your passion feels like a small, unturned stone in the pit of your belly. Nothing moves you. You stare at the body count on television and forget whether this is programming or news. You are afraid of your deadness. You are afraid of your aliveness. You eat too much or not enough. You wake in the middle of the night and the only breath you hear is your own. Sometimes you feel like screaming. Sometimes you put your head on the windowsill and pray for help.

What we need at these moments when we are raw and vulnerable is some way to begin searching for the gesture that will restore us to spiritual relationship.

In the summer of 1991, a Native American man came to participate in a writing course I was teaching in northern Minnesota. Wolf struggled to find the safety he needed to share his experiences, to believe he would be heard.[4] After the first session he phoned me at my room. "If you are going to be my teacher," he said, "I want to approach you

---

[4] The name Wolf is a pseudonym.

in the traditional way. I need to bring you a pouch of tobacco. Do you know what this means among my people?"

I had read about Native American traditions and had several friends in the Native American community in Minneapolis. "I think I understand," I told him. "Tobacco is a sign of respect, that you come for teaching. If I accept the tobacco, it means I take your request seriously." I expected a little bag of Bull Durham, the kind of offering I had made myself when approaching a Native American teacher. He brought me an elaborately beaded deerskin pouch.

The day he left the class, we stood together outside. "I want you to continue to carry the pouch," Wolf said. "I have received what I needed." At first I was hesitant, but I stood with him in the daylight and listened as deeply as I could. "If you keep the pouch, it comes with an obligation. Every day you must go outside and pray. The pouch needs to be taken out to greet each day."

Now he was my teacher. I thought of my usual life, sitting at the computer and writing to the hum of the air conditioner. I thought of Minnesota winters, when I dressed in wool socks and sweatpants and avoided going outdoors for days at a time. Every day was not an easy commitment to make. "You do not do this for yourself," he said. "You do it for the pouch, for what the pouch carries."

"When I'm outside," I asked him, "then what? What do I do?"

"You open the pouch and sprinkle a little tobacco as an offering. You say your prayers." What prayers? I wondered. The Lord's Prayer? Or "Now I lay me down to sleep"? Wolf must have seen the confusion in my face. "The pouch will teach you to pray," he assured me.

It has.

For me, the ability to make an authentic spiritual gesture has grown out of the gift of the prayer pouch. Every day I go outside, no matter what the weather, look at the day, and pray for blessings and guidance. Into a quiet bit of morning I whisper, *"Creator of All, thank you for this day."* Some days I'm at home praying in my own yard; some days I'm on the road. *"Thank you for the sun that rises and sets, for the air that I breathe, the food that I eat, the sustenance that You provide."* Sometimes I'm standing by a struggling sapling potted into concrete on a city street. *"May all that I do today contribute to the healing of the world, and may my heart be open enough to allow the world to contribute to my healing."* Some days I have the luxury of wild surroundings. *"Bless the earth and all her creatures.*

Bless the loved one and the stranger. Keep us safe through times of danger. Make us ready. Hold us steady." And then I stand still and simply breathe in the morning air.

After this preamble, I speak the names of my beloveds and ask direction and holding in all our concerns. I ask for guidance in the issues of my own life. I pray for peace, for the gathering of our kind that we may make the leap before us. This ritual takes about ten minutes and changes my relationship to the entire day.

Prayer is a practice in choice. Every day I must choose to follow this ritual or ignore it; there are days I do ignore it—out of haste, carelessness, or irritation. Sometimes it's midafternoon and I notice some foundation is missing in my day, and so I stop and go pray. Sometimes it is midnight and I open the window and speak to the moon, because I cannot say good-bye to the day until I have said hello. Through this practice I am learning to experience Somé's understanding of the one web: I feel responsible to the community in reciting these prayers. Some mystery counts on me to take these moments and hold the Sacred in the midst of the secular world. If I don't fulfill my obligations, a strand in the web is torn. This obligation is not something I was taught in church school, it's *older* than church; I just know.

I have friends who meditate an hour a day, and friends who sing in the church choir, and friends who walk the labyrinth. I don't think it matters what we choose as the ritual with which we hold on to the center of our lives, only that we choose something that honors Spirit and has meaning for us, and that we do it consistently.

Spiritual centering is not the practice of perfection—it is the practice of persistence. Again and again, despite our distraction, we return to that gesture which reopens our relationship with Spirit. This is the private core of a spirit-based life: little moments when we stand heart-naked and say to Spirit, "Well, okay, then—I'm back." The ancestors sing within us and we remember who we are.

The spiritual gesture is not in conflict with religious practice or training. All religious people have, I hope, discovered for themselves a core authenticity that makes their religion personally meaningful. There is a centeredness that radiates from those who have found the authentic gesture within their religious tradition. Read, for example, the writings of Mother Teresa, and one is struck by the absolute realness of the relational presence of Jesus. Because the connection is open and available to her, the gestures of Roman Catholicism are imbued with spiritual meaning. And while speaking, writing, and practicing her spirituality within a churched form, her understanding of the one web of life is obvious. I have spoken here of finding an authentic gesture outside formal religion because I believe it can occur either integrated into religion or independent of religion, and I want to offer everyone permission to find their way.

When we have rooted ourselves in a meaningful spiritual gesture, we have begun the journey of rooting ourselves in our life circumstances. Some mornings in my prayer space I have intense flashes of how my life fits into the web of life. My spirituality anchors me into the larger pattern and roots me in place.

Becoming Indigenous

The word *indigenous* means "belonging in place"; "native." At the beginning of the twenty-first century, an increasing number of people are on the move around the globe, either voluntarily shifting in search of better life conditions or dislocated by political upheaval or natural disaster. When Malidoma Somé wishes that we will find the indigenous person within, I think we must interpret this as finding our rootedness, honoring the lineage we come from, reclaiming what is native about human spirituality in all its variations.

To learn how to be an indigenous person in the midst of Second Culture requires a shift from letting our lives be moved along at the pace of the Machine to insisting that our lives incorporate the pace of our origins—the pace of nature. Somé states, "Indigenous people are indigenous because there are no machines between them and their gods. There are no machines barring the door to the spirit world where one can enter in and listen to what is going on within at a deep level, participating in the vibration of Nature."[5] I have the good fortune of knowing someone who understands this act of listening to the vibration of nature: my partner in the evolution of circle work, Ann Linnea.

---

[5] Malidoma Somé, *Ritual, Power, Healing and Community* (New York: Penguin, 1998).

When I first met Ann, she was a woman in deep transition. Shaken by the swift death of her closest friend, Betty, she and her colleague, Paul, decided to fulfill their longing for midlife adventure by taking a kayak trip around 1,200 shoreline miles of Lake Superior—the largest and most dangerously changeable inland body of water on the planet. They honed their paddling skills for four years, and finally shoved off in four- to seven-foot seas from Duluth, Minnesota, on a June day in 1992, both admitting they did not fully understand what was driving them on this journey.

Ann has always been a person who relies on nature for her deepest learning. In the aftershock of Betty's death, it made sense to her to go into nature for healing and guidance about what to do with her own midlife dilemmas: "I was deeply aware that my leave-taking from Duluth meant letting go of more than just special people. I was a woman raised within solid, Protestant, midwestern values. They had served me and limited me. I knew, vaguely, that I was approaching the end of some kind of life cycle, and I was hoping the trip would teach me what that was and where I might be going."[6]

In spite of her years as a naturalist and educator, Ann did not begin her journey knowing how to move at the pace of nature. Paul and Ann had carved out exactly sixty-five days of summer vacation—when Paul's wife and Ann's husband would be available to care for their children and households. The adventurers needed to resupply, and so they set up rendezvous dates with family and friends at various points around the lake. This schedule, which made sense from the perspective of planning, sometimes forced them into a grueling pace and a dangerous position once nature took hold of the journey.

In the coldest, stormiest summer in a century, Ann and Paul fought the lake for survival. Every morning, unless they were trapped by wind and storm, they got up at dawn, broke camp, and headed out in seventeen-foot kayaks to brave the lake. Hour after hour they paddled for their lives. At twelve hundred miles, divided by an average speed of three miles an hour, their journey equaled roughly four hundred paddling hours.

These endless hours of paddling gave Ann the opportunity to review her whole life: to revisit scenes, choices, relationships, decisions,

<hr>

[6] Ann Linnea, *Deep Water Passage* (New York: Little, Brown and Company, 1995), p. 6.

and consequences. She underwent a degree of mental clearing that few people accomplish. Sometimes Paul was a quarter mile away; sometimes they disappeared from each other's sight in the long troughs of waves; they took days of solo time. Alone on the lake, removed from all the machinery of modern life, totally responsible for her physical, mental, emotional, and spiritual survival, Ann entered into direct connection with the Sacred.

Writing about her discovery of a lichen-covered native stone artifact on a cold, buggy night, Ann says: "In this secret place beyond the reach of mosquitoes and night chill, I began to glimpse my life purpose, my connectedness to all things past and present. It was a fleeting glance. . . . But I know I saw it."[7]

While I carried my pouch outdoors, day by day doing the best I could to make myself available to prayer, Ann opened her connection to the Sacred through the heroic journey. When, by design or happenstance, a major event propels any of us into tremendous growth, it attracts all our attention, as well as the attention of the larger community.

Looking back, Ann says, "The lake trip was extremely catalytic, and it gave me a story for explaining change. As I left my marriage, moved from Duluth, got more deeply involved in teaching circle, I could say, 'I'm doing what the lake told me I needed to do.' And other people could say, 'Well, of course she's changed—look what she's lived through.' But the grand experience is only temporary Grace.

"The paddler, the mountain climber, the cancer survivor—each comes back into the framework of our lives charged with the responsibility to hold on to our spiritual awakenings. As life returns to its ordinary patterns, we are faced with countless decisions about how to sustain connection and change."

In the daily challenge to sustain spiritual connection and change, those who live through the heroic journey and those who live through incremental openings to Spirit find their commonality. "Oh, I see," I said to Ann after her return, "I went through the same kind of process writing *Life's Companion* that you went through paddling the lake."

"And what was that?"

---

[7] Ibid., p. 78.

"I had to allow myself to be stripped down," I replied. "I had to humble myself before the task, stretch myself beyond what I knew how to do. Writing a book may not strike anyone else as dangerous or heroic, but to write about the spiritual quest, I had to enter the quest. I pleaded with God for help, sentence by sentence, just as you pleaded for safety, paddle stroke by paddle stroke."

By the time Ann came off the lake, she was, in her words, "as close to becoming a woman of primitive culture as a white, middle-class woman could be in the twentieth century." Years later, she is still often moved to tears by the beauty of nature. She is a single mom finishing raising her children, a moderate athlete grateful for her health and stamina, a gentle-hearted, steadfast teacher, and a hardworking business partner. In the midst of the same kind of busyness we all struggle with, Ann fiercely maintains her connection to wildness because it is the source that feeds her whole life.

I do not need to find a group of isolated aboriginal people in order to understand how to live on the planet—I see our ability to retrieve this knowledge alive in Ann. This retrieval is alive in a woman who grew up in the same ways I did, in the same cultural mix, going through school in another Minnesota town a hundred miles down the road from my childhood home. I see that it is possible to reconnect with our First Culture way of knowing, and to carry that connection from the wild world to the human one.

Since coming off the lake, Ann has chosen to bring her hard-earned knowledge about the sacred in all life into circle work. She is very clear about the source of her dedication: "The wild realm is counting on humans," she says, "to come back into meaningful community with one another and with it. I believe the circle is teaching us how to take our place in the natural order."

Circle as Spiritual Practice

Having worked to create a sacred center at the core of our lives, we may move outward carrying that centeredness each step of the way. The children are scurrying to make lunches before the school bus comes; we do our best to tuck calmness into each lunch sack.

We're stuck in rush-hour traffic and refrain from blowing the horn; instead we turn on the classical music station, or listen to calming tapes, or use the silence to make a mental transition from home to work and back. The boss comes in to say that a report is due twenty-four hours earlier than we thought; we submerge our desire to curse, and say we'll do the best we can. Calmness begets calmness; panic begets panic. Each thought we have, each action we take has the potential to create a situation differently.

We choose. We choose what carries energy in our lives. We choose what we pay attention to. We choose what mental and emotional impulses and responses drive us. There's a sign on a Post-It placed over my writing desk, and placed also by the telephone, and also on the bathroom mirror, that asks the question: "Into whose hands do I commend my spirit, thought by thought, action by action, in this moment?"[8]

To claim our connection to Spirit on a daily basis is a radical act in our secular culture. It is an act that both liberates us to live in dramatically new and creative ways and pushes us to find like-minded companions. Circle itself becomes a spiritual practice—a celebration with others of the beauty and wisdom of living the sacred life. And as we remember that in each of us resides direct connection to spiritual guidance, we can claim our personal authority to serve as coleaders on the rim of circle.

---

[8] Thanks to Carolyn Myss for framing a version of this question in her work as a medical intuitive and teacher.

Community.
Somewhere, there are people
to whom we can speak with passion
without having the words catch in our throats.
Somewhere a circle of hands will open to receive us,
eyes will light up as we enter, voices will celebrate with us
whenever we come into our own power.
Community means strength that joins our strength
to do the work that needs to be done.
Arms to hold us when we falter.
A circle of healing. A circle of friends.
Someplace where
we can be free.

STARHAWK, *Dreaming the Dark*

CHAPTER 4

Holding the Rim

From center we must move to the edge. The skills of circle begin with removing ourselves and our self-interests from the middle of any group. When we come into a room and rearrange the seating, it causes us to rearrange our expectations also. Creating the space for council is the way indigenous peoples have come together since time immemorial. Moving our bodies from rows to circles, and our self-interests from the center to the edge, enables each of us to reclaim our innate knowledge of circle and carry it forward consciously.

This is our challenge: to rediscover this innate knowing of circle and to fit that knowing into the realities of the modern world. Though the circle has been marginalized to survive in Western culture, within native traditions it has remained the ceremonial core that has held their lineage together. In recent years a number of indigenous teachers and visionaries in the Western Hemisphere (and I suspect this is happening globally) have started releasing the teachings of the sacred circle, as held in their traditions, in valiant attempts to help rebalance the world.

There are a number of native myths that speak of the breaking and reunification of the circle. In Hopi oral tradition, the story says that once the truth was a whole body of knowledge known by all beings— people, animals, stones, plants; there was no separation. Then an imbalance came. The circle was broken and the whole truth divided. Each clan was given responsibility for a portion of the truth. They were instructed to care for this truth until such time as they could remember their wholeness and reunite the circle.

Of course, after a period of time, the clans forgot that they carried only a fraction of truth and began to think they carried the whole truth. They began hoarding it, protecting it, trying to impose it on others. Their spirituality became religions that divided them and caused disrespect for other ways of life. They began dividing up the land and claiming the clans of the animals, plants, and stones for themselves. Scarcity began to dwell among the people. Masala, the messenger of the Hopi people, prophesied that there would come an eleventh hour when all people would have to choose: to remain divided and destroy themselves and the planet, or to reunite and restore the balance of life. Certainly we are at that hour.

And so the circle is spontaneously arising once more, being reintroduced by a growing number of teacher-carriers and practiced by growing numbers of people. In the early 1990s, after Ann came back from her transformative lake journey and I came back from my awakening at Women's Camp, we joined these pioneering efforts and began exploring the applications of circle. Many similarities exist in how people are verbalizing and presenting the revival of the circle. We travel and study and sit in circle with as many carriers of this form as we can.

We donate our efforts to the reunification of the clans and the recognition of the need to bring our partial truths back into wholeness/holiness. And we honor those who are carrying the circle—some are named throughout this text, some are listed in the "Resources" section in the back, but every day more people are called by the circle to bring it forth through their own work and language. The circle is a body of knowledge in great flux and dynamism. Once we have identified our longing to simply sit down and face each other, speak honestly and listen openly, we see opportunities for and examples of the circle everywhere.

As Ann and I and our circle colleagues have clarified our vision of the piece of this work we feel called to carry, we have evolved a structure for the circle that is peer-led and spirit-centered. We call this structure the PeerSpirit circle.

The basic experiment in PeerSpirit circling is to invite groups of people to become self-facilitating. PeerSpirit is an all-leader circle that counts on all members to assume increments of leadership, according to their skills and the needs of the moment. PeerSpirit is a form of collective accountability that trusts all members to share responsibility for the functioning of the group on every level, from interpersonal respect to accomplishing the work that binds the group together. PeerSpirit encourages people to relinquish part of our commonly held autonomy to the center, so that all members may rely on spiritual energy—collective group synergy—to act as a force of cohesion and guidance.

This is a tremendous leap of faith on the part of enculturated Second Culture citizens. We have been trained to look for or assume leadership, but not to share it; to take responsibility or deny it, but not to hold ourselves accountable; and to separate our spiritual/religious practice, should we have one, from the ways we interact in most spheres of our lives, and from what we expect as support in secular settings. Nevertheless, we find that this experiment works. We are inspired constantly by the courage that arises in circle, and humbled to contribute to the evolution of an idea.

The word *PeerSpirit* was given to us—it is a name that emerged out of the work itself. We offer this word with the hope that it will come to represent a standard of conduct in which people may trust that certain principles, practices, and agreements are understood and applied within the circle.[1]

In 1994 Ann and I decided to merge our respective careers to form a business dedicated to helping people call circles. We moved literally

---

[1] The word *PeerSpirit* is used two ways in this book. Primarily, it names the methodology being offered throughout this book, and *in this usage* it is given freely to all who are interested in exploring this form of circle. People who are calling a PeerSpirit circle are encouraged to adapt and apply this methodology when using the name "PeerSpirit"; people being invited to join a PeerSpirit circle are encouraged to look and to see that this structure is in place, and is being utilized.

PeerSpirit™ . . . In Service to the Circle is also the name of our business, located and registered in the state of Washington. In this usage, you will see a trademark bug on stationery and business papers. The primary work of the business is to educate people in PeerSpirit methodology through written materials, seminars, and consulting provided by ourselves and other colleagues.

from the center to the edge—from the central state of Minnesota to the coastal state of Washington—conscious that we were carrying the wisdom of four-plus decades of centering out to the edge for new growth and learning. We decided our business, also named PeerSpirit, needed to be located where land meets sea and Canada meets the United States.

Moving to the Edge

In March of that year, Ann and I stopped at a rest stop near the Washington border, nearly 1,800 miles of snow-covered mountains and frozen prairies behind us, to make ceremony in a small grove of trees. It was a Friday afternoon and we were following the sun through changeable weather, watching storms on the horizon sweep toward the interstate, envelop us in rain and hail, and move on. The sunset was brilliant under black clouds. Rainbows sprouted to the southeast, a double arc that seemed to extend all the way back, back, back to Minnesota, and all the way forward to the Pacific coast. We had driven under this sky bridge, happy and stunned, and decided to pull the car over in order to cross this line with intention. I had the tobacco pouch, and we each carried symbols of what we were leaving behind. We walked among trees. Willow, our Welsh corgi, was rooting in the tall, dry grass. Ann's children were still in Duluth and would fly out a week later.

Third Culture is created by *how* we carry on our daily lives. If we want to live in a culture that validates the circle, then Ann and I had better sit in council when we are crossing the border. If we want to live in a culture that honors the sacred in the everyday, then we had better get out of the car and show our respect. So we prayed—two middle-aged women in wool sweaters, jeans, and hiking boots—that our days would be filled with sacred presence, that we would find new community, that we would go through the rigors of resettlement with confidence in our choice of new place. We poured a libation upon the ground and left small trinkets at the roots of a tree. We called friends in California and shouted exuberantly into their answering machine, "We're here!" But of course it takes a while to get anywhere. Especially, it takes a while to create Third Culture.

As I unpacked in my rented house on Whidbey Island, I spread out an altar on a corner shelf beneath windows where the sun and rain reflected on all that had been gathered in the journey here. And day by day, coming up from adventures of discovery on the beach, I laid out a circle of stones at the entrance. I could not come in or go out without stepping through the circle.

In April, a month after arriving, I invited to dinner some of the people who had helped us make this move. My cousins Bill and Donna; neighbors Sally and Bob, who'd hosted us during house-hunting expeditions; our friend Laurie, whom I'd met at Women's Camp; my mother, Connie, visiting from Vancouver Island; and Ann. We ate supper and chatted in twos and threes as the pace of the evening meandered comfortably along. And then, after dessert, I asked if people were willing to sit in council. "We've just made a tremendous passage," I told them. "And I wonder if we might hold circle for a few minutes to honor the passages in all of our lives." I brought a rattle from the spread-out altar, introduced the idea of a talking piece, and suggested for our topic that we share something about change.

Gathered around me that evening were mostly people I didn't yet know well, though our connections seemed solid and comfortable. I wanted to thank them in a way that would convey the spirit of my gratitude and would allow us to glimpse how our relationships might develop. Inviting sacred center into the evening and putting ourselves at the rim seemed a good idea.

We had met Sally when she came to a circle in Taos. She had returned to Whidbey and invited women from her church into a writing circle. Over and over she remarked, "I can barely remember my life before circle. The externals have remained the same . . . but inside I feel like I've turned into a new person."

I imagine that her husband, Bob, had watched this change with a mixture of support and apprehension. Dinner was the first time we'd met, and earlier in the evening he'd greeted us teasingly, "Ah, the phantom circlers are real!" There was a smile on his face, and we shook hands warmly, but as we dimmed the lights and brought candles to the center space amid the circled chairs, I did not know how either of the men would react or what they were thinking.

Watching my cousin Bill in the circle, I remembered us as children. When I was seven and he was twelve, he'd played his violin for me when I visited his home in Missoula, Montana. When I was thirteen and he was eighteen, I had a crush on him and he sweetly took me on my first date. I see that Baldwin stamp to his features, which my brother and I also carry. And as I notice his square hands holding the talking piece, I remember our grandpa's hands, and my father's, his mother's. We belong to a lineage that has good, solid values and traditions coded within it—which we must now go beyond if we are to respond creatively to the challenges facing us and the next generation.

The particulars of what we said that evening in the heart of council have long since melded into the stream of many circles: The importance is that it happened. We had moved two thousand miles, were starting over in the middle of two professional lives, were uprooting two children in our wake. We needed more than symbolism. And so to dinner came this collection of ordinary people—a child psychologist, a teacher, a geological engineer, an office manager, a former school board member, a piano teacher, a naturalist, a writer. Awkwardly, but willingly, we formed a circle that included family, friends, and bare acquaintances; a circle that included people practiced in this form and people new to this form. And by the end of the evening I could see: The middle had come to the edge, and we would be able to continue our work.

The Circle as Social Practice

Just as we need to remember how to make an authentic spiritual gesture that imbues the center of the circle with authority, many times we need help to remember how to behave in respectful ways that bind the rim. There is no intent to shame or blame anyone in this sentence. Much of our lack of respect is unconscious and unintentional modeling of the disrespect and power plays that have become the social norm in Second Culture. It is a common cultural idiom that achieving the goal is more important than how you treat people along the way, and it is often said—almost admiringly—about our leaders, sports figures, and other heroes that they got where they are by "taking no prisoners" or by negotiating a minefield of discarded relationships. Western culture is a warrior culture. We are a conquering political system, an economic dominator. Implying that how you treat people is equally important as what is accomplished challenges the supposition of "winning at all costs." Overconcern with the quality of interpersonal relationships has been considered weak, effeminate, and ineffectual.

These attitudes may be shifting, but they are deeply ingrained. Perhaps the greatest work the circle can do in the Western world is to teach us how to combine and balance the need for respect and the drive for accomplishment. There is a great hunger in the midst of our fast-paced life to feel in charge again of the ways we treat—and are treated by—each other, and to create settings that honor our contributions.

People rush into business and faculty and committee meetings (and sometimes even to the family dinner table) still talking on cellular phones or responding to beepers; they carry on side conversations that create alliances and rifts right in the faces of those being excluded; they gossip about the organization, its leaders, or members who are absent. People glance at the agenda, slap papers out on the table, go get coffee, leave and return, leave and return, until nobody's sure who is present or not. Finally someone looks at his watch and commands, "Let's get this ball rolling." And the free-for-all begins. This is disrespectful group process, even if it is the current social norm.

The circle as social practice asks us to be willing to arrive, to pay attention, to speak as clearly as we know how, and to help action and accomplishment arise out of the group. Angeles Arrien, in her work on the Fourfold Way, has distilled these social practices to four memorable phrases: Show up; pay attention; tell the truth; remain unattached to outcome. However, it's nearly impossible to show up at a meeting that never really gets called to order; impossible to pay attention within chaos and domination; impossible to speak clearly or tell the truth when nobody's listening; and impossible to remain unattached to outcome if outcome has already been determined by those in power or if the process is diverted away from accomplishment.

At its most basic, PeerSpirit circling is a framework for paying attention. No slides. No overheads. No fifty-page position papers full of charts and graphs. Just five or ten or fifteen people alone in a room, facing each other and the task that calls them together. Just a group of people, holding the balance between attention to task and attention to respect. A group of people admitting they will accept help as it becomes clear to them what they need. One hour, or two. No interruptions. A minute of silence going in and coming out. A few commonsense agreements binding how they treat each other. A shared intention. Imagine what we might get done. . . .

Once, at the beginning of a two-day training session where people had erupted into arguing about whether or not they needed structure, I grabbed a water pitcher from the conference table and tipped it, letting a trickle of liquid and ice cubes head for the carpeting.

"Hey! Watch out!" the man closest to me yelled, and pushed his water glass under the pitcher to catch the flow. I smiled and filled his glass. We had the group's full attention.

"Thank you," I said. "This is what we mean—the circle is social energy *contained*. The interpersonal structure of PeerSpirit is the glass; you and I are the water. The purpose of the principles, practices, and agreements is to provide a respectful social practice so we can decide what to do. Once the water—our energy—is contained, we can drink it, heat it or freeze it, wash in it, make a pot of coffee, make soup, but without the glass, all we have is a wet spot on the rug."

The suggestions for interpersonal structure that fill this chapter provide a kind of skeleton that shapes the circle and helps us understand the social practice involved. As much as possible, PeerSpirit is presented in terms that are culturally and spiritually neutral so that the culture and spirit indigenous to many different groups can flesh out the process in ways that seem comfortable and familiar.

I hope a person introduced to PeerSpirit in the workplace can understand this structure and apply it to call the circle at home or in his/her neighborhood. I hope a person who practices PeerSpirit within his/her family can adapt the structure to work, or church, or conflict resolution, such as the already explored example of Carol and John's school system. The intention of PeerSpirit is to serve as connective tissue, creating a confidence in self-governing and spirit-based communication between widely diverse groups. In many groups, this skeletal structure practically disappears. The purpose of the group is what remains, and yet, when wobbles occur, which they will, the members of the circle have agreements to call upon, and a container to hold them, so that they can come back to purpose and continue on.

The Three Principles of Circle

PeerSpirit is not a leaderless group: It is an all-leader group. The power in PeerSpirit arises from within the circle. As each member assumes and shares authority with the support of the whole, the circle functions as the basic unit of community.

Three principles serve as the foundation of PeerSpirit experience:

- rotating leadership
- sharing responsibility
- relying on Spirit

These are not new ideas. Twelve Step and other self-help groups meet with a rotating facilitator; committees and task forces share responsibility for the accomplishment of goals; and from the business prayer breakfast to Bible study groups to meditation retreats, people convene with acknowledged reliance on Spirit. PeerSpirit circling combines these elements and commits to bringing all three of them into a wide variety of mainstream settings.

Rotating leadership means that every person helps the circle function by assuming small increments of leadership. In PeerSpirit circling, leadership shifts moment by moment and task by task. Rotating leadership trusts that the resources to accomplish the circle's purpose exist within the group, and that the quality of experience is enhanced when many voices are heard.

For example, in a community task force exploring local food production, each member of the circle chooses one aspect of the issue to explore: supporting a local produce market, helping people learn organic gardening, changing patterns of land use, developing community garden plots, getting free produce to families in need, and so on. Each person facilitates the portion of the meeting focused on their topic, presenting their research, asking for help, soliciting the creativity of the group to consider what to do next.

Sharing responsibility means every person pays attention to what needs doing or saying next, and participates in doing their share. In PeerSpirit circling, responsibility also shifts moment by moment and task by task. Shared responsibility is based on the trust that someone will come forward to provide whatever the circle needs next: helping each other take action, calling for silence, or offering the next meeting space.

In the community food group, people share responsibility by cosupporting the issues they have collectively chosen to research and develop. They attend to each other's stress and busyness, as well as to their dedication—refusing to abandon each other to the workload that needs doing between meetings. They show up and help in each other's gardens, bring potluck desserts to the meetings, pass around research and recipes.

Relying on Spirit means that people perform simple ritual and consistent refocusing to acknowledge the highest intention of the group. The center of the circle literally and figuratively serves as sacred space, a place where everyone's commitment to cooperation dwells. And when we don't know what to do next, in circle it is appropriate to stop the action and create an environment in which people, each in his or her own way, commit themselves to asking for guidance. We grant ourselves permission to slow down, watch for what is needed, and see how we might do our part.

The food group opens with a minute of silence. A candle is lit in the center. The members create a "harvest center," which varies by meeting and season—offerings from their homes, symbols of their studies. They often use an edible talking piece—a carrot or celery stalk. They close with another moment of silence.

Forms of Council

In PeerSpirit, we use the word *council* to mean the verbal level of what is happening in circle. We ask the word *circle* to serve as an all-encompassing term referring to everything that is happening in a gathering—words, energy, and actions of people together. We call the circle to respectfully contain the council.

In PeerSpirit, we commonly use three forms of council: talking piece, conversation, and silence. These are introduced briefly here, and are illustrated in depth in the following chapters.

Talking piece council is a formal pattern of meeting. A talking piece is a designated object that is passed hand to hand and grants the holder of the piece the chance to speak without interruption. One person at a time has the floor while other members listen attentively. The purpose of using a talking piece is to guarantee that people are heard, or have the opportunity to be heard. The presence of a talking piece controls the impulse to pick up on what a person is saying, to interrupt with humor, sympathetic remarks, argument, commentary, or diverting questions. The first time a new group uses a talking piece, it raises our awareness of how customary it is for us to interrupt each other, consciously or unconsciously overpowering each other's words, instead of holding them within the container of the group and letting them sink in as individual contributions.

Talking piece council teaches us to trust the process, to not carry on when we have nothing to say, and to have the courage to take our turn when a contribution wells up inside us. It is acceptable to take brief notes to remind ourselves of what we want to speak about or questions we want to add, but the most powerful use of the talking piece is to hold it silently a few seconds, settle into our own breath and body, and see what comes forward as our piece of the contribution. In many settings, the most immediate gift of talking piece council is how it slows us down. We begin to see the synergy of the circle at work: We see that not any one person needs to speak the whole story or provide all the information needed.

Most often, the talking piece is passed around the circle so that all the participants know when their turn is coming. If someone is not ready to speak when the piece is handed to him or her, it is perfectly good protocol to pass it on, either silently or with the words "I pass." After a complete round, the person who spoke first may hold the piece out, offering those who passed a chance to speak, or the piece may be placed in the middle.

In smaller groups, the talking piece may reside in the middle and people reach for it as they are ready. When the piece is residing in the middle, it's important to note when talking piece form is being employed and when the group is open to discussion. Whenever someone picks up the talking piece, s/he has the floor, and the members of the circle need to take notice and see what is being called into form.

A talking piece may be any object designated to serve this function. In many indigenous traditions, a talking piece, or talking stick, is a revered object of ritual. I first saw such a talking piece while on a trip to Vancouver Island in the late 1980s. In a shop of Native American carvings, a cedar pole caught my eye. Carved with ornate totem animals, the staff is five feet long with a firm tip, like a cane. At chest height there is a smooth rounded section the width of a hand. To wrap one's palm around this stick is to experience a sense of the power of council: what it means to have the floor, to hold the attention, to stand with spirit helpers. Standing with this stick, I could feel the tradition that has come down through the lineage of the artist—an ability to call up what the earth has to say, to pull down the spirit message, and to speak from the body and heart. We have used this staff in PeerSpirit councils when its presence is a needed reminder of the long tradition with which we stand.

Since the practice of using a symbol of power that passes from hand to hand has been used in councils since earliest times, and artifacts identified as talking pieces have been found in many First Culture excavations, I can only conclude that the desire to interrupt each other is as ancient as council itself—and so is the desire to be heard without interruption.

Talking piece council is appropriately used to gather information, insight, and story. Passing a talking piece shows respect for each person's presence, honors wisdom without bias toward status, and can help a circle keep collecting people's thoughts and concerns until the group reaches consensus regarding action. The talking piece is a great equalizer between people who hold different status outside the circle.

Many circles use a form of talking piece council as a check-in, when members one by one put something into the center that relates to this circle and then take a minute or so to speak to the group about how they are and what they bring to the meeting: "My daughter made the winning goal for her soccer team last night, and as a proud papa I place her photo here this morning," or "My wife's home sick and I'm a little distracted today," or "I'm aware of the resignation of the vice president and the turmoil that's creating around us in the organization. Perhaps we can place a mental image of him in the center, and offer the energy of this circle to help us hold together through this time of transition." Such statements take only a few seconds to say, but articulate what is being brought into the container of the circle.

When calling for a round of talking piece council to consider an issue or topic, the person holding leadership at the moment may want to set parameters about time and content. A little math is useful: Divide the time agreed upon for addressing the issue by the number of speakers, figure in some leeway for passing the talking piece, for silence between speaking, for a bathroom or stretch break if the council is long, and suggest what the length of contribution might be. Some people may speak a little longer, some a little shorter, but it helps tremendously for people to have a sense of timing before they take the talking piece in hand. The group guardian (whose function is introduced in the coming pages) may serve as timekeeper, and may be granted authority to gently interrupt someone who is long-winded, though it is every person's shared responsibility to help the process flow within the agreed-upon parameters.

Not every conversation in the circle needs to be held with the talking piece, but it is an excellent way to heighten attention and slow down interaction so that circle members really pay attention to each other.

Conversation is a more common and informal manner of meeting. In conversation, people pick up on what others are saying, react, interact, brainstorm, agree and disagree, persuade, and interject new ideas, thoughts, and opinions. The energy of open conversation stimulates the free flow of ideas. Conversation can also overwhelm those who aren't comfortable leaping into the verbal fray. There are times when conversation is essential to group process and times when process will work better if it's slowed down a bit, allowed a calmer pacing and a more formal sense of completion.

To combine the quickened responsiveness of conversation with freedom from interruption, use a talking piece that lends itself to being tossed around the group. A Koosh ball, a sock, a balloon, a paper airplane, or other small object can energize a tired council and bring levity into a conversation while still observing helpful council forms.

If conversation starts feeling chaotic, it is possible for any member of the group to call for the talking piece, and if using the talking piece feels laborious, it is possible for any member of the group to call for open conversation. The purpose of acknowledging the different forms of council is to help us hold the focus and understand what is expected of us at this moment in the life of the circle. And sometimes spontaneously, or at the request of one or more members, there will rise the need for group silence.

Silence is not usually considered a form of meeting, but in a circle where ultimate reliance is spiritual, it is an essential element of council. Depending on the setting and purpose of the circle, people may speak of group silence as meditation, prayer, waiting for guidance, supplication, time-out, or centering. Silence allows the members of a circle to call on spiritual presence without dogma. Silence gives each member time and space to attend to that mystery which has been put in the center of the circle, and which we also contain in the center of ourselves.

Several minutes of silent council can serve as an effective centering tool before a longer talking piece council. And in some longer circle seminars, several hours, or a whole day spent in silence together, while people reflect, write, or carry out a common and shared task, such as food preparation or gardening, has a profound impact on how the next session of council works.

There is a simple ritual for silence that seems to work almost universally. Take three breaths: one to *let go* of whatever energy charge was commanding us; one to *touch the still* mind; and one to *ask*, "What would Thou have me do?"—or, if that language is too formally spiritual, simply to ask, "What?"

The use of three breaths is a way to introduce silence into business circles, committee and board circles, and other settings where a more formal mention of meditation would seem foreign. Stopping to breathe is also a useful intervention if discussion has become overheated, or at a moment when it would be helpful for the entire group to pause and consider what's happening.

To gain clarity, it's almost always helpful to come back to a new position. Over and over again I practice the Three Breaths as part of my contribution to holding the rim.

Inhale—*center*—exhale
Inhale—*stillpoint*—exhale
Inhale—*now what*—exhale

To be of use to the circle, both on the interpersonal and spiritual levels, we need to be centered within ourselves. Native tradition refers to this as "being able to sit within one's own hoop." The energies of a circle, even in the pace of a talking piece council, can become pretty intense. One person's speaking can release unresolved issues into the group. Suddenly people aren't sure what just happened to the focus, or what to do next, or how to recover from a flaring of two opinions. Silence, in these moments, is golden. It gives us the opportunity to bring ourselves back to personal center, then to bring ourselves back to the circle's center, then to attend to the rim.

Silence serves not only as crisis intervention—it generates great wisdom. One minute of silence, in a setting where none is usually allowed, has profound impact on the clarity of a group in heated discussion. When coming into circle to address a complicated issue, in business, in community, in family, silence can alter everyone's perception of the possibilities for conversation and resolution. Silence gives us breathing room, and breathing room gives us the inspiration we need to proceed more clearly.

The Three Practices of Council

Our ability to pay attention to each other in whatever form of council we find ourselves is largely dependent on three practices:

- speaking with intention
- listening with attention
- self-monitoring our impact and contributions

Intentional speaking means contributing what has relevance, heart, and meaning to the topic of the moment. Story, rather than facts and figures, is the heart of intentional speaking in circle. We introduce ourselves through story and develop a sense of knowing another person through his/her stories. What we remember about each other, after the facts and figures have faded in importance, are our stories.

As speakers in the circle, story does not mean we ramble on, but encourages an equality of risk taking and self-revealment among circle members. Story is an invitation to share our real selves as we share our contribution to the circle.

Story grounds ideas in personal relevance, so as listeners in the circle, we understand the importance to the speaker and can hold his/her contribution with respect.

In circle, as it comes my turn to speak, I practice asking myself: "What do I want to say? Why? What story do I carry that would contribute to the current focus of conversation (or help refocus us on our stated intent)?"

The definition of intentional speaking can be adapted to fit the requirements of the moment. In a large circle of social activists who meet to sustain an environmental protest project, the group uses a digital kitchen timer, granting each person a minute to check in, and passing on the unusual talking piece when it rings. The group also finds this quick round very helpful when gathering every person's response to an idea or proposal.

Of course, for intentional speaking to serve the circle, the rest of us need to be listening.

Attentive listening means focusing clearly on what someone else is saying. To listen attentively, we need to reprogram ourselves to listen without competing for attention or preparing to interrupt. Whether using talking piece council or conversation council, we all need to refrain from interrupting, interjecting, questioning, and commenting. In a culture of sound bites, the circle teaches us to listen again to the unfolding of a complete thought.

A circle is strengthened by strong, supportive dyads. Various exercises that pair up members of the group and invite them to take turns speaking and listening to each other help build cohesiveness as we come to know each other better. Such pairing experiences give us good practice in intentional speaking and attentive listening. Even people in positions of authority, accustomed to having their opinions taken seriously, are often aware of a different quality in how they are heard in circle.

These practices are interactive and interconnected. It's been my experience that as long as people are speaking intentionally, it's fairly easy for others to listen attentively. But if trust in the speaker's intentionality begins to waver, so does attention. As we speak and listen, make decisions, and take action in the circle, we count on others, and others count on us to pay attention to how we are impacting the group dynamics.

Conscious self-monitoring is the ability to consider the impact of our words and actions before, during, and after we interact. Self-monitoring is the internal awareness that we have an impact on the group and the capacity to notice this impact while we contribute to the dynamics of the circle. A split second of deliberation before making an impulsive remark or taking action, and the willingness to self-correct, to say "oops," or to apologize before we go on, is an incredible asset to the circle.

Sometimes people think self-monitoring means self-censoring. For me, conscious self-monitoring is a commitment to repeatedly ask a few simple questions:

- What is the intent of the circle in this moment?
- Is what I am saying or doing contributing to that intent or distracting from it?
- Are my contributions based on a sense of "guidance" or am I inserting my ego and personal needs for attention?

As members of a circle, we need to have enough sense of self-boundary to be able to keep track of ourselves in the energized field of the circle. I experience my personal boundary as a fairly consistent check-in process going on in my mind and body, a sort of "How am I doing?" When I'm not sure how I'm doing, I may go up to someone on break, for instance, and ask for a little feedback. The tension or relaxation in my body is another way of tracking the impact of my contributions and the impact of other people's contributions on me.

Perfection is not the issue in circle: Practice is enough. When we come together with a commitment to practice PeerSpirit, we are ready to make a rim of self-governance that frees us to go about the business of our circle.

Generic PeerSpirit Agreements

When the rules are placed in each member's hands, examined, discussed, adapted, and agreed upon, we are empowered to take full membership and responsibility for how we behave, interact, and contribute in circle. This is a radical redefinition of how groups form, make decisions, and accomplish their work. When power is shifted to the rim and shared among all participants, the circle becomes a democratic experience.

The following generic circle agreements are listed here so that they can be read all in one piece. They are elucidated and explained in the context of a gathered circle in Chapter Six.

1. What is said in the circle belongs in the circle.
2. The circle is a practice in discernment, not judgment.
3. Each person takes responsibility for asking the circle for the support s/he wants and needs.
4. Each person takes responsibility for agreeing or not agreeing to participate in specific requests.
5. Anyone in the circle may call for silence, time-out, or ritual to reestablish focus, to recenter, or to remember the need for spiritual guidance.
6. Agreements are adaptable. If something is not working, revise the agreements and maintain the process.

Other agreements that have been suggested in PeerSpirit circles include:

- Ask before touching.
- Refrain from violence, threats of violence, or violent language.

It is always helpful to have circle agreements written down, available to all members and new members, and to bring agreements up for review after the circle has met for a while.

As part of agreement four, a circle needs to reach consensus or vote on actions. Often circles vote by using a "thumbs-up," "thumbs-sideways," or "thumbs-down" signal on decisions and actions that require approval. Thumbs-up signals agreement. Thumbs-sideways indicates that someone has further questions to raise, encouraging ongoing dialogue that can have an impact on the decision that emerges. Thumbs-down is used to indicate disapproval but may not necessarily block an action. A person can give a thumbs-down to state, "I don't support this action, but the group may proceed if it chooses." This needs to be clarified conversationally.

Guardian of the Circle

The single most important tool for aiding self-governance and bringing everyone back to spiritual center is the role of guardian. The guardian is a person who volunteers to watch and safeguard group energy. While serving as guardian, a person does his/her best to be extraordinarily aware of how group process is functioning, no matter what form of council is being observed. To employ a guardian, the circle needs to supply itself with a small bell, chime, rattle, or other object that makes a pleasant, distinctive sound loud enough to be heard during conversation. Then, usually rotating on a meeting-by-meeting basis, one person volunteers to serve in the guardian role. *The guardian has the group's permission to interrupt and intercede in group process for the purpose of calling the circle back to center, to task, or to respectful practice, or suggesting a needed break.* The guardian often serves as the one who carries out agreement five, but even when the guardian is in place, all members share responsibility for initiating a call for recentering, for example, and for helping the guardian fulfill her/his functions. In the midst of discussions, where attentive listening has been lost, someone's voice may rise above the rest: "Ring the bell! Where's our guardian?" and the guardian, who had been waiting for a polite moment to break the flow, rings out the call for silence.

Conversation may have become heated and nobody's listening to another; the momentary council leader may be struggling to respond to too many questions; someone holding the talking piece may not be aware s/he has rambled on and lost the attention of the group; or someone may share something the group needs to sit with respectfully before another person speaks. At these moments, the guardian calls for silence by using the agreed-upon signal. *Everyone* falls silent, and waits for further instruction.

Three breaths, says Thich Nhat Hanh, is enough to call us back to center. Breathing and waiting, the circle calms itself. The guardian, depending on his/her intention and the norms of the group, holds that silence anywhere from fifteen seconds to several minutes, and then releases the silence so the meeting may resume, by resignaling (with the bell or whatever) and a brief statement as to the intent of the pause: "I called the silence to remind us we are speaking without interrupting." The guardian may also keep track of time, and of physical needs for breaks and exercise—to raise or lower energy levels or to relieve bladders.

Covenants of the Circle

Agreements in a circle are made with careful thought. They are an intellectual process—agreements of the head. Covenants in a circle are made on faith. They are an intuitive process—agreements of the heart. When an agreement needs to be changed, we can often get together and think about it; when a covenant has been broken, emotions are often unleashed that are very hard to articulate.

All relationships that contain heart energy activate covenant. When any two people assess their relationship, whether it is business, personal, or circled, and agree to do certain things and not to do others, they are covenanted. It doesn't matter if they have gone through this ritual intentionally or not. Covenant generates loyalty and belief in the good intentions of ourselves and others.

If we are in a setting where we cannot acknowledge heart energy or use covenant language, we may ignore the presence of a covenant, but that does not remove its bonds. In both business and personal realms, people remain committed to extremely difficult relationships and situations because the covenant is still intact for them, and people leave what appear to be easy relationships or stable situations because the covenant has been broken.

By its definition and structure, a circle is heart-held space. This is true even when the circle is established in settings where covenants have never been discussed. *A PeerSpirit circle, with its sacred center and a rim bound by principles, practices, and agreements, is, by nature, a covenanted arrangement.* We need to raise this to attention as we go into circle—though the impact of this arrangement may not be felt until the circle has established its energetic life, and we begin to respond to the effects we have on each other. In many examples and scenarios of people in this book, the unspoken element that heals or hurts is the stretching of the covenant bond.

My basic covenant with the circle is: *"I dedicate myself* to holding this circle and helping it accomplish its task. *I take responsibility* for my words and actions. *I will listen* to you, and I will listen for guidance."

This is way too formal a statement in many settings, but I make it silently and offer it to the center. It's very helpful at the beginning of a circle to establish, at least inside ourselves, what it is we offer and what we expect. Sometimes, after a circle has met for a while and the heart-based energy is obvious, the group may want to use a round of check-in as an opportunity to articulate their covenants: "You can count on me to do my part to reach our goal *and* pay attention to how we get there. I want to be able to count on you for the same things."

These are the conditions in which the human heart thrives: clear social agreements, a collective act of centering, and the inspiration of shared purpose. We shouldn't be surprised when we feel gratitude, relief, and celebration at finally being in a place where the heart's conditions are met.

Body Practices

The clarity of interpersonal space on the rim of the circle is sustained by our ability to be empathetic to one another *and* hold our personal boundaries. The body needs to find and offer a level of trust in the circle as much as the mind does. Most of our conversation so far has focused on clarity of mind and spirit, but the circle is an embodied meeting. We are all vulnerable, the soft tissue of the belly exposed—there's usually no table to hide behind, no back row, no way to sneak out. Coming into circle, our bodies signal us with all the instinctual perceptions we still carry.

Several practices of touch help sustain the circle. What is appropriate is determined by the setting and by the clarity that happens within a particular group. Everyone shares responsibility for establishing the norms of touch in a circle. Men and women, many with histories of physical or sexual abuse, can have very different understandings about touch as comfort, manipulation, domination, or seduction. Touch is an area where asking, showing respect, and healthy hesitation help establish trust.

The following body practices may happen spontaneously. It may also be necessary or helpful to discuss what norms are comfortable in a circle, and how these norms are different from or the same as social settings. For example, if someone accepts a hanky and a squeeze of the hand during an emotional moment in circle, it doesn't mean s/he wants to be touched every time we pass in the hallway.

Eye contact and sound: At the beginning of the circle, we can be silent, look at each other, and listen. Listen to our inner selves. Listen to the center. Touch down. Center down. Come into our bodies with stretching exercises or deep breathing. We can hum, sing, chant. "Om" is said to be the sound of the universe; it has a special resonance when sounded in a group, or we may choose another phrase, perhaps repeating each other's names.

Songs create a wonderful link within circle experience, and keep people connected to the circle while it's not in session. Many chants and simple rounds are composed for circles, or we can create our own. Days later, in the shower, in the car, there is this little tune circling around in our minds. I often find myself singing silently in the circle. Some fragment of a tune becomes an internal prayer, a focusing device that brings my attention more fully into the circle.

Heart drumming: The drum is a circle. The drum is a universal instrument that has always been in the circle and comes from First Culture. We don't actually need a drum to try drumming. The body is covered with skin, like a drumhead, and makes a pleasant resonating thump when played. Thighs and calves are satisfying to slap gently. *Lub-dub-dub* or 1-2-3-4 are basic rhythms. Fingers snap. Hands clap. Some of the best musical improv sessions I've ever participated in have been played on the body only, waking ourselves up after lunch.

Drumming is a good way to reestablish harmony after time apart. Playing off one another's rhythms, following first one person and then another, coming into shared beat, losing it, laughing, refocusing—all bring the circle together in a profound way.

Touching: Hands are powerful tools in a circle. With or without actually touching palm to palm, we can pass energy in a ring, ground energy beneath ourselves, extend hands into the center, or reach out and pull energy in. We can summon energy down from the sky or send it spiraling upward. When we reach out and offer each other a hand, it is a profoundly understood gesture.

While we are learning our personal and collective levels of comfort in a circle, it is always wise to ask before touching someone with our hands. It is also wise to tell others if and how we wish to be touched. People who are comfortable with their bodies and fairly intuitive in how they reach out for others may consider such a conversation unnecessary; others, who have been invaded in the past, may be thankful to have the topic raised. Always assume there is a wide range of comfort and personal history in every circle.

When something happens in the circle that "touches our hearts," we can be literal about it: Touch the heart. There is a place on our bodies in the center of the breastbone called the high heart, or the spiritual heart. This is considered the source of compassion, empathy, and released heart energy. We may stroke or pat this part of the body gently when we are aware of tender emotions. It can be a great comfort for someone who is in a vulnerable state to look up and see others with hands on their hearts in a gesture of understanding. Heart touching is nonintrusive; it simply lets someone know that they are not isolated in their feeling or insight. This helps the speaker remember to touch his/her own heart, to be tender toward his/her own emotions and experiences.

Backing: One way of being touched that can feel literally and symbolically supportive is backing. We have all used phrases like "Would you back me up on this?" or "I could use your backing."

In the circle, backing has several variations. The idea is to literally stand or sit behind someone and support or touch their backs. *Upon direct request,* resting the palm of the hand flat against a person's spine, with the heel of the palm between the shoulder blades, is a subtle way to provide meaningful touch. *Upon direct request,* in a public setting or business environment, simply standing right behind someone, without touching them, will provide significant support.

If we are in a circle setting that is more informal, or where people are comfortable with touch, *upon direct request* we may back someone by scooting our torso behind him/her, arms and legs making a kind of chair, and letting the person lean against us. Both people remain facing into the group, engaged with the whole circle. This kind of backing provides tremendous support and is usually considered non-intrusive because it allows both people to stay in equal relationship to each other and to the circle. It probably cannot be provided in business or professional settings, but may work well in same-gender groups, spirit circles, and families.

Circle members may request this kind of backing when someone is having an emotional response and doesn't want to leave the circle; when two people engaged in conflict resolution ask for physical support while they talk through an issue; or when someone is in need of extra energy in the middle of a meeting.

Circle Energetics

As is true in any gathering, much of what we experience in circle is based on the nonverbal environment. We call this environment *circle energetics*.

Most of the time, most of us arrive at the beginning of circle full of confused and scattered energies accumulated from the pace of Second Culture life. We are counting on the circle to center us, slow us down, and help us be present. We should not be surprised if our landing in the intimate lap of circle is often a little rough.

Each person enters the rim of a circle as an independent energy body capable of phenomenal nonverbal influence on the group. The "vibes" we emit are a combination of mental attitude and expectation ("Do I want to be here?" "Do I expect something beneficial is about to happen?"); physical well-being ("I didn't get enough sleep." "This is my four P.M. slump." "I just won a racquetball game and am really pumped."); emotions we are aware of ("Oh, wonderful, Jerry's here!" or "Oh, no, Jerry's here!") and emotions we are not aware of (———); and our level of spiritual commitment ("Do I trust this process and the lessons it will teach me?"). As we come into a circular space and face each other, the energetics emanating from each other and the energetic mix of the group accompany us into the container.

In a basic, instinctual way, our brains are wired to read energetics. There are times our lives depend on our ability to accurately sense and react to the nonverbal energetics of another person or a situation.

Though we think of these as times of recognized threat, there are also times we need to recognize safety. We often overlay our gut reactions with tremendous rationalization and projection, seeing a situation as more benevolent or malevolent than it really is. However, the instinctual body response to energy is still going on.

I've been in circles with people who kept saying they were fine, but my stomach was in a knot the whole time I was around them. And I've been in circles where people were expressing fear or anger, but energetically I felt their committed presence holding steady and my body stayed relaxed. The more we can be aware of our own energetics, and able to trust the energetic reaction we are having to another person or within the group, the more consciously we can address the nonverbal elements of circle, harnessing and coordinating them to serve a supportive function.

Accurately reading energetics is a highly intuitive function, and therefore it can be highly inaccurate, skewed by the preconceptions in our own minds. In Chapter Eight, "Challenges in the Circle," we will revisit the question of energy, but it needs to be introduced here as one of the subtle skills of holding the rim.

In our teaching circles, Ann and I sit opposite each other and often ask someone who we know has experience with circle or energetics to sit at the quarter marks. We hold the points of the wheel steadily in place. In the opening meditation, we help the group become energetically aligned by calming and deepening the breath, grounding ourselves from below in an image of sending roots into the earth; anchoring ourselves from above in an image of making a cord from our heads to the sky; calling in support at our backs; and from this steady placement offering our support to the center. This manner of being in place honors both the self and the circle. It creates home base, the resting place we return to when the guardian calls for recentering, when we are relaxing in a sense of spiritual communion, or attending to decision making and problem solving.

Below-above-behind-before: centered in body and in heart, able to attend to the principles, practices, and agreements. In those moments when we hold all this, we are beings of great power—not competitive power but cooperative power.

Even in the most harmonious group, people do not enter the circle energetically in sync, and it is extremely helpful to call in the energy, to articulate its presence and function. The idea that we are calling in energy as we come into circle may be unaccustomed language in a number of settings where the circle is newly introduced, but I've been surprised at people's ability to understand and acknowledge this phenomenon.

One group that surprised me was a gathering of fairly traditional church-based families who had come to help my cousin Don turn sixty. Don, a parish minister, had rented space at a retreat center in the redwoods of California and invited friends and family, covering the span of his career, to spend the weekend celebrating with him. My Whidbey cousins, Bill and Donna, and I traveled south to help him call the circle.

It was a big group, ranging from toddlers to octogenarians, and filled the hall. We stood in a large circle; I lit a candle and placed some redwood boughs in the middle of the floor. Don had set the stage the previous evening, asking people to think about why they had come and what they hoped to receive for themselves that weekend. I invoked our First Culture heritage, explained the principles and practices, stated the agreements, and looked around. The circle consisted of three or four different parish groups, including a dozen couples Don had married, children he'd baptized, friends from seminary days, and family who knew each other but didn't know anyone else.

"Okay, Don," I challenged him, "you called us here. And your call is like a ball of energy—invisible but real. Can you imagine and then shape that ball in your hands?" Pretty soon he was fondling a "ball" about the size of a grapefruit. "Now," I said, gesturing to his wife across the circle, "toss the energy to Peggy . . . and Peggy, shape it, hold it, and toss it to someone else."

Soon we were making a great web between the people present, each one gently holding and tossing the energy. When the ball got too big, someone carried it to the middle, seeding the center and taking back enough to start the toss again. After a while, to seal the rim, we passed the ball once around the circle, from hand to hand. The energy we'd created was handled tenderly, with respect and shared belief that something was really there; and so it was. We separated into half a dozen small circles throughout the hall and held council, making center in these small groups by contributing some object from our pockets. For the rest of the weekend, the energy that had been called into being and touched by every person in the community held the group through laughter and tears.

The structure was simply presented and understood. The energy was acknowledged and made manifest between us all. The rim held.

Everything the Power of the World does is done in a circle.
The sky is round, and I have heard that the
earth is round like a ball, and so are all the stars.
The wind, in its greatest power, whirls.
Birds make their nests in circles,
for theirs is the same religion as ours.
The sun comes forth and goes down again in a circle.
The moon does the same, and both are round.
Even the seasons form a great circle in their changing,
and always come back again to where they were.
The life of a [person] is a circle from childhood to childhood,
and so it is in everything where power moves.

BLACK ELK, *Black Elk Speaks*

CHAPTER 5

Preparing to Call
the Circle

PeerSpirit is a methodology for circling. A methodology has under-lying principles and rules of organization based on a philosophical system. The philosophical system is what we've been exploring in the first four chapters; now we explore the applications. And so we come to circle, ready to offer an authentic gesture arising out of our spiritual practice; ready to sit fully on the rim, bringing our bodies and our interpersonal skills; ready to apply the circle to real life meetings.

Carol and John, who spearheaded the crisis intervention in their neighborhood school system, were successful with their first applica-tion of PeerSpirit circle. Though hastily called, the small group of earnest parents and teachers heard each other out and stayed creative in their thoughts and suggestions. Before they went home that night, the group had come up with three alternatives to the strike and the proposed budget cuts, and Tom, Arlene, and Bev Ebble volunteered to communicate with the PTA, the teachers' union, and the school board. They set another meeting for ten days later and left with quiet confidence. Nobody was "in charge"; instead, the whole group carried a sense of charge that grew out of its purpose.

Bev ran into immediate resistance, but she was not alone. When she went to the next meeting of the teachers' union, she was accompanied by two other members of the circle. "Who the hell authorized you to talk about this outside the union?" the head of the strike committee asked her angrily.

Bev paused a long time before answering. "You know, Joe, I've been teaching for thirty years. I still like the work and I still like the kids. This alone amazes me. I've been through two strikes and two threats to strike. Each time, those have been tremendously difficult years. I don't look forward to taking the wrath of the parents, dealing with the confusion of the children, and listening to the bitterness of the board. Our little ad hoc meeting was the first time anyone has tried to make a cooperative plan. You were invited and didn't come. So now we've come to you—parents and teachers working together. Do you want to pick a fight or listen to us?"

Put on the spot in front of his peers, Joe chose to listen. Actually, the strike committee thought the proposals were pretty good and joined in their support. Later, driving home, Bev found herself talking aloud in the car: "Well, I'll be . . . this stuff actually works."

Later she joined Arlene and Tom when they presented ideas to the PTA. "We're a self-selected group of parents and teachers," Arlene began. "We just want to help the school. Parents are an essential part of keeping this system vital. To sustain some of the extra activities we want to provide our children, we have to find volunteer support out there and organize it. People say they're too busy, but if they get asked to do something manageable and specific, we think they'll come forward." The PTA agreed to survey parents and hold interest group sessions.

A month later, the entire circle went to the school board, along with the strike committee, the PTA officers, and a petition of support signed by three hundred parents. The teachers offered a signed agreement not to strike if the board would begin to carry out the suggestions. A new PeerSpirit circle was formed made up of representatives from all these groups.

Applying methodology doesn't mean pedantic stuffiness—it just means offering structure to fit the needs of the situation. Everyone who came to Carol and John's first circle quickly found themselves in positions of leadership as other circles formed to address various related issues. They distributed one page handouts of their basic circle agreements, so every group functioned with similar guidelines, and used the school logo and other commonly recognized memorabilia to create common centers. A candle was lit and blown out to signal the opening and closing of sessions, and a Day-Glo pink ruler became the standard talking piece and staff of authority. These circles addressed real needs and were presented in ways people were ready to try.

Preparations for Calling the Circle

Circling is a transferable skill we learn by practicing with each other and learning as we go. PeerSpirit circling can be introduced into already existing groups that are ready to shift from a designated-leader model to an all-leader model, and also into new groups as the basic form of governance and guidance.

To start a circle, somebody needs to make the suggestion, offer the basic structure, and be ready to model circle skills while others become accustomed to how a circle works. This person is the caller of the circle. These next three chapters are addressed to readers as potential callers of a circle. *You are invited to imagine yourself in any of these situations and ask yourself where you might introduce the circle in your own lives.*

Before the first meeting, three preparatory steps are helpful: setting intention, gathering feedback, and envisioning the group.

Two months after her school board experience I phoned Carol on my next trip through Minneapolis. "Hi! Let's do lunch," she said. "I've been trying out circling at the office and—"

"At your office?" I interrupted. "At the software company?"[1]

"Sure, why not? I have a theory about technical wizards—when they finally get the connection between head and heart, they arc. I think the circle will work for them, but I must admit, I'm having a little trouble figuring out how to convince management."

Carol is a human resources manager in her company—"the token people person," she calls herself. It's her job to keep interpersonal communications functioning while others engage in programming or

---

[1] In the interest of client privacy, the following narrative is an amalgam of several business experiences; but the process of calling and sustaining the circle is authentically presented.

sales. She likes her job, but sometimes wonders if the others quite understand her role.

Over lunch a few days later she filled me in. "After our success with the school crisis, I decided to bring just one aspect of circling into the office to see what would happen. I brought a candle." She smiled mischievously. "Simple enough, one taper in a silver candlestick. I put it on my desk and didn't say anything. Only, whenever someone came to see me with something important to say, I lit the candle at the beginning of our conversation and blew it out at the end. I think they were afraid to ask what I meant by it, but after a week or so I noticed a few people would come in and light the candle as a way of signaling they wanted my careful attention. Pretty neat, huh?"

I smiled at her inventiveness. "Pretty brave, barging right in and starting with spiritual center . . . Hasn't the fire code gotten you?"

"I didn't ask permission. And I guess nobody has tattled," she laughed. "Now management wants to develop a new product," she went on. "Something revolutionary. They're going to pull a creative team together and turn them loose for six months of R and D. They want to be innovative in how the whole project is carried out, but don't really know how. At his last job, my boss saw an R and D team destroy itself because no one was communicating, so he's asked me to facilitate team meetings. I want to introduce the circle. What do I do?"

"Well, you need to get really clear about what the benefits of the circle are in this situation and how you see its application for this group. You need to articulate a clear intention."

Setting Intention

Intention is the statement of a circle's purpose. Setting intention begins by asking: "What is this circle about? Why am I calling it? What do I want?"

In a community action effort after a woman was attacked on a neighborhood walking trail, several women put up posters stating: "This is our path! We will not lose it to one violent act or person. All fierce women and gentle men are invited to meet at the fire station this coming Saturday at 2 P.M. to discuss safety options, to arrange escorts for vulnerable people who want to continue enjoying this trail, and to design a ritual to reclaim and cleanse the space."

This intention statement invites people to assume leadership and share responsibility as part of their attendance and to participate in a spiritual ritual. It clearly states the purpose of the gathering and who is invited.

A church looking for a new pastor formed the customary search committee with cochairs and ten members and began going through résumés. After several months, they realized they had not taken enough time to articulate possible new directions for the congregation and therefore weren't clear what kind of pastoral leadership they needed. As a result of their confusion, factions were developing. One member decided to call a council. He created a centerpiece with a candle, a loaf of bread, a chalice of wine, some flowers, and the church directory. He said to the group, "I think we need to take a step back and begin by framing a vision for our community so we know the kind of person we want to call. May I suggest we take turns each speaking to our vision of this church, listening to each other without interruption?"

This call for intention addresses the root cause of group confusion without blaming anyone for causing tension, and offers a process that invites people into renewed cooperation.

Carol knew that upper management at the software company wanted an innovative design team. Carol said, "I think a project team is almost a circle, only they don't know it. After our school experience, I see the value of clear structure, additional tools to help people self-manage, and the idea of containment—that there are boundaries that make the process run more smoothly."

"Last time," I reminded Carol, "you put together a circle on a wing and a prayer. You barely had time to write an intention paragraph and get on the phone. With a project of this size, you'll need to be really focused. Setting intention means getting clear about what you want to change or accomplish."

Carol tried to articulate a clear intention statement. "I want these guys to succeed. . . ."

"Too vague," I said.

There is nothing wrong with broad intentions; they tend to be highly educational. Broad intention provides the basis for reconsideration and self-education. The open conversation will be framed by questions such as: "What do we think (or feel) about this? Where and how do we begin?" A circle called with an expansive intent will be a good think tank and discussion group, but is not likely to take action until its intention has been narrowed in focus. This clarifying may be able to occur only after the members of the circle have gathered and started dialogue. But the circle can't gather without some idea to serve as a focusing tool.

"I want to keep the team off my back and out of my office, so I'm not arbitrating every little competitive squabble," Carol offered.

"Too narrow and negative," I said. "Intention is a vision of what you want to create, not a statement of what you want to avoid. If I ask you what you want to get out of the day, and you tell me you don't want to get run over by a truck, there's nothing to guide you except a reminder to look before crossing the street."

"I want to use the circle to provide an environment that helps the project team think creatively and act cooperatively for the purpose of product development."

"Much better," I said.

Focused intention provides the basis for action. Carol's intention that she wants to provide helpful tools that allow the project team to think and act creatively will help a specific plan of action develop out of the circle. Certainly people in this circle will focus on product development, but their conversations will be held within a context that challenges the group to take action while supporting each other. The opening conversation will be framed by questions such as: "Specifically, what do we want to do? How do we proceed? Who needs to do what, and how do we all help?"

Intention is the most powerful foundation to PeerSpirit circling. Clear intention is the fundamental service a person provides as the caller of the circle. As people respond to intention and a circle gathers, the caller can take his or her place on the rim, letting leadership rotate, sharing responsibility, and allowing Spirit to guide the group, knowing intention will hold the circle together.

Though they had yet to meet, one of the women who would join the project team was also starting a circle in her private life. Demetria, an interface specialist, wanted to call a Tenfold circle for women that would meet monthly in different members' homes.[2]

Demetria's ideas about a circle had started off unfocused. "My mother used to have a bridge club that met every Thursday afternoon and was the underpinning of her week. God help any child or spouse who made a demand or set up a time conflict with those card games! I wanted friends like that, but we all have such busy lives, I didn't have time to cultivate friendships. 'Let's do lunch' just wasn't doing it for me." She began reading, and talking with women at business luncheons, at the health club, and on-line, looking for a way to meet her need. Pretty soon the word *circle* started coming up repeatedly.

While Demetria gathered information outside the office, Carol got her intention clear inside the office. Then she faced the next step of preparation. "I know I want the circle to change my relationship with the team," she said, "and for the circle to change their relationship with each other. I see how the circle can impact our work process, but not how process positively impacts the end product in a way I can easily explain."

"Maybe the reason you can't answer this is that it's not just your circle. Maybe you need to be talking with some of the people involved."

Gathering Feedback

A story explains our thoughts, feelings, and actions to others. A story helps other people understand why something is important, what significance it has, what our hopes are, and what the plan of action is. A story inspires others to think, feel, and act with us. Sharing our story is good practice for clarifying intention. When we talk, we practice putting our intention into language that communicates with others, and also practice responding to people's questions, concerns, ideas, and additions.

---

[2] Tenfold™ circles were started by Ann and me in 1992. Tenfold is grounded in PeerSpirit structure and is facilitated by teaching colleagues. See "Resources" section for more information.

When we are planning a circle, we need to talk to a number of different people:

- people we are pretty sure will understand, be supportive, and are interested
- people who think very differently and will challenge our thinking
- longtime colleagues who have previously seen us work ideas through stages of implementation
- new colleagues, on a hunch that they might be interested
- friends and family, even those we assume are far apart in their thinking

Carol's story ran like this: "I'm going to be part of a project team working on a very innovative software product. My boss wants me on the team, but I don't want to be defined as the caretaker while the engineers and programmers do all the thinking. So I want to design a peer-group circle as the basis for team management where *everyone* is committed to sharing leadership and responsibility, and acquiescing to group wisdom. I think working in a peer circle will help ensure that the project goes smoother and faster. It also introduces innovation into the process as well as into the outcome. What do you think?"

Every time people asked her questions in return, Carol wrote them down.

- What do you mean by "a circle"? Is this just semantics?
- What is your function if they don't need you to play the caretaking role?
- What do you want this experience to provide for you?
- What do you want this experience to provide for the rest of the team?
- What do you want the team to do for each other?
- Is the circle composed only of people who are on the project? Who else might be useful?
- Why are you trying to combine human-potential stuff with a high-tech project?

- Is the team still going to be part of the company, or will you go off and cloister yourselves?
- How is the team being picked? Will they know the circle is the organizational model before they sign on?
- What if someone wants to work on the project but doesn't want to work in the circle? Will s/he have a choice?
- Is it going to be all men except you? What about some diversity?
- What dynamics are you trying to protect? What are you open to changing?
- How will the circle contribute to a better product?
- Will use of the circle reduce costs?

Demetria's story ran like this: "I want a way for the wonderful women I know to meet, provide support in both our professional and personal lives, and to help each of us hold on to some kind of dream while we are going through all the busyness women attend to. I want a mix of people, married and single, mothering and not, working in business, working for themselves, working at home . . . like a neighborhood used to be. And I think it has to be a structured commitment, and that something has to happen for each of us that's so compelling we keep coming back for more.

"So I'm thinking of calling a weekend gathering I heard about on the Net where two facilitators come in and help us get clear what we want and teach us some ground rules for holding a circle and seeing where we go from there. What do you think?"

Every time people responded, their questions helped her hone her ideas:

- Why only women?
- What happens at the first weekend?
- What do you want to happen after?
- How will you deal with diversity in people's goals?
- Is this an open or closed circle?
- Can someone come in later? Can someone leave?
- Do you expect it will meet for months? Years?

- What's *your* need you're trying to fill? How will you find out if this is a shared need?
- What if the experience succeeds beyond your wildest dreams—what does that look like?
- What if it all falls apart—what does that look like?

As Demetria responded to these questions, she got a clearer idea of the conversation needed to gather her group and wrote out an intention statement: "Please join me in forming a circle of women who provide each other ongoing support and spiritual center. I've been in touch with two women who facilitate a weekend-long process called Tenfold, which is designed to teach us circle skills and define our next life goals within a spiritual context. The first step is a commitment to gather for the weekend, go through the introduction, and then decide if we want to remain together in a circle of peers."

As Carol responded to the questions, she got better prepared to bring the idea to her boss. "Will you come with me," she asked, "and talk to Stuart, the head of product development? I'm still new at trying to explain this." Two weeks later I found myself in Stuart's office trying to explain the circle myself. It's not easy to do as a sound bite.

"So what's PeerSpirit . . . In Service to the Circle?" he asked, looking at my business card.

"It's my business partnership, and an informal consortium of people committed to introducing the circle as a form of self-managing meetings."

"Never heard of it," he said, "not that I stay up with the latest business trends. Does the circle come out of OD work?"

"The circle didn't start in organizational development," I replied, "but it's impacting OD. People who were defining the team concept twenty years ago are now beginning to look at the circle. I believe the circle requires a different level of commitment than most teams." Stuart looked a little glazed, but I went on. "A commitment that can put the spirit back in business. Let's explain as we go," I suggested. "What do you want to do?"

Stuart is a bright manager in his late thirties, still on the rise. "This product should create new market share for us," he said with conviction. "The concept is experimental, though it's a natural extension of what we—and a lot of other companies—currently provide. I hear hoofbeats in the industry and I want us out in front. I'm willing to take some risks in how the team is managed as long as it fosters creativity—quick, efficient, cost-effective creativity."

"What's the nature of the team you're trying to put together, and what environment do you see them in?" I asked next.

"I think they need to be cloistered. They need to be fascinated by the problem. They need to be just plain smart. They need to be creative risk takers who are still accountable to budget and timeline concerns. And they need to work together and value each other's contributions."

"Why add Carol?"

"Because every now and then you put a team like this together and it crashes and burns. Disaster costs money. We need a solid product to come out the other end, and I want somebody in the inner circle who speaks plain English and can liaison out to me."

"So you're already thinking about a circle." I smiled innocently and pulled from my briefcase a paperweight model of a geodesic dome. "Here," I said, handing it across his desk. "Recognize this? What's so unique about the geodesic dome is that nothing appears to be holding it together. The strength is all carried at the joints and extended into the curve. Each joint supports its share; each is connected to the whole. It's very strong."

"Bucky Fuller, nineteen sixty-something?" Stuart said, and nodded. "I tried building one out of toothpicks in the fifth grade. My model fell down. I get your point, but how does anything get done? Who's taking the lead?"

"The *group* takes the lead, by rotating leadership," I said. "Every person helps the circle function by assuming small increments of leadership that carry out the group's defined purpose. Imagine a person standing on each of these joints, each holding one perspective, responsible for one piece of the puzzle. You and I can see how everybody—and everything they know—is connected, but *they* can't see it, unless you give them a tool that grants perspective.

"The circle is a tool for giving a team a more holistic perspective," I continued. "It redistributes relationships so people can really function as a team. My niece plays a lot of sports, and I know when you put a bunch of teenagers out on the playing field they *all* had better know whether they're playing soccer or softball. So the circle comes with rules of the game, and *you* come with the goal. The combined energy creates that mysterious something extra we call team spirit."

Carol leaned forward. "On a team, every person takes responsibility for their part of the action and for the success of the mission as a whole. It's very pragmatic. As your human resources person, I don't want the way people treat each other to be separated from the work of production. I want the whole team to take responsibility for itself."

"In a PeerSpirit circle," I added, "shared responsibility means that everyone pays attention to how they treat each other and to who needs what in terms of support. People learn to think before speaking, to consider the consequences of actions, and to get consensus in setting directions that will have long-term impact.

"There's one more element to the circle," I told Stuart. "People have the opportunity to draw on the center to keep themselves focused and supported. It's that team spirit phenomenon—creativity contained within the circle develops its own energy and contributes back."

"Yeah, I've seen that." Stuart nodded. "That's the most unpredictable aspect of teaming. Group dynamics can be an incredible booster, or it can get so negative it pulls people down. In this circle model, what's to prevent that?"

"Well, if we agree that what's held in the center is essentially spiritual energy—maybe we call it wisdom or higher purpose, or mission—people have a source to call on that's nobody's turf," Carol said, and we held our breath waiting for his reaction.

"Center may be called by whatever name is comfortable," I assured him. "In another corporation where PeerSpirit consults annually, a circle of eighteen administrators meets around four placards on which are printed their corporate values. These remind everyone of the philosophy underlying their tremendous workload. They refer to their values when making decisions."

"Just a minute," Stuart said. "This is a software company. We value market share. Being first. New ideas."

"Stuart, how would you describe the ideal team dynamics that will produce the product you want in the time you have?" I asked.

"Good team playing. Smart team members. No infighting. Each

one doing what he or she does best . . . group ownership of the idea, instead of ego fights."

"That's exactly what the structure of the circle fosters. Besides making good people choices, what would have to happen for these conditions to exist?"

"Some kind of containment so the group could set aside their usual duties and focus on the problem to be solved."

"The circle *is* a container," I continued, pointing to the little geodesic model on his desk. "Look at it."

"Okay, I get it. But nothing hokey, nothing religious, nothing New Age."

"Wisdom," I said.

"Group process," Carol said.

"All right," Stuart said. "What do we do next?"

"Well, you and Carol, and anyone else in the loop, need to decide who's on the team. And you need to make sure they know that the team will function a little differently than usual, that they're signing up for the whole package." I made him a gift of the paperweight, and left them to carry out the third step of preparation.

Envisioning the Group

The initial intention statement addresses the issue of what people need to know in order to decide if they are interested in responding to this invitation. As intention becomes clear, the next question is: "Who do we know that we hope will be interested?"

There is a synergy to gathering groups—an attraction that occurs when "the call" is clear. Sometimes we may be in charge of creating a list of potential participants, as Carol was when she called together the school group. Sometimes we will hardly be in charge at all, as Carol was at the public meeting. In both instances, synergy is still at work.

The dictionary defines synergy as *the interaction of elements that combine to produce a total effect that is greater than the sum of individual elements.* In calling a circle, synergy means trusting that resonance will occur between the clarity of the intention statement and the readiness of a person to participate. The caller of the circle is like the candle flickering on the windowsill. We put out as clear a statement as we can, and see which moths are attracted to the flame.

Over the years we have learned to respect synergy and not try to control it. Dozens of times after a seminar fills at the last minute, one or two people pull out. Their reasons are valid: A family member gets sick, a work deadline looms large. Sometimes they just get scared, and they call and say, "I don't know if I should do this. . . ." We listen and try to provide counsel without interfering in the synergy. Just as often, at the last minute, someone wants in to the circle. We sit with the energy before responding: Is there still room at the rim? What level of call is this person responding to?

Synergy occurred in who chose to come to Carol and John's on a Saturday night. Synergy also occurred in the church search committee, especially after they backed up and reappraised their task. The member who had stopped business as usual and called for a council introduced the basics of PeerSpirit in such a clear way that the committee adjusted its operating structure and became a circle. Two members from the original group left; three more joined. They set a clear intention and called a gathering of the full congregation to gather feedback, and set a shared vision for the church.

For Demetria, paying attention to synergy meant listing people she thought would be interested in the circle, people she wanted to develop a close relationship with, and people she thought would mix well with each other. She drew a spiderweb on a big sheet of paper, putting women's names and little biographical thoughts about them at the web's connecting points: "Rachel, thirty-seven, lots of energy, wants to leave her stable office job, look at a new career, but she's thinking of having a baby in the next year or two; Valerie, forty-nine, therapist, good people skills, kind of a loner, probably could use a group; Deb-'n'-Judy, their hyphenated name says it all—they're a package deal . . . Judy is shy, and Deb is a wild woman, so should they be in the same group? Do the two of them want to break the mold? How could I talk to them about these issues?"

Inevitably, we bring our own foibles to this point in calling a circle. We have been the carriers of an idea, but that idea cannot come to life until we bring in the rest of the circle. And as we bring in the rest of the circle, we lose our solitary relationship to the idea, and our control over what's going to happen—and how. We often confront our own comfort zone and learn a lot about ourselves as we go through this sorting.

Like any one of us, Demetria had to decide how much control to try to exert over the formation of the Tenfold circle, and how much to trust the synergistic process of gathering. Because she was calling a circle that would have the potential to become quite intimate and be together for a long time, Demetria decided to spend several weeks having lunch or tea with various women and introducing the idea face-to-face. "I wrote about myself, too, in the spiderweb, trying to see my own contributions, and questioning the ways I might clash with some of the other women. It made me very compassionate. Basically, I was looking for compatible levels of clarity—an understanding of personal boundary, as well as openness to new ideas." Later, after the weekend had introduced her to PeerSpirit language, she acknowledged, "I didn't have words for it, but I knew I wanted circle members who could practice self-monitoring: women able to hold the rim and participate in the necessary corrections of growth and intention without draining or overpowering others. And women who would stand up to me, help me grow, too."

After our conversation in the office, Stuart and Carol made a list of people they could imagine working well together, who might find this new way of doing things intriguing, and who would contribute needed skills. They came up with twelve people who had the right technical talent and who reported to Stuart, so he could make them available. They decided they wanted eight people on the team, and prioritized the order in which they interviewed so they could keep adjusting the mix.

When we are in a position to formulate the group, we may already have some people in mind who seem natural for our circle, perhaps people we've talked to during the intention-setting process. We need to consider honestly both the rational and intuitive reasons we want them in circle. We also need to consider any hesitation or ambivalence that arises so that we can dialogue about it in writing to ourselves, with others on the calling team, or with the individual person.

Around the conference table in the human resources department, we expect Carol and Stuart to have frank discussions about team members, but away from a business setting we may be uncomfortable dealing with the idea that some people are in and others out; we may be overly controlling or overly casual, fearful of introducing people with differing points of view, or of not taking the fragility of circle energetics seriously.

If we have trouble with the idea that we are making decisions about people's inclusion, it may be helpful to remember that the people we invite are making similar decisions about being in circle with us. The evaluation of interest, of readiness, of choosing a good match in personalities, works both ways and sets the synergy in motion.

Synergy is highly intuitive, and it can be clouded by our own hopes and fears. As callers of the circle, we need to do the best we can to help fulfill the intentions by considering people who have the ability to hold that intention and work within circle process. It is far easier to be discerning up front than to discover down the road that we have called or joined a circle that cannot fulfill its intention because the membership is not clear enough to function. Later chapters are devoted to handling the interpersonal issues that arise in circle— this is the moment when an ounce of prevention is worth a pound of cure.

After her round of teacup interviews, Demetria set about preparing for the Tenfold weekend. And after a week of across-the-table explaining and negotiating, Stuart and Carol had their team put together. Besides Demetria, they called in three top-notch programmers, Bill, Chen, and Mike; a marketing person, Doug; and two technical writers, Lindsay and Philip.

The circle was called.

There is something magical about any intense, tightly knit group of people working together and playing together, a feeling of being in the world while at the same time being apart from it, apart together. We believe that even those of us who have not experienced that magic hear its distant music, feel its ancient call. A transformative community is a nearly indispensable launching pad for transformation. Such a community can create the context and the confidence for a transforming journey.

GEORGE LEONARD and MICHAEL MURPHY,
The Life We Are Given

CHAPTER 6

The First Gathering

Once we were Brownies or Cub Scouts. Once we were elected to student council. Once we sat in a church or synagogue study group. Once we served on a committee at work or school, or helped with a co-op day care center, or headed a task force. The vestiges of circling that have been adapted into the larger culture are familiar to many of us, but PeerSpirit may be our first experience with intentional circling.

The first gathering of a PeerSpirit circle needs to put the three principles in place, and to show by example and format how Peer-Spirit circling is different from other forms of meeting. As people arrive and settle in, they may be wondering, "What's happened to the table and chairs? Why didn't s/he just ask me to sit on a committee, join a task force, or implement an office directive? What is this circling concept, anyway?"

It's our role as the caller of the circle, or as an experienced circle member, to help others understand how circles are different. We need to model the process of coming into intentional circle in a clear manner, so that people will know what PeerSpirit structure offers. In each new circle we have the opportunity to create an environment that supports our words—to make the circle manifest.

While Carol was setting up the first circle of the project team, Ann and I were calling a Circle Practicum on Whidbey Island.

Circle Practicums are five-day seminars for people who want to gain confidence in their skills of circle participation and leadership. The groups are usually eclectic gatherings, representing careers in human resources, teaching, the arts, social service, and health care, or they may be gathered from one organization in order to seed the company, social agency, church, or community group with circle practitioners.

In this session, participants ranged in age from late thirties to early sixties. Nine women and three men had gathered from five states, eager to leave our usual routines for a week in the circle. Telephone calls went out to spouses, to partners, to children, to someone at work: "I'm here, I made it safely . . . have a good week, call you later." We sank into a kind of timelessness, exploring the buildings and gardens of the retreat center tucked in the Maxwelton Valley on the south end of the island.

The evening of our arrival, we ate supper together and came into first circle in the Marsh House, an exquisite octagonal teaching room reached by walking on a wooden bridge through an alder marsh. The spring peepers greeted us from their hidden crevasses in the tree trunks, and the skunk cabbage unfurled its single yellow petal. At the edge of the marsh, the land opens into meadow, and the Marsh House sat aglow in evening light, guarded by a single towering Douglas fir. Seventy-five feet tall, a hundred years old, the tree stands as the elder here. People picked up the hush of nature, slowed down, breathed deeply, and readied themselves to enter consecrated space.

Sitting in Circle

The need to literally make a circle is essential. We cannot understand the circle if we are sitting in rows, being lectured at. Even when our minds have forgotten the power of the circle, our bodies remember. Half the work of comprehension is accomplished when we find our place at the rim. Sitting in circle gives us time to notice who's here, greet each other, say names, get comfortable with the energetics. The circle begins with some ritual that draws a boundary between social space and council space.

As people entered the Marsh House, they left their shoes in the vestibule. Ann held a small ceramic bowl of smoldering herbs, and people walked through the veil of sweet-smelling smoke. Holy smoke is used in many spiritual traditions as a way of cleansing the energy field around the body. I remember Sunday mornings in my little Episcopal church, the priest swinging the censer full of frankincense over the heads of the kneeling congregation, her arms arcing in great crescent sweeps. Ann is more subdued. In whispered tones she explained the ritual to each person, asked their permission, and spoke of reconnection to a more earth-honoring time. This circle consisted of a therapist, a clergywoman, two business consultants, two corporate executives, several teachers, an accountant, a musician, and a real estate broker. All came from busy Second Culture lives, where such ritual does not happen, but they stopped at the threshold and said yes to entering Third Culture space.

In daylight, far away, the project team first convened on a Saturday morning at a conference center located twenty miles outside Minneapolis. The meeting room faced into a courtyard. Light streamed in the open space and illuminated a small pool with koi carp floating under water lilies.

Since the team would be making many decisions about how to work together, Stuart and Carol chose to hold the first meeting off site, away from usual routines and distractions. They wanted to break precedent, and help people get a sense of the difference using the circle would make in how they managed themselves as a group.

Carol arrived early to arrange the room and make sure last-minute details were in place. The padded, comfortable chairs were set in a circle with a sense of spaciousness. She placed a coffee table in the middle, arranged a vase of flowers, put out notebooks, pads of paper, new pens, and her now-familiar candlestick. At the perimeter of the room, several easels were set up with large pads of paper, markers in the tray. Over a portable sound system, she put on synthesizer music.

Stuart arrived. "Gosh, it's awfully . . . I don't know . . . casual in here, or something."

Carol turned and smiled. "It's Saturday. It's not the office. Relax. The music was composed on computer. I thought it fit."

"Where am I going to sit?"

"Any place you want—as long as it's in the circle."

Stuart tried out several chairs, one by the easel, one nearest the coffee service, one facing the courtyard. "I feel like Goldilocks—one chair's too soft, one's too small, one's too hard . . ."

"They're all the same, Stuart, exactly the same."

"Oh, well then, that's the problem," he laughed. "No throne."

"Right, no throne," Carol responded. The door opened. "Morning, Chen, Mike, Bill. You guys ride out together?"

"Of course," said Bill. "Programmers are shackled at the ankles. Didn't Stu tell you? That's how he got all three of us to commit."

"Boy, this had better be good, or I'm outta here," said Chen.

"What, the circle?" Carol was nervous.

"No, the coffee. I'm not starting anything without gonzo coffee." Chen, twenty-four, is the boy wizard in the company, straight from MIT. With a small build and boyish looks, he takes a lot of ribbing from the older men. Mike is thirty-five, introverted and serious. Bill is fifty, confident of his track record, the oldest in the group. They're an odd team, but they've worked together before and get along.

Soon they are joined by Doug from marketing. "I only drink Pepsi, you know," he said, rummaging through his pocket for quarters. "Can you get some from the kitchen, Carol? I suppose this is a nonsmoking room."

Lindsay and Philip, the tech writers, arrived with laptop computers tucked under their arms. Bill greeted them with immediate ribbing. "Geez, are you going to write down every brilliant thing I say?"

Lindsay blushed. "Habit, I guess."

Philip admitted, "Security blanket. I never go anywhere without this puppy." He is tall, angular, African American. They fell silent. Demetria was late. They waited.

Doug came back with two cans of Pepsi and the last vapors of a cigarette still clinging to his clothes. "It's seventy-five cents in the machine," he said into the room. "You get hold of the kitchen yet, Carol?"

"I'm not the gofer," she said. "There's a phone on the wall; I'm sure someone will bring down sodas if you ask." The momentary tension was broken by Demetria's entrance.

"I'm sorry . . . I'm sorry . . . this place is farther out than I thought," she said in a fluster. She set down a large canvas bag and pulled out bottled water and the remains of a rice cake she'd been eating in the car. "I know I've held us up, so let's get going." The others settled in and turned expectantly toward Stuart. He waved his hand and pointed to Carol.

Telling the Story of the Idea

At the beginning of a PeerSpirit circle, whoever has called the circle, framed and held its intention, now sets the tone for what is to come. Our willingness to talk first gives people time to get comfortable, and models the kinds of things they might want to say in a few minutes. We set the context that helps everyone see this circle with similar expectations. This is not an expectation we impose—it is a model of storytelling, helping people understand *how* to come into this particular circle.

At the Marsh House, once people are seated, with backrests and floor pillows, we began to invoke the circle by recalling its ancient roots. I talked by candlelight, playing my role as caller. "Once upon a time the circle was central to life in community, not something rare, exotic, or faraway. Once there was commonality between the cultures scattered over the face of the world—the commonality of the circle."

People were tired from travel but alert to being here. "In the time of First Culture," I said, "when something needed doing, everyone joined together in doing it. When the salmon were running, everyone fished. When the rice or grain needed harvesting, everyone threshed. When the lodge house needed constructing, everyone built. In this week of learning circle, everyone speaks, everyone listens."

Ann, seated across the circle from me, picked up the narrative. "A circle has specific purpose, focused task, tangible work, and tangible results. We know why we are here. We can tell, by the nature of our agreements, how to behave. We can figure out how to fit our skills into the overall process and task at hand. We can measure accomplishment. We can tell who our community is by who supports and helps us. We can see the spiritual core by how ritual is shared, how thanks are offered, how we tend each other's vulnerabilities."

Through our words, we include people in the net of intention. We tell our story and invite others to bring forth their own stories. How this first council is modeled depends on the setting and the purpose for which a circle has been called. In a retreat setting at the beginning of a Circle Practicum, we can do "high circle" with elaborate ritual and meditation, and then drop into personal story. In her business setting, Carol has to begin with practical background and a brief introduction of circle concepts.

She cleared her throat. "A few months ago I had my first experience using something called PeerSpirit circling to respond to a crisis in my children's school. The teachers were about to strike, community intervention had failed, the board was stalemated, and I felt helpless. At the suggestion of two friends, Christina and Ann, who teach Peer-Spirit circling, I asked a group of parents and teachers to my house and called them into a circle. I knew we needed to break the pattern of how the different groups were relating to each other. We experimented with holding a simple kind of council: passing around a kid's ruler and letting whoever had the ruler have the floor. We worked with three principles: rotating leadership, shared responsibility, and reliance on group process to provide guidance. In one evening, we talked out the differences within our group and came up with some creative solutions to present to other groups involved."

Doug popped the tab on his second can of Pepsi. "How does that apply here? We're not in crisis. We don't have differences." Demetria shot him a withering glance, which he totally missed. "We've got one thing to do—design a product."

Stuart leaned into his line of vision. "Give it a minute, Doug. Carol explained this methodology well enough for me to get interested in seeing if it can positively impact how fast and how well we get the R and D done here. If it doesn't work, we'll adopt the usual team procedures."

"That experience of the circle changed my life," Carol plunged quickly on. "I believe now that small groups of ordinary people can create constructive change and have powerful impact. We averted a teachers' strike and laid the foundations for a stronger school system. When Stuart asked me to sit with this team, I convinced him to let me introduce the circle as our structure for self-management because the circle allows us to create a team that can do an effective job and avoid crisis by taking care of how we treat each other in the process. If we're going to come up with something that revolutionizes the industry, I thought it would be exciting to experience a revolution in *how* we designed the product."

"It'll make a good story," said Lindsay.

Making Sacred Center

Demetria, with the weekend of her Tenfold circle fresh in her mind, dug deeply into her bag. "Are we beginning?" she asked Carol. "Is the circle called?" Carol nodded. Demetria slid forward off the chair, a book of matches in her hand. She lit the candle. "What a lovely centerpiece you've laid out here, Carol, thank you. It's the little things that begin a meeting well. Look at this, you guys. Every binder has a name on it. Philip . . . Lindsay . . . Mike . . . Bill . . ." She passed out the notebooks, offered each a pen. Leadership was rotating already.

Sometimes in new groups Ann and I sit in the center, unpacking a basket that has traveled with us since 1993, sharing stories of circle as we pull out one small treasure after another. Sometimes we light a candle and place neutral and natural objects around it—a shallow bowl of water, a small vase of flowers, rocks, shells—to create a sense of center without reference to any specific religious tradition. Whatever the setting, we aim to create a focus that can hold the spiritual gesture.

In a large business conference where the sponsors wanted to integrate PeerSpirit circling as an interactive small-group experience in the midst of keynote addresses and facilitated breakout topics, the center was a large draped circular table. The center served as a symbol of inclusive replenishment, designed so two hundred people could contribute to it and interact with it. One candle, flowers, bowls of fruit and fine chocolate, and spirals of business cards from all those present reflected the tone of the gathering and acknowledged the conference theme—"Igniting Purpose and Spirit in Work."

The centering aspects of circle may also be introduced in a quick, on-the-spot manner. "Sneaky circles," like the one business consultant Lorilla Banbury described trying to help two warring colleagues come to compromise, can be surprisingly effective. "At my wit's end," she told me, "I invited the two women to lunch, shifted the restaurant candle and a plastic daisy into the space between us, and announced, 'This is neutral ground. While one person speaks, we other two are going to stare at this candle and ask the question "How is light trying to come through here? What is light trying to help me understand?" No interrupting. First Clarissa, then Diane—go.'"

Through her sheer confidence, Lorilla imbued the center with energy, gave each woman a way to start using circle practice, and then held the rim so they could talk. However we call in the center, we then need to call in the rim—to articulate the agreements that provide the self-governance of PeerSpirit circling.

Setting Circle Agreements

Before the first check-in at the Circle Practicum, we read the Peer-Spirit agreements aloud and formally committed to living by them for the week. We called for a vote by showing thumbs: thumbs-up meant yes, thumbs-down meant no, thumbs-sideways signaled questions or the need for discussion. When the vote was unanimous, the interpersonal safety net was set in place; people could speak, and know the covenant in which their story would be held. By this time it was dark outside, and the room was lit with soft background lighting so we could see each other's faces. Using a talking piece, we each spoke our names, put an object in the center to hold our place, and shared the first pieces of our stories.

Back in Minnesota, Bill asked, "Stuart, are you going to be part of this, too?"

"Nope, I'm here to get you started, and to talk about the project specs, then I'm going to turn you loose with Carol."

"No, turn us loose with each other," Demetria interjected, "to learn to be a team."

"Right. I can't be on this team, but I came for the opening of this circle so I could understand what I'm asking of you."

Carol's attention snapped back into focus. "The first page in the notebooks," she pointed out, "is a list of agreements under which a

PeerSpirit circle functions, so we know what to expect from each other, what's appropriate."

Michael looked puzzled. "What's usually appropriate is to focus on programming. Aren't we going to get to that?"

"Yes, as soon as we have the structure in place."

"Wait a sec," said Philip. "I'm new to this. Usually nobody calls in the writers until much later in the gig. We end up trying to explain what you all thought made perfect sense. If we weren't doing this process stuff, how would the meeting begin?"

"Last time I was in a skunk works," Mike said, leaning forward eagerly, "we covered the conference table with sheets of paper, put our goal at one end, our current state of information at the other, and tried to fill in the gaps. We divided into groups of two and three, went directly to the hardware. I don't even see a computer around here. And it's Saturday and I'm missing the game."

"Whoa, I've got something to say," said Stuart. "It's a story that may explain why I let Carol talk me into this. And before I tell you, I realize I want to know if you're going to tell anyone else. . . ." There was a murmur, a few shaking heads. "Now that I have something kind of personal *I* want to say, this list of agreements makes sense. So—you want to hear my story? Let's agree on the ground rules. Carol?"

"All our social interactions occur with mutual expectation," Carol explained. "For example, we expect people to respond when we speak to them. We expect people to drive on the right side of the road. It may seem strange this morning to state our agreements straight out, but the circle works most effectively through contracted social understanding. That Stuart is waiting for the agreements before he speaks says a lot to me about how important they are, and how much we need them."

"We've all signed noncompete clauses," said Doug, "and we know better than to open our mouths outside the circle—I mean the team, so why do we need agreements? It's just business."

Demetria leaned forward. "We need agreements because I don't want you blabbing some anecdote about me around the dining hall that you think means nothing and I think is embarrassing."

"Okay, I won't say anything. But I don't get why any of this is even going to come up. This is a product development team."

"Yes, and it's a circle," Demetria interjected. "In a circle we don't go in a straight line from point A to point B—we go in a circle, we go in a spiral."

"That's not efficient."

"Yes, it is. And it's like what you did before, breaking off into little subgroups huddled over the hardware, working this angle and that, trying to get into the core of the program, seeing what you could make it do. That wasn't linear thinking! It was creative, circular, tangential."

Doug reached into his pocket, began fingering his lighter. "I gotta take a break. So tell me again, why is it that we're gonna tell each other the story of our lives as part of this circular process?"

"Because maybe if we know each other better, we can work together better." Demetria struggled a second, went on. "Maybe if I know your story I won't think you're rude, and you won't think I'm pushy, and we'll have enough understanding of each other to get the real work done."

"Okay," he said. "You want to understand me—fine. Just let me grab a smoke."

"After we make our agreements," said Carol, and began reading from her notebook.

1. *What is said in the circle belongs in the circle.*
    "Confidentiality means that we hold the business of the circle within the circle. We don't gossip about each other, or how things are going between us. We deal with conflict directly. We keep confidentiality regarding the project."
2. *The circle is a practice in discernment, not judgment.*
    "Discernment means we practice listening to each other very carefully—noticing the gifts each one offers, and not cutting short our attention by jumping to conclusions or judgments or preparing rebuttals."
3. *Each person takes responsibility for asking the circle for the support s/he wants and needs.*
    "Asking for what we need allows us to avoid power struggles and drama as ways of getting attention. This applies both to asking for technical support in the midst of a task and to asking for interpersonal support in the midst of a meeting."

4. *Each person takes responsibility for agreeing or not agreeing to participate in specific requests.*
"We can support someone and not take direct part in what they need. We may choose not to support a request. We may challenge whether or not a request serves group purpose. If a request fits our task, others are likely to help carry it through. If a request doesn't fit, we need to work together to hold the focus."

5. *Anyone in the circle may call for silence, time-out, or ritual to reestablish focus, to recenter, or to remember the need for spiritual guidance.*
"We're using this form because it promotes communication, and communication promotes both creativity and efficiency. If communication breaks down, we need to stop and restore it. Later we can talk about using a group guardian—but for now, I just want us to agree to the idea of stopping to refocus when we need to."

6. *Agreements are updatable. If something is not working, we revise the
agreement and maintain the process.*
"Agreements are like our mini-constitution. If trouble develops, we search together for an agreement that better supports how we're treating each other and what we're getting done."[1]

Carol glanced around. The faces of her colleagues looked closed to her, unreadable. "I had no idea how strange this language would sound in business," she thought. Then Demetria nodded. "I'll live with these agreements," she said.

"So will I," said Lindsay.

"Yeah, I guess . . . ," said Philip.

"Okay by me. Now can I have a cigarette?" Doug stood up and broke the circle and the group took a stretch break.

---

[1] See Appendix A for a complete statement of PeerSpirit circle agreements.

Fears and Expectations

Carol barely made it into the bathroom before she broke into tears—the release of her own nervousness. Demetria found her there, reached out a hand, paused. Carol nodded, and the tall, intense Greek woman put her arm across Carol's shoulders and gave her a brief hug. "You're doing great," she said. "This is hard stuff. I couldn't believe it when you and Stuart said you were going to try a circle in this project. It's the reason I signed up."

"It is? Boy, I feel like everyone else is just barely tolerating it."

"They don't know what it is yet. It hasn't really started happening."

"Thanks for getting me back on track a couple of times this morning. You know something about this, don't you?"

"Well, I started my own circle a couple of months ago," Demetria said. "It keeps me balanced."

"What do you do?"

"Some friends and I mentor each other about career stuff and personal dreams and celebrate women's spirituality. Since that started, you should see my house—it would surprise everyone here, maybe even you. There are little altars everywhere."

"I don't know you very well, do I?" Carol said.

"Well, you will, if the circle works. I'm sorry I lost my temper with Doug. He's going to be a challenge for me. I get so tired of taking baby steps. I want us to give up our precious control mania and get into circle so we can start communicating, let down a few walls. . . . I don't know if this is going to work with Doug, but *I'm* sure glad to be here," Demetria told her.

"You know so much more than I do, you should be leading this group—not me."

"No, I shouldn't. Leadership rotates, and responsibility is shared. . . . Listen, we need to get back out there and help everyone start leading this group."

The first fifteen to thirty minutes of the initial meeting are often difficult for the caller because the principles haven't clicked in, agreements haven't been set, and, unless people have been in circle before, no one is quite sure what to do. The more we can let go of worry and control over how this first meeting will go, the more synergy will be available to help the group coalesce. This doesn't mean we—as callers—withdraw energy and attention; it means we call upon clear intention, gathered spirit, and common interest to help everyone come forward. It's new for other people, too, and all their fears about loss of control are also rising.

For the first few minutes of a new circle, sometimes the whole first session, we are *all* in turmoil. We are between cultures—trying to let go of our Second Culture assumptions, not yet able to see how Third Culture is going to work. Our minds are sending us all kinds of messages: "This will work. . . . No, it won't. . . ." We are looking for something to trust, a rock to stand on. One of the greatest helps is to look at each other, to begin to tell and listen to each other's stories.

Story—oh, yes, we remember how to do this.

First Time Around the Rim

Stuart brought the perfect talking piece to introduce to the software team—a wand made out of a diskette and a slide rule. After some good-natured ribbing about his arts-and-crafts work, the group settled down to listen. Stuart held the talking piece while telling his own story, and nobody interrupted.

"Well," he said, "upper management views this project as my baby. If you guys produce, we'll all be heroes; if you don't, I'll take the rap. This makes me a little nervous, as you can imagine." He brushed his hand through thinning hair. "I think I'm a good manager, but I'm not going to be in here managing. I can't. I don't have the time and I don't think you really need me. What you need is a way to manage yourselves and build team spirit.

"In my last company I pulled together a team like this, gave them a pep talk, and sent them on their way. I checked in weekly and they kept telling me things were fine, but the team blew up. One guy refused to finish the project. Another man quit with the R and D in his head, took it out of state to a competitor. A woman had a nervous breakdown. Careers splattered. I saw a lot of pain come out of what I thought was a very ordinary process.

"I'm a little haunted by this mistake." Stuart's voice cracked for an instant. "Those people were my responsibility, and I let them down. I didn't read the distress signals, and the project was hemorrhaging before I even knew it was bleeding." Stuart looked around, noticed their silent attention.

"My first thought was to stick Carol in here as my safety valve, the person designated to keep everyone communicating and to communicate with me. Much to my surprise, Carol didn't want the job and came back with this suggestion to try managing by circle. We've tried out enough aspects of total quality management that this didn't sound too weird. So here we are. Carol says that leadership rotates, responsibility is shared, and the group finds its own wisdom. Sounds good to me. I want to thank you all for agreeing to give it a try as part of your commitment to project development." He took a breath and passed the talking wand to Chen.

"Well, that puts a different slant on things." Chen gulped. "This is my first job, and unless you guys tell me otherwise, I haven't made any big mistakes yet. I'm as eager as anyone else to get down to work, and I love working with Mike and Bill. I'll try anything that can build a team between all of us as good as the team we three have already got going." He passed the talking piece to Lindsay . . . and so they went around the rim.

At this point, group dynamics have been set spinning: The circle has come alive. No one person knows everything that will happen. We may have spent months jelling the ideas that brought the group together, but it's not our private plan anymore. Right before our eyes, the council calls itself into being.

Without anyone needing to mention the structures of PeerSpirit all at one time, those structures begin to activate within the circle. Stuart's plea that the team take seriously its attention to process, as well as its drive for product, invited everyone to make a covenant with the team—even though in this setting the idea of covenant may never be explicitly articulated. And as the day progressed, they worked toward a first understanding of how to lay out the work before them. They defined tasks, with one person assuming leadership for each task and asking for help from other members. They devised a work plan and created a schedule.

Sometimes they forgot they were in circle rather than the usual teams—they forgot to feel awkward in the newness of the learning curve. Every now and then Carol or Demetria would interject, "Hey, you guys, we just rotated leadership and shared responsibility." One time Mike asked, "Isn't this in agreement three? Listen up—I'm asking for what I need!"

"So what?" mocked Chen. "Agreement four is I get to say yes or no."

"Not on my list," Mike responded in kind. And every now and then, someone would call for a round of talking piece to slow things down, heighten attention, make sure everyone had a say. Every now and then Carol would suggest a few seconds of silence and three breaths.

By Sunday noon, they had a grid in place for setting out their task. They were exhilarated and tired, wanting to go home and rest before returning to work. Stuart gave them Monday off and his managerial blessing. They were ready to close the circle and to let each other go.

Closing the Circle with Respect

To hold the rim—paying attention to task *and* process—requires a high degree of attention. We need to be more alert than usual. One reason for opening and closing the circle with simple ritual is to signal each other when this level of attention is required, and when we may relax, have a cup of tea, and make light conversation.

In a Circle Practicum, when we are living together for several days, closing the circle is especially important so that people can relax between sessions of council. People take turns offering some kind of centering for the group, often a meaningful part of their own spiritual practice. The guardian watches over our energies and calls for stretch breaks, breaths, and silence. And at the end of every session we stand in circle, pause, and someone says something like, "Thank you for the teachings of this session. As we shift from ceremonial space to social space or private time, we release each other from the intensity of council, and let the rim expand." People tend to scatter slowly.

Someone may sit back down to write, someone does tai chi or yoga stretches, a few stroll slowly across the meadow and back up the marsh trail.

Circle business needs to happen while the circle is open, when people are expecting to have their attentiveness called upon, not during transition times. Even the standard phrase "Meeting adjourned" acknowledges this need to signal the end of business. It feels good to close a circle, to signify that the experience has been successfully completed. Closing a circle that has met for only a few hours usually requires only a simple and short acknowledgment. At the end of a long seminar or ongoing group where the circle energy has deepened, the closing needs to reflect the atmosphere of intimacy that has developed.

Energetically, what has been called in needs to be released. At the end of the planning weekend, Carol called for attention one last time. "I know we all want to get home," she said, "but I think that instead of just splitting, it's important to acknowledge what a terrific start we're off to. What if we pass the talking piece and each say one thing we learned about the project or each other that was a positive surprise?" A few minutes later, when the piece came back to Carol's hands, she said, "I learned what a techno-peasant I am! And that you're going to find ways to use my ignorance—like, if *I* can understand it, you must be getting clear! I look forward to the education and to getting to know you. Thanks for coming. Thanks for taking this risk. See you Tuesday." She leaned forward and blew out the candle, grateful that Demetria had remembered to light it.

An epiphanal community
of two or more people
expands the imagination of the culture around them.
The more organic, less structured the community is,
the more powerful the pace of change.
A group of people who are inspired
from an imagination that has been illuminated by Nature's presence,
and has contact with the Voice of the Sacred within each of them,
generates a great deal of power
to move through large, rigid organizational structures.

DAVID T. KYLE, *Human Robots and Holy Mechanics*

CHAPTER 7

Sustaining the PeerSpirit Circle

When we bring spirit-centeredness and peer leadership into the meetings-meetings-meetings of Second Culture, we introduce a radical shift in business as usual, no matter where we're calling the circle. The circle will adapt and work in whatever setting we call it, but it will be influenced by the people, the place, and the purpose of the group. What remains the same is the structure that underlies what appears on the surface.

On the surface, if we are passing a talking piece to gather stories at a family reunion, or opening and closing with prayer in a church committee, or rotating leadership agenda item by agenda item in a staff meeting, circles might not appear to have much in common. The subtlety of PeerSpirit structure is intentional, so that it may be integrated and adapted into the subculture of many groups, providing a skeletal core for process and accomplishment.

Think for a minute about the skeleton inside your own body. Basically, we all have the same structure. When you hang flesh off our combination of bones, you get a being that stands and moves about and is capable of certain kinds of action and reaction determined by the nature of the skeleton that supports us. Line up a hundred people and you begin to see the variety of our embodiment, the beauty of our diversity. PeerSpirit serves as the circle's skeleton; we are the circle's body. To sustain the circle, we put the skeleton in place and practice embodiment of the form. Bones don't move until they are fleshed out: Momentum in the circle comes from its applications. And when we need it, the structure is there to call on.

I believe it is important for those who are learning the circle in business to gain understanding of how the circle emerges in the private realm, and for those who come to circle practice through its expression in women's or men's work, healing, spirituality, and celebration to see its applications in business. Throughout this chapter, we will continue to trace the embodiment of several circles that share PeerSpirit structure but sustain themselves differently because their settings and intention are different.

The first meetings of a new circle, or the first meetings after the switch is made to circle process, can be very dynamic. As people work through their initial awkwardness with the form—remembering not to cross-talk when the talking piece is used, placing something in the center without embarrassment—the usefulness of the circle starts to become obvious. Voices are heard that had been silenced; the workload is lifted from the overburdened shoulders of those who had carried the group or called the circle; the values, mission, and philosophy that activate a particular circle are articulated and honored; and containment has been created that allows people to take risks in truth telling and coleadership. Most of the time, this is an amazing relief.

Energetically, there's often a rush of enthusiasm—"We get it!"—and a willingness to try circle in an ongoing way. As the circle progresses, questions soon arise about how the container is held and how things get accomplished. These questions might be divided into two categories: how the circle functions as an interpersonal environment, and how the circle functions as a tool for action. The combination of these aspects allows the circle to be inward-facing and outward-doing.

One integrating tool that helps the members of a circle keep track of both these elements is the circle logbook.

The Circle Logbook

When the project team reconvened after their weekend retreat, they had established an agenda for action. They had developed a shared and articulated intention. They had defined goals. They had formally opened and closed their sessions and developed a basic familiarity with each other and their task.

Back in the office as they started work, Philip walked in with a present for the group. "I thought we did a great job over the weekend," he said during check-in. The group wasn't using the talking piece yet, just sitting in a circle of comfortable chairs with a coffee table in the space between them, placing their objects—reflecting on the weekend. "It seems we ironed out some of the process and defined the project's actual work and timeline. So, to keep us on track, I took the liberty of taking the stuff Carol gave us and notes from the meeting and putting it all together in a cyber-notebook." He opened his laptop. "If I may offer Exhibit A—the project team logbook." With a flourish, he booted the circle's private interactive site onto the screen.

A logbook holds the historical record and future projections of a circle together. Even though the technical wizards of the software team chose to do an on-line rendition for their circle, most groups find an old-fashioned notebook a highly satisfying artifact of circle. The logbook holds the group's memorabilia—everything from the collective intention to personal commitment statements and photos and notes. At times of review, the logbook plays an important role as it reminds people what the circle set out to do and how they agreed to participate, and it may help trace the roots of conflict as well as how resolution occurred and new vision developed.

Most of the time, circle logbooks are standard three-ring binders divided by index tabs with topics adapted to suit the group. In the case of the project circle, the tabs were electronic. Philip flipped through several screen options. "Tab A: Group agreements and other foundations—in here I downloaded the agreements page Carol provided. Tab B: Circlemates—bio pages on each one of us. My page has a photo animation sequence of my dog, Samson, and me—say hello to the nice people, Samson." He pressed a key and the on-screen dog barked obediently. "Of course there's every phone, fax, E-mail, and pager number I could think of. Samson has his own separate line. I have a page formatted for each of you, and I am sure you'll get creative in your additions." The group nodded at him.

"Tab C: Minutes of our council sessions—Lindsay and I slipped into scribe mode over the weekend. It was a good way for me to stay comfortable, but I don't want to be the one doing it all the time. However, I do think a consistent charting of our progress is necessary. Private tracking, just for us. Tab D: Action items—who's working on what, with whom, what the timelines are, et cetera. Tab E: Outcomes—a place to note the completed tasks that lead up to fulfilling our project intention. I don't know about you, but tackling something this long and complicated, I need to see the steps and have some way of checking them off."

"And celebrating!" said Chen. "I think we ought to come up with some definite blowout points along the way."

"Obviously Tab F," said Philip, "needs to be designated for celebrations. Tab G is open."

"Wow!" said Demetria, "what a great setup! Thanks, Phil. I can hardly wait to get in there and log on." And so they began their first day combining circle and task.

Time and Commitment

Another issue that arises quickly in most groups is all the questions about time and commitment: What is the length of time the circle will meet? How are meeting times handled? What is their frequency? If a person agrees to join at the first meeting but later wants to leave, how should that be handled?

Every circle has a life span: a time period of existence. In Carol's parents and teachers circle, the time frame was set by the immediate crisis. The group united to face the crisis and get the job done. The original group met only a few times, but disseminated into the system circle skills that may be widely used for a long time. If circles continue to meet to support students or to organize volunteer activities, interpersonal issues will assume more importance as the circle shifts from the cohesiveness of crisis management to reckoning with the complexities of the interpersonal environment. The more "leisure" that exists in a circle, and the longer its time frame, the more attention will need to be placed on the interpersonal. Take, for example, Demetria's Tenfold circle, where the time span is indefinite and open.

Circles like Tenfold, with a long-range time commitment, need intermediate points where members can carefully reconsider their commitment to the circle. During these periods of review, every member is invited to recommit, or to withdraw with the blessings of the group. For example, a Tenfold circle of women friends who have been meeting for three years review their logbook every January, rewrite their personal covenants, and update their intentions. One member left for a year and returned; one member has left permanently, without hard feelings. This circle has evolved into a major source of support in each member's life. The evolution of their circle has depended on their ability to openly negotiate time and commitment.

A specific time contract creates immediacy in the circle—a sense that we need to get things done because this isn't going to last forever. The right balance between the time we have and the size of the job, or the meaningfulness of the experience, creates a sense of backing that helps coalesce the circle.

In the project circle, the time frame is set by the deadline for research and development—they expect to have a working prototype in six months. "This could mean a lot of late nights," warned Bill.

"I'm willing," Lindsay agreed.

"So am I," said Demetria, "except for the night of the full moon—I have another meeting to attend."

"What, you're a werewolf?" asked Doug.

Demetria laughed along with the rest of them. "No, but one more comment like that and I'll lace your Pepsi with eye of newt and toe of frog!"

In Demetria's Tenfold circle, the group decided to spend the first session after their weekend of formation laying structures in place to help them stay in balance. They compensated for their broad intention, "to define and pursue their life dreams in a spirit-based circle," by making a strong commitment to the exploration process. They laid out intentions for how they wanted to be with each other, and vowed to stay together while going through the first wobbles.

By the end of the evening they had decided several things that surprised them—decisions Demetria would not have thought of by herself. They chose to meet two times a month: once on the full moon, when they would explore and express their spirituality, and another time to be decided month by month, when one member could call on the group for active support and they would get to know each other's lives and circumstances. They voted to paint Valerie's kitchen and agreed to take all their collective children to the park. They decided to stay together for six months and then to review their intention and commitments.

The Importance of Familiar Ritual

What holds the circle together is a sense of being a distinct group. Circle identity is set in place through familiar ritual and routine—how a circle runs itself. While ritual may take only a few minutes in a business setting, it can be quite elaborate in a private setting.

In Demetria's Tenfold circle, there are twelve women, ranging in age from early thirties to late fifties. At a recent meeting, when Rachel volunteered to host the next circle, she folded up the group's altar from Demetria's living room floor and took it and the logbook home with her. In the group's fifth month, routines and rituals were both established and evolving.

When members arrive at Rachel's house bearing potluck entrées, salads, and a tray of brownies, they hug and chat and help set out supper. This is an informal time to talk about pets or children or local news, suggest books and movies to each other, and generally catch up. The women are friendly, but they wait to share the deeper issues on their minds until the circle is gathered, when they know they can have—and offer—full attention to each other.

A Tenfold circle opens and closes with ritual that honors center. In the living room, away from the clutter of supper, Rachel has already laid out the basics of their centerpiece. This circle has its own basket with a collection of small treasures representing each one of the members. It is dusk when the circle convenes. Rachel starts a tape of soft music and lights a stick of incense. The women filter into the room and settle down in silence. Rachel removes a ball of red yarn from the basket. She passes it around the rim, and the women unroll it hand to hand, laying the outline of a circle on the carpeting. They sit on the rim of a circle of their own creation, honoring rituals of their own design.

Demetria sighs deeply, grateful for the balance of both circles in her life. Rachel lights the center candle and reads a quote she's found to share. There are thoughtful nods, and the women fall silent for a few minutes. Before they pass their talking piece, Rachel asks, "Who will be our guardian this evening?"

"I'll do it," says Val, and she takes a small brass bell from the center and sets it in her lap. Once the guardian is in place, every member knows that her check-in will be held within the full structure of Peer-Spirit circling. The shift has been made from social space to circle.

Doug would not yet be comfortable here, though if he ever wandered into a men's group he might find that the rituals are not significantly different. At the office, the team also puts an object in the middle and checks in with a brief statement about something going on in each of their lives beyond the project work. It seemed a needed balance, since so much of their time and talk is focused on their shared task.

Check-in is a common ritual for beginning many circles. It allows each member to present him/herself in an anecdotal way. In these few minutes of verbal gathering, everyone learns what may be asked of his/her attention during this council.

The Importance of Real Dialogue

After check-in, the women break into dyads, scatter around the house in nooks and crannies, and take turns speaking with a listening partner. Each woman has fifteen minutes of uninterrupted time to speak her mind. If she falls silent, her partner simply remains in an attitude of receptive listening and does not prompt, interfere, or interpret. At the sound of Rachel's kitchen timer, they switch roles and the second woman talks. They do this at every meeting to build interconnection and help each woman articulate her spiritual journey.

At the end of the evening, they meet again in full circle, and each woman shares an insight or makes a commitment to some change she wants to pursue in her life. There is often a lot of emotion: tears and laughter, requests for backing, spontaneous song. The interpersonal environment contains much affection and mutual support as the women grow comfortable with each other and the process.

What is going on in Rachel's living room may seem foreign to those immersed in business-as-usual or accustomed to more traditional forms of meeting, but the circle is following stages of group development that have been widely studied and documented in the last thirty or so years. This information, expressed in the vocabulary of psychology, business, or social theory, has been streaming into the culture in narrow bands that have not necessarily cross-communicated. Each band has developed its own language for explaining what happens to people in groups.

Anthropologist Riane Eisler takes on five thousand years of patriarchy and challenges people to reclaim a "partnership way" that balances power and radically alters communication.[1] M. Scott Peck talks about group process as starting with pseudo-community, proceeding through chaos, then achieving authentic community.[2] Group development models, based on the work of Bruce Tuckman, William Schutz, and Wilfred Bion, refer to stages of a group's life as "formin', stormin', normin', and performin'."[3] Sam Kaner's work with Participatory Decision-Making defines a group as beginning with divergent thinking, heading into "the groan zone," where differences surface, then being able to experience convergent thinking and come to closure.[4] David Bohm's Dialogue Process invites participants to throw ideas and issues into "the open space."[5]

---

[1] Riane Eisler, *The Chalice and the Blade* (San Francisco: Harper San Francisco, 1988), and Riane Eisler and David Loye, *The Partnership Way* (San Francisco: Harper San Francisco, 1990).

[2] M. Scott Peck, *A Different Drum: Community-making and Peace* (New York: Simon and Schuster, 1988).

[3] W. R. Bion, *Experiences in Groups* (New York: Basic Books, 1961); W. C. Schutz, *Here Comes Everybody* (New York: Harper and Row, 1971); B. W. Tuckman, "Development Sequence in Small Groups," *Psychological Bulletin* 63 (1965), pp. 284–99.

[4] Sam Kaner et al., *Facilitator's Guide to Participatory Decision-Making* (Philadelphia: New Society Publishers, 1996).

[5] David Bohm, *Unfolding Meaning* (Loveland, CO: Foundation House, 1985).

All of these theories, including that of the PeerSpirit circle, are attempts to work with the energetics of the interpersonal field in creative and respectful ways so that a group can come into existence, define its purpose, and live through the process of being together without shedding blood.

One widely known integrator of much of this theory is MIT scholar Peter Senge. He synthesizes in business language much of what we've been exploring in circle language.[6] For teams to function in an organization, Senge says, they need to hold three critical dimensions: to think insightfully about complex issues, to innovatively coordinate action, and to seed similar insight and behavior throughout the organization.

I see the circle supporting these dimensions and, in PeerSpirit form, adding the focused center as a way to help orchestrate the rise of collective alignment. "Wisdom," I had said to Stuart when we were trying to convince him to give the circle approach a chance. "Group process," Carol had said. "Okay," Stuart had said, because there was something familiar about the circle—familiar in its ancient roots, and familiar in its current applications.

This is not just a dialogue about how circle looks different in its applications in business/organizational settings from its applications in personal/spiritual settings; this is a dialogue that often occurs between men and women as we strive to understand the nature of circle itself and how it can be broadly integrated into our lives. The more we can see the commonality in the skeletal structure of the circle, the less afraid we will be to try the circle in a new setting, or to validate the use of the circle in ways that look different from our own.

It's heartbreaking to me how many times people (usually it's women, but not always) admit on the last day of a Circle Practicum that they have no idea how to speak to their spouses or business partners about what they've been learning. I hope that as the application of the circle spreads, this sense of the "otherness" of circle will

---

[6] Peter Senge, *The Fifth Discipline: The Art and Practice of the Learning Organization* (New York: Doubleday/Currency, 1990). Senge reassures anyone who still thinks "spirit" is out of place in the work environment that he considers synergy a real force and acknowledges the ability of a group to experience "collective alignment" that empowers every individual while simultaneously empowering the team.

diminish. Meanwhile, it's fascinating to me that people who do not seem to have heard of circle are nevertheless applying circle structures. This should be greatly calming to people in business who think the circle is strange, and greatly calming to people outside business who fear a form with heart could never be accepted there.

Peter Senge acknowledges dialogue's ancient roots, crediting both the classical Greek period and Native American societies as sources that have taught us the necessity of truth telling and listening with objectivity. In his own vocabulary, Senge validates the forms of council I describe in Chapter Four of this book: "The discipline of team learning involves mastering the practices of dialogue and discussion, the two distinct ways that teams converse. In dialogue there is free and creative exploration of complex and subtle issues, a deep 'listening' to one another and suspending of one's own views. By contrast, in discussion, different views are presented and defended, and there is a search for the best view to support decisions that must be made at this time. Dialogue and discussion are potentially complementary, but most teams lack the ability to distinguish between the two and move consciously between them."[7]

To put this in circle language, the commonality in the circle—whether it's occurring in Rachel's living room, or in a suite of offices in the back corner of the software company, or in any of the other places cited throughout this book—is that dialogue has been reintroduced into a culture that had ceased to value anything deeper, or slower, or more meaningful than discussion.

What initially confounds people accustomed to the percussive pace of sound bites and snappy comebacks is the circle's emphasis on dialogue and on techniques of council that deliberately slow down and alter the pace of conversation so that it can transform into dialogue. The good of the circle, in business, in community, and in our homes, is the reintroduction of deep listening. The circle holds us in place long enough to draw out what is trying to get said.

In many business settings, the time people spend in circle may be the only hours in a week or month that move at a pace where people can have a thought and time to express it. The nurturing within this experience fosters a level of dialogue that has profound and far-

---

[7] Ibid., p. 239.

reaching impact. And out of this fertile ground, our decisions and tasks emerge within collective support.

The Importance of Real Accomplishment

In Chapter One, I suggested that the circle is waiting for us to apply it broadly and boldly. We know the circle can serve as a forum for healing and for clarifying communication, and to join the mainstream in ways that influence Second Culture, the circle must also facilitate our ability to get things done. We are a people with much to do if we are going to respond to the crises surrounding us, and we are in need of better ways to do things.

PeerSpirit circling is a transformative tool for staff, board, and committee meetings. The ritual elements of the circle (calling in the center and using some form of check-in to help people to gather and focus) can be adapted to fit almost any setting. The guardian is put in place as an observer of group process. Then leadership rotates by building an agenda where one person at a time sponsors an item.

We often help a group design an agenda-building sheet similar to the model below.[8]

Date:_____

Time session opened:_____

Time closed:_____

Facilitator (if used):_____

Guardian:_____

Sponsors by agenda items:_____

Name:_____

Item:_____

Negotiated discussion time:_____

Work needing to be done/by whom:_____

_____

Date of next report, outcome or completion:_____

---

[8] See Appendix B for a more complete format of this checklist.

The sponsor of an item contracts for a specific amount of time within the parameters of the meeting, decides how best to present the issue, facilitates conversation or dialogue using forms of council, and asks for the task support needed to do this piece of work. While acting as the facilitator of the moment, this person has the watchful help of the guardian (who often acts as timekeeper) and the support of all the circle's structure to help the group take thoughtful action. Depending on the nature of the agenda item, this may be twenty minutes of talking piece council to gather ideas for upcoming decisions, or dialogue leading to the need to assume responsibility for specific tasks. Consensus or the thumbs-up/thumbs-down/thumbs-sideways form of voting may be called for. At the end of the time, people volunteer to take on parts of the task as needed.

Inside the confines of the software company skunk works, much of what started off as formal circle was now happening while the group huddled in front of a computer screen trying to make the machines respond to their ever-evolving programming efforts. Carol, an outsider to the techno-jargon, kept watching for ways to adapt the circle to help the process. She brought in a Koosh ball that got tossed hand to hand, followed by shouts of "Wait, wait, try this . . . I know what might work!" It kept the cross talk down enough so they could hear each other, and kept the energy up enough to facilitate their innovative thinking.

Twice a week, or anytime a member requested an hour of stop-action, they met for council without the machines and talked to each other about progress, frustration, and how particular tasks and assignments were going. Chen and Mike were overseeing subteams assigned to the project from engineering. "I need ten minutes," Chen said, leading into his agenda item. "I need to know how to direct the guys in engineering. Lindsay, start the clock," he said, referring to her role as guardian of this council. "I want three minutes to talk it out, and seven minutes of brilliant response."

In an interdepartmental administrative group Ann and I consult with, the circle addresses long-term agenda items for many meetings. One person carries an item and reports progress month after month, informing the rest of the circle about current developments going on in the wider organization and carrying guidance from the circle back out to that part of the organization where decisions are implemented.

They have decided to write position papers, claiming responsibility for their words going out from this circle into the organization. And now they are coaching other groups within the company who want to start meeting in circle.

As people in business circles respond to their needs to have a container for heart and spirit as well as task, people in more private, spiritual, or interpersonal circles discover their need to balance the richness of their intimacy with task.

The members of a Tenfold circle that has been meeting since 1993 illustrate this balance beautifully. The members have been through many celebrations and challenges and have developed a strong core commitment to circle, to each other, and to service. An older friend of two Tenfold members, a woman who sat in another circle with them, had a tragedy strike her life. Her daughter was assaulted and left with permanent brain damage; this woman and her husband, both in their seventies, were being emotionally and physically exhausted by the sudden and unrelenting return of parental care duties. As the situation continued, the Tenfold circle made a commitment to provide respite care for the daughter, and to become a supportive presence willing to advocate for her, even after her elderly parents are gone; people used the agreements to sort through their own levels of participation. A long-range commitment like this is dependent on the stability of the circle.

The Importance of Authentic Conflict

Everyone participating in a circle is on the learning curve. We bring differing backgrounds and experiences, strength, vulnerability, and confusion to the circle. As an energetic container, the circle itself is constantly shifting. The next two chapters address the interpersonal challenges that arise in circle and various ways to respond. But before we leave the project team, they have something to teach us about successful conflict resolution using the principles and practices of circle. It wasn't a great surprise when Demetria and Doug got into conflict; the surprise was how they—and the circle—handled it.

Though tension had been accumulating and dissipating during the first two months of R and D, there was a moment when Demetria was making a point, talking piece in hand, and Doug cut her off. Instead of smoothing over the moment and going on, the two locked horns.

"I get it, Dee," Doug interjected. "So let's stop talking about whether or not we can make the program work and get back on the machine."

"Dammit, Doug, I know you're frustrated, but don't take it out on me—you've cut me off every time I've had the floor for the past week."

"No, I haven't!" Doug countered.

"You just did it again!" She thrust the talking piece toward him. "The purpose of this thing is to give me the chance to finish my thoughts without having to worry about interruption. But lately I've come to *expect* interruption."

"You're just touchy," said Doug, pushing his chair back from the table, as though wishing to eject himself from the situation.

"Stop!" said Mike, who was acting as guardian. "If we're going to use the form, let's use the form. Either respect the piece, or put it down!"

Demetria paused for a moment. "I want to put it down—all down," she finally said. "Especially the way Doug and I go at each other." She took a deep breath. "I have a point I want to make here and I need to know if you're ready to listen." She looked at Doug pointedly. "For my part, I promise not to attack—and I want the same assurance from you."

Mike rang a bell they used as the guardian's signal; the group fell into a few seconds of silence. Then Mike rang the bell again and said, "I suggest we take a five-minute break and reconvene away from the conference table in a circle of chairs."

There are really only two kinds of conflict: conflicts with people who will step forward and work to resolve the issue, and conflicts with people who escalate the issue. The actual issue is far less significant than our attitude toward problem solving.

This is the moment when both Doug and Demetria have to decide what their attitude will be toward conflict within the team and toward each other. However the situation crystallizes, it's important to remember that Doug and Demetria aren't having a problem; the whole circle is having a problem. As commonly occurs in the circle (or in a team or other group), two members are poles for the frustration inherent in project development. Chen can look energized, Bill can look relaxed, and Philip can remain detached because Doug and Demetria are carrying the collective load. As such polarization develops and comes to a head, everyone in the circle needs to support those who have brought an issue forward and to help them release the polarity in order to redirect group energy. Such polarities exist in all groups—and in every circle.

After the break, the group regathered in circled chairs, a centerpiece of accumulated project memorabilia placed between them. Doug announced, "I'm willing to spend five minutes on this. No more. I'm not interested in getting into some kind of big feeling session with anyone, but for five minutes, I'll listen and speak."

Maybe a particular circle isn't the cozy home base of like-minded souls we thought it would be. Does that mean it isn't functioning, or does that mean we need to look realistically at its intent and purpose? Maybe a particular circle is getting too personal for our comfort. Do we wish it would just handle business and not ask us to speak or act from the heart?

Chen moved his chair over next to Doug's. "I don't want you to get the feeling that you're being cornered," he said. "So if it's okay with you, I'd like to sit next to you." Doug looked surprised, but nodded.

Demetria asked Carol for similar support, and Carol sat next to her with her arm across the back of the chair, her palm about an inch from Demetria's shoulder blades. "Does this feel okay?" she asked. "I don't want to distract you." Demetria nodded.

Bill sat in the point halfway between them; Lindsay was across the circle from him. There was a sense of four points being held with attention around the perimeter of the group.

Every circle has its more and less dominant personalities. Every circle has people who are more and less aware of their behavior, or the impact of their behavior on the circle. Every circle has a matrix of affinities: people who respond and resonate with each other easily, and others who aren't quite sure how to fit. These affinities tend to shift and change, and partly depend on how different individuals handle themselves at moments like this.

Bill took up the leadership and said, "While Mike's being guardian of the whole group, I volunteer to hold the rim. Lindsay's going to help me. We're going to act like referees in a boxing match—though that isn't the image I want to convey. You guys aren't in opposite corners; you're both on our project team. One team. Doug, if you get hot under the collar, Lindsay is going to say one word to you—'Halt.' That's your signal to stop talking and think about what you're saying. If Demetria gets hot under the collar, I will do the same." Lindsay nodded. "If five minutes doesn't do it, then I'm going to ask us to consider the next option. Each of you gets to make a statement and the other responds, back and forth, until it's clear what *you* need to do differently and what *we* need to do differently. Who wants to start?" He held up the Koosh ball, and Doug gestured to receive the toss.

"I'll start," he said. "Um, I'm not comfortable with what everybody calls group process. I like to take charge. It makes my day to get things done. To make a list and check off real items. It's a sport with me—how much can I do? I'm on this team 'cause I love the idea of this product. I want us to beat the competition to market. I want something I can be proud of, a feather in my career cap. When the brainstorming is rolling along, and this Koosh ball is flying back and forth, I love how we work together. But when we veer off focus, it drives me nuts. I just want to get up and running again. So that's where I'm at." He tossed the ball to Demetria.

"I know you like momentum, Doug," Demetria began. "So do I. You don't know this about me, but I used to ride bicycle marathons on weekends, and can still get out and do thirty miles on a Saturday. I know about the exhilaration of speed. I also like to come in first. I don't have any differences with your goals. But what happens when I'm the focus of your frustration is that I wind up waiting for you to interrupt me instead of thinking about the point I'm making. So I'm not giving my best thought to the project because it's divided between our goal and the way we're getting there. Does that make sense?" She tossed the ball to Doug.

"Yeah . . . but I'm just impatient. It's not about you. Why do you take it personally?"

"Because your impatience seems to be expressed more openly when I'm talking. You don't always verbally interrupt me, but you look at your watch, you flip through papers, fiddle with your cigarette lighter. It may be just a chemistry thing between us. I don't care if we ever get to the root of it—that's not the kind of colleagues we are—but what you're doing distracts me to the point where I'm not being the best member of this circle I could be. I keep being pulled away from making my best contributions."

"So what do you want me to do?" Doug asked.

"When I'm the one holding the circle's attention, however that happens, I want you to be more conscious of your impatience than you are when Mike or Chen is holding the circle's attention. They don't seem to bug you the way I do. If a little flag went up in your mind that said, 'Hold still, listen, support this woman and we'll move along faster,' that's all I need," Demetria replied.

"Mind if I write that down?"

"Nope. Whatever works."

"Hold still. Listen. Support Demetria. She's a speed demon, too, if I don't undermine her momentum." He smiled in relief. "I think I've got it."

Bill interjected, "Five minutes are up. Anything else?"

"Yeah," said Demetria, fingering the ball. "Doug and I, well, we both probably feel really okay right now . . . and that's a little unnerving, because this kind of project *is* frustrating. There's no way around it. So if *we* relax, somebody else is likely to get less relaxed. I want our team frustration level to be talked about, not acted out. I want to let you know I'm available for backing or bike racing if anybody else in this circle besides Doug and me needs to let off steam."

The circle agreed and went back to work.

The ability to maintain PeerSpirit is based on our ability to communicate without shame or blame, pulling out of polarity and seeing the underlying issues. We are building a new skill, exercising a different kind of energy and patience. If we aren't going to call for someone or something else to come in and act as the authority to fix our circle when it's not working to our satisfaction, then we are going to need to call on ourselves. We need to trust that we—*all* of us in the circle— are willing to preserve the integrity of what we have created, to see our process through to completion.

When Carol met Bill in the parking lot after the meeting, she said, "Thank you. You were great in there this afternoon. I have to say, I was surprised. Where did you learn to do all that?"

"I don't know. I could see this big mess coming, and I didn't want a fight any more than Doug did—or Demetria either. But I couldn't figure out how to sidestep it."

"But how you handled it was genius."

"Maybe wisdom works," Bill said, scratching his head. "It did for me last weekend. . . . My son, BJ, got suspended from college for cheating on a chemistry exam. He didn't want to come home, of course, so he hid out at some friend's place, drank beer and got picked up for underage DWI. Last Friday night, at ten o'clock, the cops called me and told me to drive down to Iowa to get him.

"I was so scared for my boy. All the way down, I was huffing and puffing just to keep from crying in the car. When I saw him, I flipped out and practically hit the kid. I paid his bond, signed a bunch of papers, and started driving home in stony silence. My whole relationship with my own dad kept flashing before my eyes. I was desperate to break the pattern.

"I pulled off the road to a little resort by a lake, woke up the owners, rented a cabin, and called my wife to say we wouldn't be home for a while. Then BJ and I held council. I mean, I pulled out the stops—told BJ everything I'd ever thought about my dad and what I thought went wrong between us, and gave him the chance to say the same about me. We passed a rock back and forth between us until that sucker was hot. No interrupting, no justifications. Then I drove BJ back to school, helped him get reinstated, and got back to town at midnight on Sunday.

"I figured if the circle can do that for BJ and me, Doug and Demetria were a piece of cake." Bill smiled. "See you tomorrow," he said, and walked to his car, leaving Carol standing in amazement.

The greatest trust is built when we get through the bumpy, scary, risky, and vulnerable aspects of circling. We don't know what we're made of until a circle has faced a problem, resolved a conflict, gotten several members through a crisis. Actual conflict resolution, since it's so seldom practiced, may be nerve-racking as we develop confidence and learn to say our truth, but after a while, the empowerment is positively exhilarating.

Preconflict bonding is sweet, but not as potent as postconflict bonding. The circle that has lost its innocence by coming through crisis with respect for each other and the process is a circle to be reckoned with. And out of such experiences we develop a deep appreciation for the human beings we are.

Appreciation Council

We first learned the structure for appreciation council while visiting Dennie LaTourelle in 1994, at a weekend retreat of the Council Circle Foundation, in Santa Barbara, California. "To feel bonded," Dennie says, "we must feel 'seen.' The circle can act as a trustworthy group of people who mirror back to us our own unique qualities. Most of the mirroring we get in our lives is criticism, which doesn't help us because it hurts to receive it."

In appreciation council, the talking piece works in the opposite manner of its usual use: the person holding the piece is silent and the rest of the circle has the opportunity to offer heartfelt appreciation to the holder of the piece. It is useful to begin these statements saying something like:

- "What I honor and respect about you is . . ."
- "What touches me about you is . . ."
- "What I love about you is . . ."

Dennie also has suggestions on what not to do:

- Avoid superlatives ("You're the best . . .")
- Avoid comparisons ("I'm not . . ."; "You are . . ."; "I wish I could . . .")
- Avoid referring to first impressions of another person or his/her work ("At first I wasn't sure you knew what you were doing, but then . . .")
- Avoid talking about yourself while appreciating someone else ("Your story reminds me of the time I . . .")
- Avoid interpreting his/her experience ("I see that you have worked through . . . and now you are . . .")

Appreciation council works well as an opening ritual at the beginning of staff or committee meetings by asking each person to articulate one thing they love (or appreciate) about their school, church, or company. The question challenges us to keep remembering why we work or volunteer where we do, and is especially useful to set a positive container around a council that may hold difficult moments.

When Ann and I were called in to help the board of a community action organization reestablish communication during a time of painful personnel layoffs, we started with a round of appreciation that changed the tenor of the group. People began to see each other and the situation they shared with compassion, rather than feeling isolated and picked off one by one.

Sometimes at the end of a busy circle, appreciation can be offered by having each person draw a name out of a hat and say one appreciative thing about the person whose name s/he has drawn. Or people can do a round of appreciating the person on their left. If the circle experience has been brief and individuals don't know each other well, people can appreciate one thing about the group, or their experience of the circle itself.

It may be hard to take in appreciative comments at first because we are unaccustomed to being acknowledged in this way, but if we sit still with our resistance, the capacity to hold positive feedback will increase.

We need appreciation from others because, by ourselves, we cannot accurately perceive the qualities we bring to the circle. Appreciation helps us define our place in the circle, our place on the team, and our place in the overall vision of an organization or community, and it is a socially understood way of sharing our heart connection to each other. We find appreciation, however brief, serves well as a fitting closure for many circles.

The Importance of Closure

Sometimes it's easy to know when a circle is ending. If the circle has focused on a task, its accomplishment releases the group. In a group that has reached its goal, either the circle negotiates to take on some new task or we let the circle dissolve. The software project team will have no trouble knowing when the project is over, though in a business setting it may need to design ways to acknowledge grief over the end of an experience.

When a circle is functioning at a high level, it is charged with energy that elicits participation, loyalty, priority. When a circle accomplishes its goal, it reaches a high point of energy, excitement, fulfillment. And then that energy falls away, either quickly or slowly. At this point, the circle needs to take up a new task or let itself go. Sometimes this point gets put off because it seems disloyal, or we don't want to enter our own grief. But in PeerSpirit circles, since there have been exit points and discussion about commitment all along the way, the idea of ending is not taboo.

Letting go is a time when ritual provides a comfortable framework for expressing closure and is a container for emotions. Even in a business or academic setting, some form of closure is extremely helpful. We need to be reminded of the boundaries again, that there is a difference between being in council and being in social space. We need to let go of expectations of each other that have grown up in the intimacy of the circle and resume a more casual connection. One simple ritual is to go around the rim and invite each person to recite: "Here's what I take with me from this circle . . . Here's what I leave behind for center to hold . . ."

Circle work necessitates that Ann and I move in and out of many circles. We need to be intensely present in whatever circle we sit in, and we need to be able to release ourselves from that energy and move on. The only way we can do this is to open our hearts, minds, and bodies to the experience of the moment, knowing full well that we will grieve, knowing full well that we have reason to celebrate. All of us in circle need to be able to say, "I have fully participated. I have given and received all I could. Now I release it."

There is a Navajo prayer that ends with the phrase "It is finished in beauty." This is my prayer for the circles I'm in: that we may finish in beauty, finish with a sense of fullness over what we have shared and how we have grown to love and respect each other in the process. We may love the circle, and leave it knowing there is another circle coming.

This is what endures: a heartbeat.
This is what endures: a place, a circle,
a gathering to which I belong,
which would not be this gathering without me,
without each of us,
without all the infinite,
minute causes that come to body here.
There is always reason enough.
This is what endures.

This is what endures
even though I neglect it,
devalue it,
dismiss it,
fear it,
what I steel/harden/shell myself against
to prove I can live without.

This is what endures—
joy and ecstasy
and daring to drink it in.
This is not to be resisted.
This is what endures—
to be found.
And if it's out there
I can bring it in,
and if it's inside
I can damn well let it out.
This is what endures
and will endure.

HELEN DOUGLAS, UNPUBLISHED POEM

CHAPTER 8

Challenges in the Circle

If we weave a basket, perhaps it is our first attempt and the rushes are loose and fraying at the ends, the weave full of holes; we will not ask it to hold very much. We will not entrust it with our valuables. But if we weave a basket and the rushes are strong, finely threaded, well knotted, and uniform, we will expect much of it and confidently place within it our most treasured possessions. So it is with the circle. The well-crafted circle is entrusted with our highest hopes, and the well-crafted circle is challenged and tested to see how it will support these hopes.

As we weave the strength of the circle around the rim, committing to the principles, practices, and agreements; as we focus on clear intention and set our greatest good in the center; as we look up and are present to each other and to the circle's purpose, we create a container of remarkably high tensile strength. And this strength is the source of challenges in the circle, for the stronger the container, the more we ask it to hold.

The circle is an interpersonal art form. And the challenges to circle are interpersonal challenges.

As discussed in Chapter Four, in the section on circle energetics, human beings are genetically wired to be sensitive to each other's energies. Our perception of each other's nonverbal emanations and communication is an ongoing phenomenon, whether we are aware of it or not. We often try to ignore and override these perceptions, and have much hindsight about them. We say things like, "I knew he would sabotage the process, but I just didn't know how to say no," or "Something inside me told me to invite her to join the group. Even though she looked shaky at the time, I knew she'd be just fine."

We cannot avoid influencing others and being influenced by others whenever we enter an interpersonal arena. This influence occurs in every interaction and meeting we have with other people. Our thoughts and emotions are activated and ever-changing—one moment we are relaxed, the next moment we are tense. One person's sentence can radically alter how we perceive what is happening. Often the person doesn't even need to speak; we are so sensitive to each other that one individual coming into the interpersonal field emitting anger or fear sets off a vibration in the group that impacts everything that is about to happen—even if the source of the vibration is never identified or mentioned.

In most Second Culture settings, the impact of interpersonal influence is simply not brought up. It may not be considered important, or there may be no framework for dealing with it. We cope as best we can, and then complain, gossip, and scheme behind each other's backs. If we are an underling in this configuration, we often feel helpless about getting heard or being able to make changes in our relationships to authority figures. If we are the authority, we often feel equally helpless about motivating the group, getting tasks accomplished with quality and timeliness—and so it goes.

Into this arena comes the circle to challenge our assumptions, expectations, and especially our helplessness. A circle of problem solvers, dedicated to shared intention and practicing interpersonal respect, is a fully empowered group of people. This chapter provides a framework for understanding how differences arise within the Peer-Spirit circle, and offers a protocol for responding to them.

Refuge

As differences surface in the circle, the primary source of our strength is the covenanted nature of our experience. The covenant is the heart-based connection between us.

In Second Culture, heart-based connection is relegated to the closest personal ties of family or select friends, and denied everywhere else. It's as though a billboard is posted on the front lawn: LEAVE YOUR LOVE AT HOME. We have almost no acceptable language, ritual, or gesture for showing the heart in business, professional, or community settings. This is an unnatural dislocation.

Indigenous people know from birth that they belong to the community and are interconnected. The African proverb "It takes a village to raise a child" reverberates in Western consciousness as a profound statement of what's wrong in our current beliefs about children and the nature of the family unit. It also "takes a village" to sustain a couple relationship, to support working partnerships, and to prepare ourselves for meaningful roles in the community. The covenant aspect of circle invites us to remember the ancient truth of unity and belonging—and then provides a socially prescribed container for the heart's energy.

Most people enter a new group looking for commonality and affinity. In a PeerSpirit context, our yearning for community is held by the spiritual dimension. By calling in the center and imbuing it with spiritual authority and neutrality, we create a shared source of strength that resides with us inside the container. In the meditation that Ann and I offer to open council, we first ground circle members below, above, and behind, and then we say something like, "And from this anchoring abundance, centered in the boundaries of the self, we offer our gifts to the center of the circle and receive in return the gifts the center offers us."

This is the paradigm shift: The circle is held by each of us but is not created solely by, or for, any one of us. We become participants in a process where our actions are weighted with spiritual significance. We surrender some of our usual autonomy, and in turn receive inspiration, guidance, support, and stamina from a spiritual source, as well as from each other. This is the dimension that differentiates PeerSpirit circling from other forms of group management: It can contain the concerns of the heart and help us express them in ways appropriate to the setting.

There is a reason the heart comes into circle: We come for healing. Beneath the similarities and differences of our personalities, our stories, our backgrounds, our careers, our goals, there resides a commonality based on the path of the soul. When we dare to recognize each other at this level—across the boardroom table or the family supper table—our hearts are flung open and Spirit pumps through us as literally as blood pumps through our veins. If one person can stand in the power of released heart energy, s/he is often able to help a circle turn from defensiveness to openness.

At the beginning of a Circle Practicum several years ago, a circle in which there were twice as many women as men, one of the prominent personalities was a sixty-year-old patriarch from southern California. Dean was tall, tanned, barrel-chested, and deep-voiced, and he carried a powerful presence that could easily have been viewed as intimidating by others in the circle. As we introduced ourselves in the first check-in, he took the talking piece for the first time. This was a pivotal moment when he was on the verge of either inviting other people's perceptions of him as overpowering, or finding a way to stay self-defined. His rumbling bass voice began with a brief recitation of his professional identity. "I'm a commercial real estate broker in San Diego," he said, and took a breath. "I've spent a lot of time in my life bossing people around in meetings. Six months ago I had a coronary and emergency quadruple bypass surgery. I arrested four times on the table. . . ." Tears came into his eyes, and into all of ours. "I finally got it"—his voice cracked—"I have to live the rest of my life with my heart open. Wide open. I'm grateful to be alive today, to be able to say these words to you, and to be here and find out what circle's all about."

The heart pulls, entices, and sometimes drags us into circle because we need what is waiting for us there. We need refuge from isolation, refuge from judgment and criticism, refuge from competition and power-mongering. Because the need is so great, when the PeerSpirit structure takes hold in a group—even when the circle is called to intervene in the midst of group crisis—people willingly seek refuge with each other.

Even the barest structure of circle may call forth refuge. A woman in Pennsylvania shared this example: "Tonight was the first meeting of our new finance committee for our church—I am treasurer—and I hoped to be able to put some of your ideas to work. As the meeting became more and more tense, and a yelling match developed, I stood and called for a time of silent prayer. I searched my purse for something to use as a talking piece—all I could find was a small clock. I quickly placed that in the center (I don't think I said anything about a sacred center), just put it there, and explained how a talking piece works. This one element changed the entire course of the meeting. The chairman said to me afterward that it had helped him realize more about leadership. He got the point about not interrupting and listening; we all did. And I certainly felt I was holding the rim."

The passionate plea—for order, for respect, for remembering purpose—has tremendous power to realign relationships and to help a group of people correct the course of their actions. In the circle, Ann and I have the privilege to witness miracles. We see powerful men weep with surprise at their own openheartedness. We see timid women rise and hold their point of view with great tenacity. We see staff groups and committees and boards of directors able to slough off years of difficulty and shift into alignment and clear action. We see couples and families break through accumulated defensiveness and rededicate their love for each other. In these moments, we are reminded of the circle's ability to contain tremendous shifts in human energy and to provide the format for great healing. At moments when the shift is full of tension, this healing capacity is what we need to draw upon.

The youth services director of an inner-city community center came back to work one Monday to discover that her assistant, Tamika, had gotten into an argument with one of the teens at the drop-in center. This disagreement had escalated into a shouting match, with the young staff woman asserting her authority to suspend the young man's privileges to the building. The boy and his buddies challenged her to step outside, which she refused to do, but they spent the rest of the evening circling the building and her office, making threats and gestures of defiance. Tamika had, in turn, threatened that her boyfriend and brother would come after them if they hurt her or vandalized her car.

The following afternoon, the director arranged a meeting between the two in her office. She relates, "They came in and sat at the table, sullen and self-righteous. Tamika wouldn't look at Wong. Neither wanted to speak to the other, but had agreed to the meeting hoping to convince me of his or her viewpoint and that I would punish the other.

"I lit a candle in the center of the table, without explanation. I held up my talking piece and explained the rules: Whoever held the stick could speak without interruption until he or she was finished and would then lay the stick down in the center of the table. Whoever wanted to speak next could pick it up. Interrupting would not be tolerated. Both would have the chance to tell their story completely and to respond to anything the other person had said. We would talk as long as necessary.

"They were eager to vent their frustration and wasted no time plunging deep into the issues, full of fury and passion. The stick hardly touched the table, passed hotly back and forth as they accused. Gradually, because they were allowed to speak their outrage unimpeded, their urgency faded and they began to hear what each was trying to say. Their manner changed and they began to think about what was being communicated. Now they tried to explain themselves to the other, insisting they'd been misunderstood. I started to take an occasional turn when a point had been missed, just assisting the process.

"Finally they could understand and acknowledge each other's perspective. They offered each other apologies and reassurances. Each insisted they only wanted respect and validated that need in the other. They wanted a peaceful relationship. Like the slow wobbling of a top, their dispute wound down to stillness. Animosity was gone. Without prompting, they shook hands and Tamika voluntarily lifted Wong's suspension. They came to their own peaceful solution."[1]

We may think of healing in highly dramatic terms, such as the moment between Tamika and Wong, but less dramatic moments are

---

[1] Thank you to Patty Armstrong for sharing this story.

equally significant. The conflict resolution between Doug and Demetria, modeled in the preceding chapter, is an excellent example of a
circle holding its integrity as an interpersonal container. People's responses to healing in this business context were expressed within the
norms of the group—Doug smoked a cigarette in relief, Demetria said
a silent prayer of thanks, Bill had his confidence buoyed, Lindsay
experienced herself as a powerful presence—and the team was able to
reclaim its intention and get back to work.

At work, the circle may be the only setting where people experience successful problem solving, or give and receive nurturance and
appreciation, or are acknowledged at the level of the heart. The shift
in group dynamics after Doug and Demetria had a chance to address
how they got on each other's nerves had a long-term impact on the
project team. The moment contributed to the group's sense of
strength and confidence in how they functioned, and ultimately to the
quality of work they produced. Other members trusted the circle to
let issues of difference arise, and expected themselves to work them
through with backing and solid guardianship.

When we imbue the circle with these expectations and they are
fulfilled, we develop tremendous loyalty to the form and to those who
are present and participating with us. Refuge is real; it is our reference
point. When we know communion is possible, we find ways to return
to it again and again.

Safety and Challenge

In the mid-1970s, I first called the circle during writing seminars as
a way to honor the life stories people were putting in their journals.
All I thought I was calling was refuge for myself and other seekers—
hoping for safety, without challenges to that safety. Over the years I
have come to accept that these two things are, in fact, inseparable. *For
how do we know safety exists until it is challenged, threatened, worked through, and
reestablished with a deeper sense of knowing?*
Everything addressed so far in this book readies us to hold the rim
at moments when differences arise. We are people who have made a
covenant with each other to observe a structure of respect expressed

through the principles, practices, and agreements. We are people who have arrived at common intention. We observe boundaries, opening and closing council. We take turns being guardian and have authorized the guardian to remind us of the presence of center and help us carry out all we have agreed to do. We are ready.

There are two interwoven contributions that PeerSpirit circling makes to managing interpersonal challenges. The first contribution is the sacralized center—the expressed presence of something greater than any one self in the circle. In PeerSpirit, as we address confusion, difference, and conflict, we are not alone; we are contained within a space that also acknowledges Spirit. This is an essential foundation equally accessible to each member of a circle. The center provides a place that belongs to everyone and to no one. This understanding cannot be overemphasized.

The second contribution of PeerSpirit is the belief that people are by their essence capable of self-governance, and that by adopting the basic principles, practices, and agreements, each person in the circle assumes accountability for his/her own behavior and shares responsibility for the well-being and accomplishment of the entire group.

As we bring PeerSpirit circling into mainstream settings, the combination of spiritual center and self-governance is catalytic. Through these dynamic elements, we shift the interpersonal paradigm from competition to cooperation, and from intellectualism to guidance.

Our conditioning to compete for attention, to protect our turf, and to overpower or succumb to each other at moments of dissension does not magically disappear because we've called the circle. We retrain ourselves by noticing our conditioning emerge in the circle over and over and over again, catching ourselves at it, and helping each other experience cooperation and spiritual insight. Consistent apprenticeship to the circle leads to the release of separation consciousness and the embrace of unity consciousness. Imagine the shifts in all aspects of our culture if we *believed in* and *behaved with* a sense of unity.

Experience is not always a comfortable teacher. It takes great spiritual discipline to remain steadfast within discomfort. We have a natural impulse to get back in control or reinstate conformity at whatever cost. But as we learn to tolerate discomfort and succeed at personal and collective breakthroughs, circle energy is celebratory.

There is a church congregation I know of (the pastor participated in one of our Circle Practicums) where factions had developed and the pastor felt isolated, watching this fracturing from the pulpit, not able to help. One Sunday she announced, "The vision I think we share is that of a faith community. We aren't fulfilling that vision particularly well, and I think my standing up here every week isn't helping. So I'm coming down into the circle. I invite us to reconvene as the early Christians did, to believe that the Christ Light will work through each of us if we come into spiritual council." That afternoon they held a circle of eighty parishioners, with one talking piece and the commitment to listen to every voice in the community. One of the women on the church board served as guardian, providing space for silence, prayer, and bathroom breaks. They were able to experience refuge, even in the midst of dissension and difficulty. The church is now doing fine.

We enter the circle at its heart. We experience refuge. We bond with others who hold the rim with us. We invest it with great hopes. We feel safe, energized, recognized. Then something happens that breaks for us this sense of spiritual communion. We are, at the least, surprised, and at the most, devastated. We become indignant—"How could this circle take such a disastrous turn? Why isn't so-and-so behaving as I expect him/her to? I thought being spiritual would prevent all this!"

Projection—It Ain't the Movies

Whether or not a circle is occurring in what we would usually define as an "intimate" setting, the circle itself is an intimate container. We are more vulnerable; there is less hiding space in a peer-led group. We are called upon to be present, to pay attention, to keep track of things, to be responsible for ourselves. Coming into the container, the soft belly of our psyche is exposed. Our hopes and fears come floating in with us and sit down at our shoulders: who we think we are, who we want others to think we are, who we think they are, who they want us to think they are, and all the parts of ourselves we hope we've hidden. It's quite a crowd. To handle this crowd, most of whom are invisible, it's helpful to understand a little about a phenomenon psychology calls projection.

Projection happens when we put onto others the parts of ourselves we do not claim ("You're so important to this group, I'm just a beginner") or the parts we do not want to claim ("Joe is so judgmental—I can't stand how he labels people"). When projecting onto others we may feel self-righteous in our opinions and not be able to see how we share the same quality. Our projections are often unconscious or invisible to ourselves, though they may be quite obvious to others. What we say about others when we make these projections may also be true (but not always). Joe may indeed express himself in a judgmental manner, but when other members of the circle identify Joe as "the judgmental one," then they are projecting, instead of looking at how judgment rises and subsides in all of them. This is what Demetria was addressing when she told the project team, "Now that Doug and I aren't carrying the tension, the rest of you may feel more tense." As I listen to my friend rant about Joe in the circle, I can see her own disavowed judgmentalism and can decide whether or not to bring it to her attention. Of course, a week later she is likely to point out some similar disowned aspect of myself to me.

To have genuine regard for someone and the contribution s/he makes to the circle is not a projection. If I think or say, "Tom is a strong and steady presence today," and do not put him up, or myself down, but simply make the observation, I am having an authentic reaction.

To have genuine difficulty with someone and how s/he contributes to the group is not a projection. If I think or say, "How Mary expresses herself is so different from how I express myself that it's difficult for me to wait patiently while she reaches the point of her story," I'm still having an authentic reaction. I'm acknowledging our differences—not maligning her character or touting my own.

We lay projection over our reactions if we add a judgment that makes another person a good or bad human being based on the way s/he is behaving. So if I think or say, "Mary drives me nuts! She's so self-centered, making everybody listen to her so long," then I'm projecting. I make her less than myself; I assume my experience is the same as other people's experience; I assign to her attributes like "needing attention," when I don't know her well enough to understand her motive or style.

Projection may also be positive. If I think or say, "Mary's storytelling is so lyrical, like listening to poetry. I could never talk like that," then I make her more than myself; I make her be "the poetic one," and diminish my own abilities to speak metaphorically. And if the circle needs a poetic moment, I'll wait for Mary to jump in and provide it. If she doesn't, I may even get mad that she's not playing her part, not doing the job I've assigned her.

The reason to pay attention to projection in the circle is that resentment builds when who we really are is interpreted or ignored. In the energetic realm we can sense projection being laid on us, and have a natural tendency to resist it. We get tired of being honored or despised for fulfilling other people's fantasies. If projections accumulate, the circle seems less and less holy or whole and can begin to shiver and shake with undercurrents that nobody understands.

The key task for members of a circle is to retain a sense that we are equals who are all connected. When we participate in our own or another person's diminishment, it throws the circle off its purpose and saps its strength. In a group where there is no permanent authority figure to keep the rest of us in bounds or to carry the projections we might like to throw onto "leaders," everyone has a heightened responsibility to keep the field clean.

As long as there is a basic commitment among all circle members to address and honor differences, solve problems, and get on with the work of the circle, we can use PeerSpirit structure to work through the roles we carry and the roles we expect others to carry. We do this by calling on the practice of self-monitoring, by applying the agreements of asking for what we want and offering to provide what we can, and by using the center to both cleanse and compost the energies of the group.

Handling projection in a PeerSpirit manner does not require a degree in psychology—in fact, it may be easier without one. It does require the willingness among group members to entertain the idea that projection is occurring and that certain roles or aspects of ourselves are getting played out. Finding ways to bring this phenomenon into the consciousness of the circle is part of how we keep the circle healthy and functioning.

In *Dreaming the Dark*, Starhawk's groundbreaking work on the circle and spiritual activism, she identifies ten common personas that people often assume around the rim. She calls these lone wolf, orphan, gimme shelter, filler, princess, clown, cute kid, self-hater, rock of Gibraltar, and star.[2] These names articulate a particular self-view or life stance that serves as the filter through which each person makes his/her contributions to the group. It might be interesting to ask, "What is the list of characters in our circle? How can we acknowledge this energy?" As we become aware of the roles we play in circle, we can bring them into the life of the group through positive recognition and play.

For example, after a circle has been meeting for a while, it can be very useful for members to name themselves by the attributes they are bringing to the rim: "What is the role I am aspiring to play? How could I personify the contribution I am trying to make?" Another way to play with this is to look at the roles we are shy about or try to avoid, and how our resistance impacts the circle. What we name are the parts of ourselves that support our personal style. In serene moments, I might name myself "She Holds the Rim." In stressed moments, I might name myself "Longs to Share Responsibility."

Personifying archetypal energies is an ancient and ingenious way to shift projection into consciousness and give it a voice in the circle. In native tradition, as it is carried by the EHAMA Institute in California, the council circle is represented as an eight-pointed Medicine Wheel.[3] Each person sitting in council is trained to hold a specific perspective. Together the council speaks as a whole to any issue that requires wisdom and decision making. Each of the directions offers a perspective such as freedom and creativity, present condition and appreciation, power and danger, maintenance and balance, interrelatedness and timing, clarity and action, and integrity and vitality.

---

[2] Starhawk, *Dreaming the Dark* (Boston: Beacon Press, 1982), pp. 122–24.

[3] EHAMA Institute is carrying on a three-thousand-year-old oral tradition called the Original Teachings of the Delicate Lodge. WindEagle, RainbowHawk, and six other shield carriers form the core community, bringing this way of council to many Second Culture settings.

Though different traditions may vary the attributes assigned to points of the Wheel, the spokes, or directions, ritualize a way for people to consciously assume roles. Ritual allows us to practice differentiating between holding a role and speaking from the self. To personify is to speak through the role or archetype; to express our personhood is to speak from our own deepest knowing.

My friend Jim is a business consultant who does councils with floor managers, power plant operators, and accountants. He congenially confronts the fake roles that have accumulated in the workplace and helps replace them with what he calls "the real guys." He listens as people say, "Boy did he lay a trip on me," or "He's sure running a number," or "First they put me up on a pedestal and then they knocked me down." Then he uses the circle to clear the field and gather their authentic stories. "The real guys" love it. They need it. And they follow him into the containment of the circle because it is presented in terms they understand.

If we can respond to projection with both ritual play and seriousness, we can keep the energetic field of the circle clean. Cleaning up projections becomes an ordinary part of our awareness of how we are in circle: part of self-monitoring, part of shared responsibility, part of our agreements, part of our stewardship.

Protocol for Reconciliation

As a child watching my grandfather tend his colonies of honeybees, I noticed that when he set the frames into the hive he always inserted a sheet of stamped beeswax into the corner. When I asked why, he explained, "Honeybees are driven by instinct to make surplus honey and will attach honeycomb to just about any available surface. When we insert the frames (for holding honeycomb), if we give them a uniform starting point, they will keep following the grid, and fill the forms with tidy blocks that make harvesting a lot easier." The wax sheet was already configured with tiny hexagons. The bees took it from there, patterning their own neat rows of cells, filling them with alfalfa pollen, and returning to several generations of Baldwins the sweet source of family heritage.

In this section I'm offering a grid of response—a protocol—to apply to the variations of challenge that arise in circle. We are assuming that, momentary flares aside, the members of a circle share an enthusiasm for making the circle a tidy hive and for cooperating in the sweetness of their task or intention. PeerSpirit is the embossing in the corner that lays out an orderliness to rely on—it is not imposed. There is no perfect way to apply this protocol; it's a structure to help us, but it's the people involved who choose to let it work. *What makes challenges resolvable is the willingness of the people involved to solve the problem.* A circle of people committed to problem solving can get through tremendous complexities; by contrast, a circle with even one or two people unable to let go of misunderstandings, or needing to be consistently "right," can disband over the smallest issue. The circle is designed to handle human confusion. The question is, are *we* willing to handle our confusion?

A meeting is going on in a PeerSpirit circle. X has the talking piece and suggests an action. From across the circle, Y interrupts the established procedures of the talking piece and cuts in sharply: "No way, X!" The interruption is brief, but fires a charge of disagreement into the synergetic field. Several people laugh it off nervously. Two people's heads jerk up from note taking. Two more just look away and don't notice that they've stopped breathing. X is sitting, holding the charge, trying to remember her thought. This is the instant when choice is made: to ignore the rupture in the field, or to acknowledge that something just happened.

This is the point where circles need to have a protocol in place that they have all agreed to try, or else what happens next is haphazard. In moments of tension, we feel much safer when we have a structure to fall back on—even if it hasn't been tried before. Just reading this protocol gives us a grid, a sense of being prepared. If we have no agreed-upon preparation, the circle freezes, waiting to see what X and Y will do; X and Y feel abandoned, and assumptions about what can or cannot be addressed in this particular circle get set in place. It is possible to work through these moments without protocol, but it takes tremendous personal courage and stresses the container more than need be.

The protocol offered below is generic. It needs to be creatively tailored to fit the components of any circle. (Most circles will not establish a protocol until after tensions have erupted and the need is obvious. This is not such a bad idea; a group probably doesn't know what protocol is needed until they've watched themselves wobble a few times, and once they start to wobble, any protocol will need to be adjusted to fit their personalities and situation.)

The degree of need for following a complete protocol, and the level of attention given this process, should be congruent with the depth of charge released into the group. There is no need to create drama; plenty will arise of its own accord. Verbal content is often less important to track than energetic content. A slight sharpness in voice tone takes a few seconds to occur, and a few more seconds to mend, but if the charge is delivered by cannonball, it needs more tending. And so we go back to the moment, after rupture.

STEP 1: *The guardian (or, if the guardian is immobilized at the moment, anyone who wishes to temporarily assume that role) acknowledges that charged energy has entered the circle.*

Maybe someone takes a rattle from the center (since the circle is being "rattled"), shakes it, and says, "I see trouble has entered the field," or "Opposition rises," or "I feel a break in the rim," or, simply, "Ouch." This is said without drama.

STEP 2: *Everybody in the circle comes to full attention.*

Attention is support. Attention acknowledges that what occurred impacts everyone in the circle, not just X and Y. We need to energetically snap into full presence, to hold the weave of the container and get centered. Three breaths are useful here. Everyone's mental attitude needs to shift into "Okay, I'm here, I'm available to help sort out what just happened."

STEP 3: *With the rim held, the circle decides whether it—as a holistic body—needs to deal with the rupture immediately, or can assign it to a later time.*

If the decision is made to put off dealing with the break, it should not be put off too long, for this is avoiding the problem. This negotiation is usually facilitated by the guardian or the leader of the moment.

We tend to put off dealing with energies of dissension if we assume that they will take a lot of time to address or that they are unresolvable. In this protocol, time is attended to respectfully (remember Demetria and Doug asked for five minutes), and a peaceful outcome is not necessarily dependent on resolution, but on respectful listening (remember Tamika and Wong let go of deciding who was "right").

    a. The guardian asks: "X and Y, shall we address what just happened?"

    b. The guardian asks: "Is everybody paying attention?"

Before the meeting proceeds, X and Y and the rest of the circle members need to be able to be present. If they are and want to continue with the momentum of the meeting or following the agenda, setting aside another time to respond to the disruption, fine. That time needs to be negotiated, and protocol followed at that time.

STEP 4: *The circle enters into a protocol of listening and witnessing. Each member contributes his or her attention, and energy is sent to and drawn from the center.*

    a. Everyone in the rim takes three breaths and asks *him/ herself*:

- "How are my feelings/reactions being acted out by X and Y?"
- "Where did I jump to for safety? affinity? taking sides?"
- "How can I help? Am I clear enough to listen impartially?"

    b. The group offers X and Y backing: to have an ally/ witness who sits beside them, or stands behind them, so they are not alone in holding the energetic charge of what has occurred.

    c. The entire group takes time out to be in silence. In a small altercation, three breaths is usually enough to center everybody. In a more dramatic break, five minutes of writing using the phrase "I see a circle where . . . ," will help people articulate in a nonjudgmental way what's happening. If the circle members take time to write, the guardian may pass the talking piece afterward, asking everyone to read his/her perception without comment or editing. Expressing and releasing our own perceptions of the situation clears the field inside of us so we can support X and Y.

d. Each party may also ask for a recorder, who writes down the essence of what they say, so there is a reference point to the ensuing dialogue. This also slows down the impulse to overexplain.

e. Witnessed dialogue begins.

> Y: "I got mad when you suggested . . ."
> X: "Do you mean . . ."
> Y: "Yes." (Or "No," and then restatement occurs.)
> X: "What I meant was . . ."

If there is a need, the recorder may read back to the circle what was just said. The purpose is for each person to feel heard, to have his/her differences honored, to let X and Y hear what each has said to the other. *Agreement may arise, or may not arise.* The circle can hold our differences as long as we are holding them consciously. Some unresolved issues need a long time to come fully to light. Intention and clarity of meaning will rise again and again to the surface as the circle sorts out its basic tenets and values.

f. The guardian asks: "Now that you understand what your intentions were, do we need to revisit this, or does each of you feel clear and present?"

Assuming X and Y say that they are present, the guardian may check on the rest of the circle, and call for a stretch break before the meeting continues.

STEP 5: *The circle expresses gratitude for safe passage and learning.*

After tension has lifted or conflict has been resolved, the trust level of the group may need to be rewoven. Some acknowledgment of gratitude is very grounding. The guardian—or anyone so moved—may say, "I want to acknowledge the courage of those who went through this learning on behalf of the whole circle. Thank you." Song helps to lift spirits, or someone may offer a meditation or in some other way honor the insight that has been carried into the circle.

After a round of successful protocol, we once watched a business-man open all the windows during a break. As people reconvened, he invited each one to come take a breath of fresh air before going back to their seats, and then to bring their chairs in closer to warm each other up again. It was a wonderfully intuitive ritual of cleansing.[4]

Shadow

What we project onto others, and what we often act out in mo-ments of dissension, is psychic material Carl Jung termed "the human shadow." The shadow consists of the unexplored, feared, and un-wanted aspects of our personalities—whatever doesn't fit into the ego ideal of the good self.

It's true that everything we need to know about life we learned in kindergarten: By the age of five, if there has been any successful socialization at all, the ego has formed, and so has the shadow. These are two inseparable aspects of the self: We cannot grow into who we think we are without developing a corresponding sense of who we think we are not. These are parallel identities: one that is claimed, one that is disowned. We separate ourselves into the designated "I" and the designated "not-I." "I" seeks recognition, stepping forward to intro-duce itself, shoving "not-I" back into shadow, over and over again, until we forget what we're doing.

Personal shadow develops unavoidably in the human psyche and serves as the storage closet for attributes of self we cannot get rid of but do not know what to do with. To understand this allegorically, suppose a mother flings open her child's bedroom door, casts a judg-ing eye around the chaos, and announces, "This room had better be spotless in one hour." The child scurries into action and the room gets cleaned—but where did the old gym socks, the half-eaten sandwich, and the library book that will never be seen again go? Into the closet. Meanwhile, the good child receives its praise. After a while both the

---

[4] There are other reasons to employ the protocol besides interpersonal tension. This is, for example, an excellent structure for holding people accountable to the tasks they have offered to do on behalf of a circle's purpose.

mother and child forget the closet is even there—however, it's still filling up.

Now, suppose the child is scolded for not sharing candy. "Don't be selfish!" The child dutifully passes out the candy, but where does the selfishness go? Where does "survival of the fittest" go? What does the child do with the genetic wiring of the body/mind that says one must compete for food? Into the closet. So down the road, the now grown-up child cannot think of him/herself as selfish; if selfishness is occurring, the impulse to hoard must belong to somebody else.

As what is not wanted is shoved aside by the psyche, eventually the closet may become so full it bursts open and reveals the dusty, moldy, putrid stuff of the discarded self. What makes the contents of the shadow so undesirable is that they have not been attended to in a very long time. Anything, including the very best aspects of ourselves, may be in shadow, and will at first appear repulsive because it has been disowned and untouched. The contents of the shadow have not gone through the process of maturing that the rest of us has.

We become our authentic selves by handling our own shadow material, instead of insisting, "It's not me!" At some point in our lives, we enter a process of sorting the shadow and discover that what we have disowned is not so horrible. If we bring these contents into the light and practice living consciously with them, we experience many rewards, and the tension that had been bound within the psyche is transformed into an abiding peacefulness with the self. We learn to see and accept and hold ourselves accountable.

If I can admit, "I *am* selfish. I *do* want things to go my way," then I can see that I am a lot less selfish when I am conscious of this impulse than when seeing it only in others. If I claim my own tendencies toward selfishness, I can speak of it, even joke about it in the circle, helping to release tension, helping to break up the projections and shadow material that tends to calcify around us. I can apologize when necessary, modeling the resilience of my own spirit and my belief in the spirit of the other person and/or the group.

If we refuse life's invitations toward consciousness and continue to deny the shadow, our impact on other people becomes increasingly destructive. We become a dangerous influence in our circles. We cannot enter the protocol and share responsibility in problem solving if we are stuck proving our innocence. Over time, our ability to make contributions from the authentic self becomes more and more distorted. Robert Johnson says that we tend to define the good person as the "all-right person." This simplified understanding of ourselves creates a horrendous blind spot, and inside that blind spot our destruction is brewing. Johnson suggests instead the working definition of goodness in a human being needs to be "the balanced person": s/he who is able to hold both sides of the self. One who knows both sides of him/herself is free.[5]

Studying the shadow is an imperative aspect of circle work. We can't keep shadow out of circles in business, or circles in church, or circles in the family; the shadow is not isolatable. When we come into circle and sit down in contained space, pretty soon we see the contents of our shadow reflected back to us around the rim. If we are in a circle that does not acknowledge, respect, and ritualize the existence of shadow in the group, the projections of our "not-I" material accumulate and accumulate until everybody's closet explodes.

What causes the collapse of circles full of well-intentioned human beings is not the presence of shadow but the repression and denial of shadow, the insistence that it is not among us. Denial of shadow eventually fills the interpersonal field with so much unrecognized and unresolved energy that it is released through explosion or through gradual erosion and undermining of healthy norms.

Most people do not enter the circle thinking about shadow. We enter the circle hoping for light, for shelter, for more efficiency, for a humane way to get things done. But if we do not look at shadow, we create a repeating scenario. *Time after time, there is a circle of "good" people who come together with the best intentions and dedication to accomplish a good thing. We are nice to each other. We are often polite and unconsciously conforming. Sometimes one or two people commandeer more leadership, attention, or time in the group than others want, but we don't know what to do and so we let them. If we are irritated, our dissatisfaction goes underground, covered up with more niceness, or we begin withdrawing our hopes that this will be the circle that really nurtures and protects our fragility or accomplishes our goals. If we are invested in the group, we get angry in our disappointment and begin trying to make others behave. If we aren't invested, we drift off, showing up less and less often, looking for another, better situation. Sometimes we end up talking with others about a "problem person,"*

---

[5] Robert Johnson, *Owning Your Own Shadow* (San Francisco: Harper, 1991).

usually not feeling good about our behind-the-scenes behavior but not knowing what else to do. Personalities polarize between those who seem oblivious to what "they" are doing to the cohesion of the circle and those who are intensely responsive to this discomfort and keep trying to manage "the other(s)." In many of these instances, the concept of the shadow is never introduced into the group, and people do not have the opportunity to live out healthier alternatives for dealing with accumulating energies.

Now that the practice of circle is entering a phase of widespread application and evolving maturity, our perception needs to shift from polarities of innocence and guilt—"Look what he/she/they did to me"—to consider what is happening to us, the collective, interconnected body of the circle, and how we continually learn from each other.

Psychic Housekeeping

Releasing the shadow and clearing the interpersonal field is part of the practice of a PeerSpirit circle. As with all kinds of cleaning, it works best when there is consistent attention to tidiness.

We attend to shadow by applying little corrections of course, accepting the not-perfect self, watching as diligently as possible over our projections, speaking compassionately to coax the shadow into the open between us, being willing to reconcile ourselves to each other over and over again, and applying protocols that allow us to release shadow and look at it together. It takes courage to carry the shadow, and courage to name it, to go through the work of bringing up something so disowned and despised—yet it is our only hope.[6]

A few circles ago, there was a woman present whom I experienced as demanding a lot of attention from the group. As she spoke her needs throughout the first day of a week together, I got more and more agitated—she seemed (to me) to take longer and longer, to require more time, and every time she asked me something I winced inside. By the end of the afternoon I knew I had to intervene—with

[6] If I could recommend only one book in this area, it would be *Meeting the Shadow: The Hidden Power of the Dark Side of Human Nature*, an anthology edited by Connie Zweig and Jeremiah Abrams (New York: Jeremy Tarcher, 1991).

myself—to clear up my projections and to examine what piece of my shadow she was carrying.

I went for a walk before supper and had a chat within my mind. I called home my annoyance, called home my own abandoned insecurities, called in compassion until I could visualize this woman in a new light. Instead of withdrawing from her, mentally or physically, I stepped toward her, extending five minutes of attention at supper, a special attempt to say good night, a moment to ask her how her day had been.

The next day I noticed that two other participants, both skilled carriers of the circle and wise in the ways of the shadow, were also extending toward the woman. We had not orchestrated this, not spoken to each other—our responses were just naturally occurring in response to the situation. She began to calm down, as her needs were being responded to and she was not being isolated.

By the third day, the woman felt comfortable enough to say, "I'm beginning to understand more about how the whole sense of circle works and I wonder if I talk too much. Do you think I'm taking too much time in the group?"

I stopped our walk toward the dining hall, turned, and faced her, bringing us into a kind of body council. I waited until words rose inside me. "If you are feeling more comfortable now, with all that you are receiving in this circle, one thing you can give back is more space for others to speak in the time allotted."

"What else can I do?"

"Well, I think we're heading into several sessions where we're really going to need to trust the center. If you'd like to work silently with me and several others to keep that center strong, it would be a great contribution to our process." And so the shadow came to light, and we found constructive uses for its released energy.

People revert to old patterns of behavior when we do not know what else to do. If we will admit the shadow to the circle, we can often—not always, but often—clear the field. As we experience the success of releasing shadow in the circle, we discover tremendous revitalization. Our intentions and task shine before us; we are eager to accomplish our goals, to fulfill the circle's purpose, to honor the process we are engaged in. The heart connection is restored, and the refuge we provide each other matures.

Clearing the shadow, while personally empowering, is not only beneficial in the personal realm; it is part of our obligation to the world. Wildly projecting shadow onto other nations, races, religions, and minority groups (whoever is "not-us"), Second Culture is being consumed by the havoc we generate in denying shadow. The twentieth century is one great bloody trail of shadow gone wild and out of control. In our projection and denial, we have accumulated a debt to shadow that looms over our future stability as surely as our government's financial deficits.

As we contemplate the work of the circle in the midst of Second Culture, we see that it is a form that can help us compost our accumulated cultural confusion. When you and I come into council and have the courage to ask, "Where is my negative side at this moment?" or "Where is the cast of the shadow in this interaction?" we restructure how we see interpersonal relationships, in the circle, and in the wider world.

When a circle is ended, all our energy, all that we have learned, is released into the wide field of the world. This energy becomes part of our collective consciousness. We carry every circle's experiences of pain and joy with us to the next one. The healing that circle offers us—the chance to be present, to experience our empowerment as peers, to become elders of the form—can happen even in circles that do not work very well or last very long. As we learn from our mistakes, we become wiser about what the circle requires. We discover its potential and acknowledge its limitations.

Yet there is mystery here and it is not one I understand:
Without this sting of otherness, of—even—the vicious,
without the terrible energies of the underside of health, sanity,
sense, then nothing works or can work. I tell you that goodness—
what we in our ordinary daylight selves call goodness:
the ordinary, the decent—
these are nothing without the hidden powers
that pour forth continually from their
shadow sides.

DORIS LESSING,
The Marriages Between Zones
Three, Four and Five

CHAPTER 9

When the Circle Shatters

As Ann and I crisscross the continent teaching PeerSpirit circling, occasionally someone approaches us carrying a story of anguish about the circle. The questioning usually begins tentatively. "Do you think the circle can work for everyone?" they ask. "Is it always possible to take care of everyone's needs?" "Are some things unresolvable?"

Yes, some things are unresolvable. No, it's not always possible to take care of everyone's needs. Sometimes, in the give-and-take required to be in circle, some things don't get solved. There are energies human beings hold inside ourselves that if unleashed in the interpersonal container of the circle shatter or enslave it. Most of the time this is not a conscious intention.

Much of the model of PeerSpirit has been developed in thoughtful reaction to the times I have asked these same questions myself.

The first time I sat through the shattering of a circle and had enough presence of mind to question it was during a nonprofit board meeting in the early 1990s. At this meeting we were in a called council, setting the organization's directions for the coming months, passing a talking piece. At the time, though I had already had lots of experience in circling, I hadn't begun to think about the meaning and structure of what I was doing. PeerSpirit didn't yet exist. I was enjoying serving on the board, enjoying the sense of innovation and connection. We were doing business from a very integrated place; people spoke vulnerably and passionately about organizational ideals; we made personal commitments and acknowledged each other. We were in openhearted space with each other.

Everyone knew that at noon that day a group of influential donors would be touring the facility, and the chair of the board excused himself to show them around. At exactly noon the talking piece was passed to one of the founding board members. She appeared to check her watch, and with a blink of her eyes descended into an unrelenting tirade against how she was being personally treated by the rest of us. She screamed verbal attacks at us individually and collectively for nearly twenty minutes. The content was irrational and disorganized, but contained enough grains of truth to be thoroughly confusing. I saw the donors walk by the open door, certainly overhearing this woman giving her colleagues quite a reaming.

I was new to the group and could not believe that those more experienced or more familiar with this woman than I were just sitting there. I could not believe *I* was just sitting there. She finally wound down and we somehow went on with our business. It was an incredibly instructive moment, for I realized we did not have any agreements in place to handle such destructive behavior. And so entered the dark Teacher. For months, I carried on internal conversations with myself trying to understand my own immobilization, trying to understand the woman's apparently calculated decision to go ballistic right at that moment, and trying to understand what structure might be put in place that would give a group honorable options for intervention. Out of these inner dialogues I began devising the structures and methodology of PeerSpirit.

PeerSpirit is designed so that the agreement to abide by certain standards of behavior occurs up front. The group does not commence, the meeting does not begin, until everyone present has said, "Yes, I choose to be here under these conditions." This up-front negotiation through establishing principles, practices, agreements, and intention creates a social contract to which every group member is voluntarily bound, and for which every group member takes equal responsibility.

As soon as this social contract is in place, I know what standards apply to my own behavior. I know what standards apply to other people's behavior. I know these standards are subjective, filtered through the complexity of who we are as human beings—with our personality differences, diverse backgrounds, histories, and previous experiences in groups—but they provide an articulated and contracted framework for talking to each other when things go awry.

PeerSpirit structure is a safety net. When walking the high ropes, a safety net does not prevent us from falling, but it gives us a place to land. PeerSpirit is designed to help each person coming into the circle ascertain whether or not this form supports how s/he can function, and to give those of us already in circle a language to talk about what is required for staying there. With this understanding in place, we can enter the balancing act of process and purpose that has been illustrated and exemplified throughout this book. And if we fall down, we can also get up. In most situations of circle, this is enough; we will wobble and come through, wobble and come through and go on, and get done those things which are important to us.

Unbondedness

The circle, even when highly focused on task, operates as a bonded community. First, as we are introducing ourselves, the PeerSpirit structure provides a matrix upon which we can depend. Our first bond is to the structure. Then, as we progress into our work together, the structure fosters within each of us a respect that bonds us to each other. This bonding is something many of us seek. One of the ways we measure success in the circle is that we grow in commitment and loyalty to each other as we work through interpersonal issues while accomplishing intention. For most of us, the interpersonal structure is an additional draw to the circle form.

However, within some people, it seems that the actual experience of being contained within circle triggers the need to break these bonds. They experience interpersonal containment as confining, threatening their identity. As the sustenance of the circle builds around them, they do not seem able to tolerate deepening emotional intimacy or energetic connection. They become psychologically and/ or physically agitated and activate intense defense mechanisms to "protect" their core self from the threat of this bonding energy.

Instead of experiencing the connective web of the circle as a safety net, they experience it as a fishing net and thrash wildly to escape. They are compelled to act out against the health of the group.

Most circles are not equipped to effectively address an extreme level of personal need and still fulfill their other functions. The board meeting I've described was called to focus on the needs of the organization, not personal needs. The woman's tirade could not possibly get her what she needed, even if she had been able to sort it out, because fulfillment of personal needs was outside the social contract of the group. The only possible outcome to such attack was to shatter the field and divert intent.

As painful as these outbreaks are, they can serve to restore safety or sanity to the one who discharges the chaotic energy. When the field is broken, everyone is thrown into an unbonded state. Before the break, the circle was operating as an energetic unity with one person outside; after the break, there is no outsider because there is no inside. Once the container is gone, so is the immediate threat of confinement. When the board member was done raging, the rest of us were in shock, and she was calmly ready to proceed with the next agenda item.

As a result of this occurrence I began asking if there is something about the circle's nature as container that draws out both the hope and terror that it might contain the most difficult and deeply shadowed parts of the psyche.

Explosion in the circle shows us clearly the level of distress occurring for at least one person. Any one of us experiencing life-threatening confinement would do the same; it's just not the circle that sets off this reaction. Put us in a dark corner . . . let somebody threaten a child or loved one . . . and we ought to unleash similar fierceness! In the unleashed rage I received in that boardroom, I recognized the intensity of the fight-or-flight response: I just couldn't figure out, from my point of view, why it was happening there.

If we can see through the rage, the fear beneath it is obvious. What has been covert is now an overt, in-your-face reality. When rage erupts, fear splatters all over the group. Partly this is displacement, and partly it is the reality of the threat; someone who feels cornered will do whatever s/he deems necessary to get out of the corner. We are back in the "hard-wiring" of the reptilian brain, and impulses are pretty basic: It's eat or be eaten. To understand these dynamics is not to suggest that we have empathy without taking protective action and dealing with our needs for recovery. We would not watch a grizzly bear run at us and start thinking how sorry we were that it was "really afraid."

At the beginning of the next board meeting, six months later, I suggested we articulate our expectations for functioning as a board, and I offered an early draft of what has become PeerSpirit's generic circle agreements. I walked in having given myself permission to take action if I was again screamed at:

- I would call on the newly established agreements to defend our use of time, to say, "This is not why I am here. I am not willing to have myself or my time used in this manner."
- If intervention didn't work to reestablish group direction, I would leave the circle, choosing to stand as witness from the corner of the room, or, if threatened, to leave the space entirely.

The woman never raised her voice again. I served out my term and left the board.

The appropriate bonding of the circle can also be shattered through more subtle erosion. Then the fear splatters anyway, but we may not be able to identify the erosion and why our stomachs are in such a knot. Circle is proceeding, but there's an internal "uh-oh" that won't go away. The unclaimed shadow manifests in highly creative ways and pulls us into our own shadows. In the circle, we are not outside anyone else's reactions; we are ricocheting around in the energetics, trying to discern what's happening. Invisible material is being dumped into the container not just by one person, but by all of us.

The first time I noticed the impact of invisible discharge into the center was during check-in at the first meeting of a journal-writing group. A man introduced himself and as he checked in mentioned that he had lived in San Francisco during the same time I happened to have lived there. In friendly jocularity I said, "Hey, I was there too, in sixty-nine, but I never saw you. Where were you?" Everybody laughed, including the man, but I saw his eyes widen for a split second and felt a rush of fear sweep into the circle, shocking me into awareness that somehow this teasing comment had been an awful faux pas. As his story came out in writing in the following weeks, he revealed that he had been AWOL during the Vietnam War and had been in hiding in San Francisco. I began to learn how sensitive the field is when we close the rim and face each other.

If this act of being woven into circle is terrifying to the psyche, we will try to keep an opening and an option for escape available. If we live with this terror of not being able to escape, and are not conscious of it, then all the behaviors we exhibit will also be outside our awareness.

- Someone may obsessively blame the form, coming up with explanation after explanation for why the circle won't work, rebelling against agreements, needing to word and reword them, and then refusing to abide by the rewording because they still perceive it as coercive.
- Someone may declare that other members of the circle are not safe or trustworthy and refuse to contribute fully until a number of conditions are met. These terms, however, are highly subjective and constantly shifting. No group can prove itself "safe" by the definition of one member; it can only prove itself healthy and responsive to the needs of different people over time.
- Someone may consistently undermine the self-esteem of others—being hypercritical, reframing other people's statements, competing verbally, or being overly helpful in a condescending manner.
- Someone may demand emotional attention that doesn't fit in the context of the circle; for example, crying until the entire group has stopped to comfort him/her, or raging until the entire group has stopped to placate him/her, or insisting on excessive processing interaction after interaction.
- Someone may declare him/herself so "different" that s/he can't identify with the rest of the group—or s/he removes him/herself from peer collegiality through feeling superior or inferior.
- The entire group may stay locked in the honeymoon phase for a year or more, avoiding the usual breakouts into differen-

tiation. Nope, no shadow here . . . only incomplete engagement.

And when any of these behaviors are confronted, they may be directly denied, or reframed in a barrage of explanation: "That's not what I meant"; "You're projecting onto me." Or the confrontation may be used to prove the point: Their behavior is justified.

I want to make it perfectly clear that over the years, we have all personally exhibited every one of the above behaviors (myself included); only we may not have needed to do them to the extreme. We may have been able to commit ourselves to learning from these slips into neediness, projection, and unconscious material. We may happen to be psychologically wired so that the circle is an arena where growth in consciousness can occur for us. And some people happen to be wired so that the circle is not an arena where such growth can occur for them. Even if, on one level, they are attracted to the circle and to the promise of bonding, the actual experience is intolerable.

A few years ago, at a family reunion, a couple of daredevil nieces and nephews convinced my sister-in-law, Colleen, and me to ride the Wild Thing, one of the biggest roller coasters in the world. I had started off the day on the merry-go-round testing out my stomach, swallowing little homeopathic pills for motion sickness with the determination that I would be able to accompany at least the prepubescent set on some of the amusement park rides. Why I thought I could progress from bumper cars to roller coaster in one day, I don't know.

Colleen and I stood in line for half an hour, constantly reminding each other, "We don't have to do this." But around us the teenagers were proclaiming the thrill, telling us it wasn't scary. A kind of ethic of belonging developed, and we got caught up in it. We let ourselves be strapped into the little car, and the train of cars started up the slope toward an enormously high vertical drop. We looked at each other: "Oh, no, this was not a good idea!" And then the coaster dropped us over the other side. We practically broke our fingers holding on to each other and the car. I heard myself scream with an animal pitch as we lurched and lunged around a mile of track. Colleen was shouting into my ears, "You're not going to die! You're not going to die! We'll be all right." I could hardly hear her. How did she know?

I am not wired to find roller-coaster riding a thrill. Later, Ann asked me, "What did you learn?"

"I learned what it feels like to be utterly taken over by terror. To be trapped in an experience that I could not get out of until it let me go. That I could barely hear the voice of love, though it was shouting in my ear. That I was immobilized and screaming at the same time. And I learned that this was too traumatic a setting for me to learn anything."

When someone lashes out of the bond in circle, I remember that vertical drop and try to hold on to that empathy while dealing with the detonation of the field. The shadow in the circle is an opportunity to practice compassion for what is unhealed in all of us—and at the same time to practice fierceness in protecting the delicate interpersonal bonds of community.

A Rock to Stand On

The rock we stand on is what we have agreed to. *If someone in the circle is not able to abide by these agreements, we are called to respond to the breaking of the social/spiritual contract.* This is a very challenging experience in the life of the circle, and could cause its demise. There are a number of options; none of them is easy. Any action will teach us something. We will struggle with ambivalence and ambiguity. No matter what we decide, we will most likely think about the situation and the people involved for a long time, wondering what we could have done differently . . . what the circle could have done differently . . . if there was something that could have helped that we didn't know how to do. . . . As Doris Lessing says, "There is mystery here, and it is not one that I understand."

At this point, it ought to be obvious that prevention is easier than cure. Back in Chapter Five we considered the components for calling together a healthy, compatible group to come into circle. Sometimes we participate in groups where we are not in charge of the membership, but if we are in charge of calling a circle, it is wise to arrange enough personal contact to know if each participant is ready to be there. We can talk about intention, skill building, the need to hold one's own boundaries in an interpersonal field. If we use some of the language developed throughout this book and people overreact to it, that is a helpful warning signal. It's a good idea to be as careful with those who overidealize circle experience and project only positively as with those who resist bonding and project fear or anger.

In an ongoing group, the "uh-oh" usually starts before behavior has surfaced. If we respond to our own body tension and other signals of distress, we may have time to start questioning the underlying dynamics before the eruption of full-blown crisis. Oftentimes, when a member of the circle is the vehicle for shadow or the constant instigator of dissension, it is due to his/her sense of being separate, of not belonging. We have all felt this pain, and as the tension rises in the circle we have opportunities to look at how the bonding is working and not working, and see if we can change the dynamic before getting on the roller coaster and strapping ourselves in for the ride.

Entering the I/Eye of the Storm

When I'm in a circle that is in trouble, one of the first things I notice in myself is that I start ruminating over a particular moment or interaction, sensing there is more to it I don't understand. I can't seem to let it go. Or I find that one person seems to be consuming all my energy, both in the circle and as I think back on the circle. I spend hours replaying conversations or practicing for conversations I want to have with them (or that I want to avoid having with them). Or I find that I'm making excuses for my own withdrawal from the group, start lessening my commitment, "packing up my valuables" in my head. "These people aren't so important to me," I say. "I've got other things to do. I'm tired of everybody's process." Our own unconscious material is stirred up by the agitation around bonding, however subtly it is manifesting in the group. We start to feel dissonance and respond to that dissonance in a way that is typical for ourselves. I try to be conscious enough to use these signals as wake-up calls that I am in trouble and the field is in trouble.

Once we've admitted our own agitation, our first job is to deal with our own dissonance in as healthy a way as possible for us. We need to get ourselves clear. In the middle of long circle sessions or seminars, during stretch breaks, meals, or free time, instead of using that time to keep chatting socially we may go outside, go for walks, go into silence, and listen carefully to the internal monologue, looking for clues. In an ongoing group, on the days or weeks between meetings, we can look at the circle from another perspective. We may decide this is a good time to reread Chapter Eight and start preparing to practice the protocol for dissension.

It is extremely helpful to begin the process of sorting by writing about the circle in the third person. Any of the following sentence stems will get us started shifting perspective: "I see a circle where . . ."; "In this circle is a wo/man who . . ." (this is us we're writing about; first "know thyself").

If we are having specific reactions to a specific person, we may explore those by writing: "If I were (so-and-so) I would be feeling . . . thinking . . . sensing . . . behaving . . ."

To be an effective circle member, still practicing the three principles, we need to become aware of the subtleties of disruption, and to explore how we are being influenced so we can call ourselves back to the rim. We are often in a state of turmoil—emotional or otherwise. The bigger the "uh-oh," the more resistance we may face in ourselves or others for dealing with it.

There are many questions that help in this sorting process; we may choose whatever fits and start taking inventory.

- How have I been pulled off center?
- What's my body telling me? What's my mind telling my body?
- Where do I experience these energies coming from?
- How am I contributing to them?
- What am I avoiding in the circle?
- How am I going passive instead of active?
- What am I afraid of? (What's the worst-case scenario?)
- How will I take care of myself if all this comes to pass?
- What other options do I have for myself? for the circle?
- Is my compassion intact—for myself, for others, for the process of dealing with this?
- Where have I lived this before?

- Whose shadow work is this? And how do I do my own piece with integrity?
- Who does this person remind me of? Am I seeing this situation through a filter of past memory? of judgment? of fear?

As we work through our internal reactions and thought patterns, we reestablish the circle within each of ourselves. If we discover that the agitation is arising from one person (or several) and that the circle is going into avoidance and/or placating in hopes the group doesn't have to deal with the unarticulated issues, it's time to enter into spiritual practice.

As we note the specifics of behavior that are disruptive to us, we need to ask for spiritual guidance in understanding how to deal with this disruption, because this is probably the first time we are breaking our own old patterns of response to shadow material. So we need to become clear about what is agitating us from inside ourselves (and our own shadow) and how this agitation is being stimulated from outside ourselves. One of the things I am learning about these situations in circle is that they are often complementary—there is a way that the shadow pieces released complete each other. The piece that is coming forward through someone else is there because it is matched in the circle, and it is seeking completion/release. So as I explore and articulate what "they are doing" or "how they are being" that is agitating to me, I need to hold up a mirror to myself and see the complementary piece that I am (or someone else in the group is) holding for them.

This is not easy personal work. As dear old Carl Jung used to say, "It's hard to look at the lion that has swallowed you." When our whole culture is so enveloped in unacknowledged shadow, clearing the field in our circles takes a tremendous level of personal accountability and determination.

No one teaches us how to behave around shadow, how to work with it, respect it, or release it in ways that will not ultimately harm us or others. We have no culturally or religiously sanctioned structures and occasions for acknowledging shadow. We have no protocol, no parameters of control. We have no trained guardians to see that the fabric of community is preserved.

Most of the books I've read on group process don't even mention shadow. They may talk analytically about theories of group process, even reference the psychological growth of groups, and still not mention shadow. And certainly not mention what in the world to do when a circle of colleagues is trembling before energies that it has no language to define. The situation reminds me of that now-famous cartoon that shows several scientists before a blackboard covered with mathematical equations, and in the middle is scrawled the sentence "and then a miracle occurs." One scientist is saying to another, "Could you be a little more specific about step three?"

There are times I have come home from a day in circle and pulled books off the shelves, looking for help and guidance and structure; wondering if this group is already strapped into the roller-coaster car and heading up the slope, ratchet by ratchet being carried toward the vertical drop; wondering if there is any intervention that can turn this event aside, or if, indeed, this is why this particular group has come together—to go over the drop and learn from it.

If we take the circle as our teacher, then we take these moments and this difficult person as our teacher. *We* are being offered a learning together: not me/her-or-him, not us/them. However this learning shakes out, we can take responsibility only for our piece of the puzzle.

In this internal process of self-examination, I have found the following questions useful, and there are many more:

- How can I do what is required of me to be true to the spirit of this circle?
- How can I be true to my own spirit?
- How can I show respect for the spirits of all other people involved?
- How can I honor the called intent of this circle?
- How can I stay connected to Spirit (or the sense of greatest good) as we enter the cauldron of this crisis?

During this time of sorting, each person will be holding his/her own counsel. We may feel alone, not knowing that others are also sorting. If others approach us, we may talk briefly of our own feelings without talking about someone else. "Some energy drain is happening for me," I might say; "I'm working to clarify it, and then I intend to bring it up in council." We put our intentions on notice to ourselves, and to anyone who comes to us; this has to come into the field for all to see.

As people begin signaling each other their awareness that something is going off center for them, or as the agitation erupts in the group, we may feel a great impulse to call up others and get reality checks, make alliances in our points of view, and discover who is feeling the same or differently.

In facilitated or leader-led groups, leaders may call each other up and figure out how they are going to handle so-and-so, or members may call the leader and ask, "What are you going to do about so-and-so?" But in PeerSpirit, where everyone is a leader, everyone is responsible for bringing the insights from their sorting process back to the full circle. We have agreed that what is said (or happens) in circle, remains in the circle. If we don't bring our awareness of the issues back into the circle and handle that responsibility openly, the circle is undermined.

One of the primary signals of circle distress is that people, especially those carrying some kind of leadership, find themselves talking and talking (or wanting to talk) about another member of the group. The greater this impulse to talk outside the container, the stronger the signal of collective distress. Conversation outside the bonds of the container is "unbonded" conversation, and we cannot solve the problem of unbondedness by unbonding ourselves. As we keep learning how to hold the integrity of PeerSpirit, we will learn to trust the counsel of the circle, even at our most difficult moments.

Full Council

If during periods of commonality and excitement we believe we have been graced to come together, it follows that during periods of shattering and painful learning this grace will not desert us.

There are times in circle when I am praying so hard for guidance, for help with my own shadow agitation, for the ability to see the way clear. As we come out of self-exploration we need to know how far we are willing to go in confronting the disruption and prepare ourselves to raise the issue—or speak our truth if others raise it. I look around the circle to see who is still in the weave, pray for people to stay present and use the center as our shared growth.

Holding steadfastly to this belief, we watch for the opportunity to address our difficulty: perhaps at the next check-in, perhaps at the next point of dissension. Rotating leadership means that anyone can call for a talking piece and state, "I'm concerned for myself in this circle. I experience our energies being diverted and our intention not being held. I want us to fulfill our purpose. I want to feel that we are all respecting the principles, practices, and agreements we have made. I'd like to know how other people are feeling and thinking about how we are functioning."

At this moment, widely divergent views are likely to come forward. Some people have genuinely not been agitated. Some have not thought about it. Or if they have thought about it, they may not feel safe or confident enough to speak their own truth. Relationships outside the circle may prevent or limit their level of honesty, or even introspection. There are times when no one is willing or ready to take this level of risk, so the circle will absorb the agitation and get through the meeting, or serve out the life of a short-term circle. As a consequence, whoever has brought up the issue may feel isolated and crazy.

Anyone who has initiated such a conversation has probably lived through an experience of group abandonment. Many of us react instinctively to "desert the messenger" and see if the issue can be polarized between two people so the rest of the group doesn't have to get involved. It's like watching a dogfight—we are trained to stay out of the way. But in circle we are challenged to break this old pattern, to not wait until tension runs high, to not desert each other.

The protocol for reconciliation described in Chapter Eight can be applied to acknowledge the interconnectedness of what is going on, even if we believe the polarity is real. Whoever calls for the protocol may say, "I need to talk to X. What we talk about influences the energy and efficiency of this circle, we need to have this conversation within the circle." The circle needs to follow the protocol. We provide backing, assign recorders, call for an experienced guardian, act as witnesses for each other, self-monitor, and move *slowly* through the steps.

There may also come a time when you or I are the one people are sorting and sorting about. If we find ourselves repeatedly in conflict with other circle members, if we've applied the protocol and people are still saying to us, "Please look at this," then we need to consider getting perspective and help. The circle may invite someone trained in circle skills or other group methodologies to come in as a "fair witness" and help everyone gain new perspectives on group interactions. Or personally, we may want to consult a therapist or business coach and get some help with interpersonal skills.

Remember: The rock we stand on is what we have agreed to. We have agreed to create and hold a healthy interpersonal field as part of the way we fulfill intention.

Whew! This is not easy! Every time we bring up an issue that challenges the circle's bond, we need to acknowledge that it may cost us the group. If we know this and have been working with our grief, we cannot be held hostage by this possibility. People let themselves be controlled by others because we don't want to take the brunt of a negative charge or don't trust that any protocol will help and hold us. Or we think that if we just can hold our piece intact, the circle will get through this phase. But the truth is, if there are unacknowledged energies in charge of the group, the circle is already dissolving; only its facade remains. Is this the time that we will be the one to start the truth rolling? Will we support someone else who breaks the silence?

Every two years I take first-aid classes and refresh my skills in CPR. The trainer brings in a plastic human torso and everyone takes turns learning the procedure of alternating breaths and chest pumps designed to restart the heart of an accident or coronary victim. When it was my turn, the paramedic teaching our group hovered over me. "Good rhythm," he said, "but you have to press harder on the chest." He knelt down and whacked the dummy's sternum sharply. Down went the fake chest, up to breathe, back down on the sternum, *wham*—not violently, but with measurable force.

I tried it again. "I'm afraid I'll hurt the person," I explained. "Won't this cause a huge bruise? What if I break their ribs?" I waited for comforting guidance. He looked me square in the eye.

"This is radical intervention," he said. "There is no breathing, no heartbeat; you are minutes away from permanent brain damage. The person is already dead. You decide whether or not you have the courage to try to bring him/her back."

When the circle is shattered, we are faced with the same decision: Do we have the courage to try to bring it back?

If over time we try to reinstate and hold the social contract and cannot find ways to carry out intention in the configuration of this particular circle, we may choose to acknowledge the death of this circle and leave. We may work to help the group disband with honor. We may reconfigure in another circle, at another time. We will need to grieve. And in the next circle, especially if there are members present from the shattered circle, we will need to design rituals of healing that keep our covenants of confidentiality and respect with the former circle, and yet provide ways to compost that pain.

My heart is heavy, remembering times when I've been in circles that have carried this much trouble. I remember and grieve for my own limitations. I remember and grieve for our attempts to help the charging grizzly bear in all its guises, and to cope with the rising of the corresponding bear inside each of us. I grieve for the hard decisions, and acknowledge the courage of people to keep coming through crises as best we can. I pray that PeerSpirit structure can help, and know it cannot help all the time, in every situation.

"No," I say to a woman in Chicago who looks at me searchingly, "sometimes the circle cannot hold," and without her speaking a word of her story, I see in her eyes the haunting she carries from a women's group that shattered.

"Thank you," she responds, "I just needed to know," and quietly she begins to cry.

The Sting of Otherness

The circle is a powerful form. Our energies turned upon each other have as much capacity to wound as they do to heal. Since the capacity for healing in the circle is great, we must assume the capacity for wounding is equally great. There is no one who comes into the circle without wounding of some sort; it's part of being human. We open up to each other, make mistakes, hurt feelings, decide what to carry on, decide what to set aside.

We honor the dark mystery, the dark gifts. Sometimes it takes decades to understand the lesson. There is no answer to "Why?"—there is only the challenge "What shall we do?"

Forgive. Forgive the circle. Forgive ourselves and others—without forgiving away our integrity. That is the challenge.

There are circles of darkness, circles of gangs and cults that use containment as a trap. Good people have entered circles, or been lured into circles, and lost their souls. As we bravely enter this form and light the candle again, we might pause for a moment in gratitude to those who have walked the dark way for us. Their struggles with shadow are not lost: their energy is not lost. We call in a rim of power, and remain humbly aware of its full potential.

I have spoken repeatedly of the circle as a container for human and spiritual energies. For this energy to get in, there must be an opening in ourselves and in the form. This opening creates receptivity: brings in insight, interconnection, intuition, and even a sense of spiritual inspiration. Our willingness to sit within the container gives the healing potential of the circle a place to reside. We invite—and so energy comes.

However, energy is not separated neatly into our preconceived notions of light or dark, good or bad, helpful or hindering. For Spirit to enter the circle, a threshold must be created and a door left ajar. The more we are conscious of this, the more readily we can work with what enters. Over this threshold, along with Spirit, comes the shadow, comes confusion, comes narcissism in all its subtle disguises. On the rim of the circle, our obligation to energy is to learn to stay awake, to practice discernment in the minute-by-minute shifts that break and/or sustain the weave.

We need to remember that we are powerful interactive participants with energy. We cocreate what is going on in our container and may use the threshold to release energy and send it back out of the rim, as well as call it in. Clearing the field that builds up between us in circle is an important practice, and especially necessary when disruptive energies have commandeered the group.[1]

In her energy work, Kathleen Bjorkman-Wilson teaches people to

---

[1] Thank you to Cheryl Conklin for teaching me to acknowledge the threshold, and to Cheryl, Dana Reynolds, and Kathleen Bjorkman-Wilson for ongoing teachings on circle energetics.

respectfully separate from the collective field by silently calling to mind everyone who has been in a circle and stating three differences between themselves and the other. For example, Kathleen has blue eyes; Kathleen is shorter than I am; Kathleen lives in Idaho. These differences do not imply connection or rejection: They are neutral, observable. Yet simply stating them re-creates energetic boundaries and sends everybody "home" so that the field of the group can be fully released. Kathleen has taught us to add this to the ritual of closing at the end of a session, a seminar, or during breaks when energy is intense and people need to come back in with clarity.

We invite in. We release. We reenter the spiral, for another circle is coming that has another gift. We rise up from our mistakes and lost ways and say "yes" again, and come back to the rim to reenter the experiment to make community. We keep learning. In the neighborhood, in business, at home, at church and temple, we look around and find the others who will join us as citizens of the circle.

The breeze at dawn has secrets to tell you.
Don't go back to sleep.
You must ask for what you really want.
Don't go back to sleep.
People are going back and forth across the doorsill
where the two worlds touch.
The door is round and open.
Don't go back to sleep.

RUMI, "A Great Wagon"

CHAPTER 10

Citizen of the Circle

I come from the middle—but I have moved to the edge. I'm settled into community on an island in Puget Sound. The continent backs up behind me with a great push of energy, nearly sending me into the sea. But not quite. I hold the rim.

When I was writing this book the first time, in 1993 and 1994, I felt fairly alone on this rim, an isolated voice crying in the wilderness. I remember the blank faces and polite smiles when I'd say, "I'm writing about the circle." Circle what? "It's a new form of meeting with ancient roots. . . . It's a way people can get together and share leadership instead of being led. . . . It's got a spiritual emphasis. . . ." I had as much trouble explaining what had come to reside in the center of my heart as others had trouble understanding my devotion. How fast things change. Readiness for the circle is rising in the culture like yeast. Just when I think the circle is never going to work in the midst of Second Culture, we get an opportunity to introduce it in places where I never expected to find receptivity. All my assumptions about where the circle will find its home are being constantly blown away. So while circle is not yet a mainstream phenomenon, it's headed there to help us hold the heart while we change.

This is our vision: *That so many people will experience PeerSpirit circles that any one of us can stand up in a crowd and call for a circle and people will spontaneously make sacred center, sit down in council, and rise with clear intention to do whatever needs to be done next.*

This is our vision, for whatever comes—to our island, to our country, to other countries—we intend to help instill the skills of circle in a thousand ways and places. Through writing, teaching, speaking, and living the model, we intend to introduce PeerSpirit circling into mainstream culture, helping to educate hundreds, then thousands, and then tens of thousands of ordinary citizens in the basic practices of circle so that we may participate in and call the circle into our homes, jobs, schools, religious institutions and spiritual lives, organizations, and governments. We are participating in the evolution of the circle, so that we may have a tool for fostering community as we enter the next millennium. Every day the "we" expands: More people come into circle, try it out, pass on the form, interact with the evolution of a good idea.

Becoming PeerSpirit:
Circles in Evolution

In addition to the hundreds of circles we know about that are currently using PeerSpirit as their primary organizational structure, there are thousands of groups ready to become circles. Many groups already operate with pieces of circle structure, whether or not they use the same language or have been introduced to PeerSpirit or other forms of council.

One way PeerSpirit is being adapted is by helping already established circles become more peer-led and/or spirit-centered.

Demetria's Tenfold circle is a good example where the addition of structure strengthened the women's naturally friendly bonds. "I wanted this circle so badly," Demetria admitted. "I feel as though I insisted it into existence, and then kept hovering over it in ways that weren't healthy. Now that I'm working with the circle at work, too, I have a whole different appreciation of its resilience. I'm ready to relax and let others take charge more."

Issues of leadership can be ambiguous when the caller of the circle, or the one(s) perceived to have the most experience or power, are not able to let go and allow the circle to wobble into shared leadership.

A forceful, intense participant, Demetria simply stepped in and provided the kinds of structure that made her feel comfortable. She called to remind everyone of the next meeting date and orchestrated the entrées for potluck suppers. She fussed over their rituals, wanting patterns to be consistent. Such imbalance is not unusual in many fairly informal circles—it just happens. At some point there is a perceived vacuum in how leadership is emerging, and if others want to make sure something happens, they do it themselves. Pretty soon others are letting them do it, and the imbalance is set in place.

To rebalance a group where patterns have been set, others need to start doing those things they have been letting one person do. The supportive structure of PeerSpirit allows us to rebalance without shaming or blaming anyone in the circle. Instead of saying, "I don't want Margaret to do the phoning anymore," or "I don't like how Harry is handling that job," we may call for the reemergence of rotating leadership and shared responsibility.

Demetria took some significant teasing before she got the message. "It's come to my attention," she said, checking in at their six-month recommitment circle, "that I've been doing a lot more managing than I need to—or than anyone has asked me to. I'd like to retract my willingness to carry the details and see who else would like to help. Not just one person picking up what I was doing, but all of us learning how to hold the container together."

Rachel laughed. "I thought you'd never ask! Let's all run the show. I mean, we're all trying to learn how to share responsibility, and not just go along with others." The women split up details of maintenance and recommitted to each other, and the Tenfold circle is progressing just fine.

Another way that PeerSpirit is being adapted is when groups shift from a facilitation model to a peer-led circle. Facilitation is a common and often needed leadership style in many groups—including circles. Skilled facilitators—including therapists, consultants, mediators, and teachers—often attend PeerSpirit seminars looking for ways to help groups move beyond a facilitated model, if and when they are ready.

Facilitation is needed by all of us all the time. Without facilitation, meetings wander and wobble and people get frustrated at "the lack of leadership" and the wasting of their time. PeerSpirit acknowledges the importance of facilitation by suggesting it lift from the shoulders of a designated leader and shift to the shoulders of everyone in the circle. Sometimes this shift is appropriate, sometimes not, but my experience consistently confirms that most of us can handle more leadership and responsibility than is available in many settings, and that the release of bound-up leadership in a group often brings renewal to the whole process of being together.

In the summer of 1991 I taught a writing class to a group of fourteen midlife women who simply wouldn't stop meeting, and convinced me to keep meeting with them. The class, originally held at the Split Rock Arts Program in Duluth, began reconvening about every six months, with me finding the space, organizing meal prep, and facilitating critique of their current writings. The group paid for my leadership, but as I got busier and traveled more often, there came a time when I needed to move on. I suggested they consider what kinds of responsibility they were willing to assume for holding this circle themselves.

If facilitation has been the primary model, whether it's been paid for or volunteered, when a group is ready to transition to peer leadership, the facilitator needs to get out of the way and let the circle evolve. If I hadn't invited the writers to step into leadership, they might have disbanded out of loyalty to the established form, or faltered in their confidence, but I knew they were ready.

After discussing the timeliness of this change, I wrote a letter to the group suggesting that at the next weekend we create an intentional circle to begin and end our time, that we acknowledge and hold sacred space and use talking piece council during reading and response sessions.

In late May 1993, people drove in from three states to meet at one member's house in the Minnesota north woods. Jan had taken over all the site arranging—including sending her husband on a fishing trip for the weekend—had gotten a talking stick, and was acting as the caller. With their accumulated experience, sense of community, and a few simple circle structures in place, the group easily began to run itself. The women passed the talking stick while responding to each other's work, the shyer ones now emboldened and the more talkative ones waiting their turn. They listened to me read some early draft material on the circle, critiqued it, and then applied it. My job was over.

They invited me to stay and join the rim. This invitation often occurs, for the affection and respect between facilitator and group are genuine and reciprocal. There are circumstances where the facilitator can successfully join the rim—and this may have been one of them—but such a shift requires vigilance on the part of all members to break old patterns of reliance, and the facilitator must truly be able to get his/her needs met in the role of peer. I had grown very fond of these women, and the offer was gratifying to my heart, but I wanted to honor their readiness to assume full authority with each other. I was getting ready to move within the year and didn't want to divert their intent only to withdraw after two more meetings.

Years later, the Split Rock writing circle is a solid core of individuals who have truly befriended each other and who care for each other's written words. They set aside two weekends a year and drive for hours between the homes of their far-flung membership. They have their own basket/altar. They have a logbook of collected writings and mailings that go out after each meeting. They have helped several members complete manuscripts and get published. And most important, they have a tremendous sense of their own power, of having moved from a traditional student/teacher model into a PeerSpirit circle.

Circle as Social Movement

How we come into a sense of our personal power is a repeating theme that underlies the applications of circle. The circle challenges us to break out of our assumed helplessness and look, again and again, for the points of empowerment where we can fulfill our own (and other people's) needs, accomplish purpose, and take a stand. The first pages of this book show a number of circles emerging at points of empowerment—many of them spontaneous, for that is how empowerment comes upon us.

If we look at the world as citizens of the circle—a birthright that precedes all current political, social, and spiritual divisions—we begin to ask: "What piece of the world's condition can I respond to? be in relationship with? dialogue about?" The first step to answering these questions is to practice seeing everything around us and within us as interconnected.

The more we live consciously in the interactive energy field of the circle, experiencing the unavoidable connection of both communion and trouble, the more we comprehend that interconnection is reality—isolation is the theory.

Isolation is a taught perception laid over the child's and the mystic's understanding of the unity of all things. This overlay of isolation is a virus that infects our natural way of life. By creating the illusion of separation, by highlighting differences, by making ideology, religion, color, gender, and affection things to fight over, isolation fosters war, famine, violence, and hatred.

Most of the time we don't see how our sense of aloneness is constructed and maintained by the machine-based society around us. The sense of isolation imbedded in our culture becomes imbedded in the family, and even within the self. After a while, we can no longer tell whether isolation is something extruding from the self, creating a society of isolation, or something intruding upon the self from an isolating society. We expend great amounts of energy trying to feel connected when the status quo is not designed to foster this experience. We get angry at ourselves and at each other—but not at our oppression, which remains largely invisible to us.

Community is universal reality. From the atomic level on up, community is the pattern set into the design of the world. Invisible circles of atoms cluster into molecules, combining in marvelous diversity to create all that is. Things group together by attraction and affinity. Two atoms of hydrogen and one atom of oxygen make one molecule of water, which seeks another, just as one human being seeks another. We live on a planet where creatures move in herds, flocks, packs, prides, families, and tribes. We thrive best in the company of others. We evolved by living in small, sustainable communities that shared in raising children, growing food, building shelter, designing work, making crafts, worshiping, and celebrating. Community is our social-genetic inheritance.

Communities have several elements in common; they are held together by specific purpose, focused tasks, tangible work, and tangible results. People join community because there they feel needed. There they experience a sense of being essential, being validated for what they contribute, being honored and sustained. People give to the community and the community gives back in a constant recycling of mutual exchange, mutual interaction, and mutual acknowledgment.

Size is an important factor in community, especially as we crowd six billion human beings onto the planet. When we are looking for the point of empowerment that allows us to activate our citizenship, we need to start with a unit that is tangible and immediate: this household, this school, this church, this company, this block. When we address a problem, we need to engage it in a size we can imagine handling: this creek, these children, this garbage burner, this city office, and so on.

We react to the personal. Show us one child, one animal, one tree, one situation, and we are much more likely to get involved. Heart energy fuels our determination to make a difference. The mind may understand yet remain immobilized, but when the heart understands, we act. Perhaps that is why, in a society that reinforces isolation, we are so careful with the heart, so armored, so defensive, for if the heart's gates open, we will let in the world. And if we let in the world, we will be compelled to interact.

Every now and then I wake up on an ordinary morning with my heart so wide open I can *imagine* that none of our problems is insurmountable. Imagination is the source of empowerment—or immobilization. The future of the world depends first on what you and I imagine that world to be. What we believe is what we see in the world, and these beliefs determine how we make the world behave. We all know people who radiate optimism and good fortune, and their lives seem to go that way; we all know people who radiate frustration and anger, and their lives seem full of mishap.

Projection isn't just an interpersonal issue—we project expectations and assumptions about reality onto the whole world. Are things getting better or worse? Are we aiming toward transformation or extinction? I don't know, but I know that my beliefs affect all my responses and choices.

On the days when I am most deeply in tune with the circle, I am sustained by hope. And the phone rings more often, checks arrive to pay the bills, letters seem full of encouragement. I feed off these moments, weaving intention strongly through the activities of the day, sending positive energy out into the world, moment by moment, action by action—thought by thought.

In increasing numbers, both philosophers and physicists are trying to explain to us that the world is mind first, and then matter; that things are energy before they are form. This book started with a discussion about context, which is another way of saying that we must be able to think about something before we can create it in the world. David Spangler writes, "We live in a strangely different universe from the one our culture assumed to be true a hundred years ago. All that was solid has melted into air, and we now see a universe vastly more energetic, dynamic, and mindlike than we had previously suspected."[1]

Sitting in our isolation, we cannot touch this universe of dynamic, interplaying energies. If we really want to come into a new relationship with the world, eventually we have to trust something or someone enough to step out and energetically engage. Along comes the circle to provide us with a form and structure to begin to experience interconnection.

Not long ago I had a dream. *I was in a large meadow playing catch within a circle of men and women. We were tossing a ball back and forth, apparently randomly, between each other. The ball left a trail of light, and soon we all could see the web of interconnection we were creating. While continuing to play, we began to marvel at this phenomenon, commenting and calling out to each other. Just in front of me was a young woman waiting for her turn to catch the ball. It came flying at her like a small comet, and as she reached to grab it, it slipped through her hands and down the insides of her arms into her body, turning her torso to light— light everywhere. I could see atoms whirling as she became filled with energy. A voice said to me, "This is the nimbus. This is where you are all heading."*

I half woke and recited this unfamiliar word to myself, and at dawn I got up and went directly to the dictionary: *nimbus, n. 1. a shining cloud sometimes surrounding a deity; 2. a cloud, aura, or atmosphere surrounding a person or thing; 3. a halo signifying the presence of the divine.* I took the dream to mean that the connections we make in circle hold the potential for

---

[1] David Spangler, *Everyday Miracles: The Inner Art of Manifestation* (New York: Bantam Books, 1996), pp. 42–43.

transformation. We are practicing now, getting ready to perceive the world differently, to know it—and ourselves—as energy.

Our experience of energy changes how we see the world; as a result of changing our point of view, we change our actions; as a result of changing our actions, the world is changed. Groups of women and men come together and dare to speak their hidden stories, work teams develop relationships as well as products, school systems and community groups avert crises. As we practice the circle, these tangible acts of citizenship contain within them the aura of spiritual presence. They contain the transformation we seek and need. And they are happening up the block and down the road and across the hall, in your home and mine as we learn how to live with each other again. Someone right now is tossing the ball—will we catch it?

An Island and the World

My home on the edge has an unusual feature to it—boundaries. One can tell where the neighborhood ends because it is there the water begins. We are held very literally in this place, and the challenges to break out of ingrained isolation and come into citizenship with each other rise over and over, as repeating as the tides.

On an island we are made aware of the interconnectedness of everything we do. On an island we are reminded that everything that didn't grow here has been carted on—by boat and truck—and must be carted off, or used up, or recycled, or disposed of respectfully, or else we foul the place we have sought out because it was unfouled. This is the great challenge—*to figure out the most honorable way to be here.*

In many ways my island is a microcosm of the world, presented in such a size that I can hope to understand the whole by interacting with this piece. The south end is reached by ferry, a twenty-minute ride from the mainland, an hour's drive north of the city of Seattle. Friends say, "I'm going to the other side, need anything?" "The other side" is mainland America—the mainstream, the mall, the Boeing factory, the freeway, the business and cultural life of the city, the airport.

From my writing desk I watch eagles glide on the updraft along the cliff that brings an abrupt end to my neighborhood. Across Puget Sound, clusters of homes, probably much like my own neighborhood, splay themselves against the hills and down to the water's edge. They are cutting the trees on the foothills of the Olympic Mountains. Every time the fog lifts I notice that another hilltop is devastated. How big are these patches, that I can see them from my balcony fifteen or twenty miles away? I will look at this deforestation as long as I live here: It will take the rest of my lifetime before those hills look green again. I want to shout at the people on the opposite shore: "Look over your shoulder! Do something!" I wonder if they are shouting at me, watching devastation that I cannot see occurring on the hills behind my neighborhood. At night our lights twinkle at each other against the blackness.

Ships go by: tugs hauling barges, container boats carrying goods in and out of Seattle and Tacoma, gray military vessels with spiny antennas, Darth Vader hulls of submarines, and long-bodied oil tankers herded by their protective tugboats. I love to watch the boat traffic, but I worry what the ships are carrying. I wonder if the crews on the cargo ships and the young men and women in the military are careful about how they make their way across this shimmering sea.

In 1963 Puget Sound, contaminated by runoff from the paper mills and other industry, was one of the most polluted bodies of water on the continent. In recent decades, environmental groups and governmental regulatory agencies have fought to keep the sound from turning into a dead sea. The fishing industry struggles and the oyster beds have dwindled, but water quality has been partially restored by citizen groups and government agencies that guard ecological standards. And guard we must. The community cannot rest assured that the laws they put on the books are being complied with. A recent study released by the Washington Public Interest Research Group reported that up to 70 percent of Puget Sound facilities are violating their discharge permits.

When people ask me how I like the place I've moved to, I say, "I love it—and to live here with awareness requires living with a great deal of tension." Ann and I can walk the beach below our houses and hardly see another human being, but this basin of land and sea is populated by more than four million people. Many of us are newcomers, threatening the wild beauty that drew us here. I believe we owe something back: attention, carefulness, stewardship.

Every Sunday morning Ann and I do an hour of council on the

beach. While her children still sleep—in the way that teenagers can zone out for twenty hours in two days—we leave the compound consisting of our homes and a small woodworking shed converted to PeerSpirit office space. We carry mugs of hot tea and pieces of toast, and head for the water's edge with Willow the Welsh corgi jumping excitedly at our heels.

This is "church." This is spiritual practice. This is constant alignment and realignment of intention. We walk a ways, find the right log and settle down, make center out of whatever is gathered before us from the wonderful detritus of the shore. We choose a talking stone and begin with two long monologues, each of us in turn speaking the deeper level of what's happening inside us. Then we enter a period of slow, thoughtful dialogue, passing the rock back and forth. We do not rise until we are calm, centered, aligned with each other and ready to enter the coming week.

At the top of the stairs is our little neighborhood of nineteen homes. Half these households are retired couples. A third of the households are empty many months out of the year. I serve on the water board, that being the typical governing body for these little areas—trying to keep the peace one block at a time.

Fifteen years ago two widowed women lived here among tall trees, orchards, and a vegetable garden, the land of this subdivision divvied up between them. They sold off a lot now and then, and someone put up a mobile home for the summer. When the old ladies died, the developers moved in. It takes five pages of fine print to read all the DC&Rs (Declaration of Codes and Restrictions), and still we don't know how to talk to each other very well. How do I ask my neighbor to trim the tree growing into my view? How does my neighbor remind me to turn off the back porch light, which shines in his house if I forget? The men gather at the mailboxes and wonder if the young builder at the end of the lane is going to sue the association for not getting the road fixed up this spring.

I am looking here for the circle. I am looking for the point of empowerment: a way to reframe the issues of even this one island so that we see all our concerns as common concerns. And this is what we all must do, those of us who hold the circle as an idea in our hearts— look for the daily, incremental applications of cooperation and communication, and have the courage to step in and introduce new ways.

The first year we were here, Ann declared a ban on television in the house. She wanted her children to get out and look around, explore their new setting, have impetus to make friends and stay engaged with each other. A year later, when the moratorium was up, Sally, then age twelve, brought up the issue at the family supper table. They called a family council, each one ready to make their point.

Ann spoke first. "You kids know my bias. I don't want a TV, and if we do decide to get one, it can't be in the living room." She put a talking piece down in the middle of the table.

Brian, age fifteen, spoke next. "I don't want one, either," he said, shocking his mother and sister. "I can't control my impulse to watch it, and I don't know if I'll keep doing my homework if it's around."

Sally took the talking piece and held her own. "I can control my viewing, and I don't think it's fair to be punished if Brian can't. If you don't want it in the living room, Mom, then I suggest we get a little one and put it in my bedroom. Brian and I can work out his access to my room and he won't be tempted all the time."

Despite the occasional, inevitable squabbles that have resulted, the compromise works fairly well. And a round of appreciation council on a regular basis keeps Brian and Sally acknowledging their affection and trust for each other, as well as reminding them that the circle can be used for something other than problem solving.

At the end of my first year serving on the water association, the president of the board asked if I'd sit in while she talked to a neighbor. "I think you have some skills that might be useful," she said. I am heartened that she has registered the vibration of the circle I hold at the rim of her dining room table while she graciously pours tea and offers cookies and makes a centerpiece of extra pencils and papers for taking notes. I don't know if I can help, but I walk up the block with a candle stuck in my jeans pocket, a small beach rock in hand, and my Tibetan bells, ready to be guardian.

Last winter we were guardians of a different sort. A friend was having a baby after many years of trying to conceive. Deb and her husband, Karl, both forty, wanted a blessing ceremony as they embarked on their parenting. Before the birth, expected the week after Christmas, they summoned a group of midlife friends, many with years of experience, some whose children were already grown. Ann and I were invited and asked to share the circle.

What might have been an ordinary party shifted into sacred space. We placed a baby rocking chair in the center. We used a teddy bear as a talking piece, and though most of the couples in the group had never "done circle" before, their love for Deb and Karl moved them into honest and heartfelt storytelling about their own initiations into parenthood. Everyone received something significant that night, and one friend suggested that we make a telephone tree so we could call each other and send support to them when the day of labor came.

Two weeks later, with a freak snowfall of over two feet lying on the ground, Deb woke us at seven A.M. "I'm in labor," she announced, "and none of our planned support can come. Karl's been sick with the flu, is barely up and walking. Can you get out to the highway and come help?" Deb and Karl hiked out of their back road to a neighbor's house; he put them in his four-by-four and began maneuvering to the local hospital.

By the time we arrived at the hospital, after several hours driving up the slushy, unplowed highway, Deb had laid out a centering altar in the room, including objects from the blessing ceremony. While the obstetrical nurses monitored and coached the labor in their own competent ways, Ann and I took up the role of doulas—spiritual helpers to the mother, and respite for the father. We called in the circle and energetically surrounded the birthing bed with prayer energy, directed it toward the safe delivery of this child. Thirty-six hours later baby Kaj joined the island family. Maybe Kaj will grow up in the circle.

The primary classes in the local school system are being taught through the Tribes program, where children work in "tribal circles" of five to six students, with five to six tribes per classroom. The program, designed by California educator Jeanne Gibbs in 1978, is used in thousands of schools across the United States and Canada. The purpose of Tribes is to give each child a tangible sense of belonging and accountability among peers. The circles foster higher achievement levels and make students and teachers coresponsible for their learning. Tribes functions with four basic agreements: attentive listening; no put-downs; right to pass (the talking piece); and confidentiality. Perhaps these children will learn to be citizens of the circle, and perhaps their parents will learn to honor the circle in the larger community so these children have a place to take their circle skills.

Ann's son, Brian, the year he was captain of the junior varsity soccer team, called a circle one afternoon after the team had suffered yet another loss to a bigger school. "I thought we needed to talk about how it felt to be having a losing season. And they wouldn't say much with the coaches around, so when we were alone on the field I told 'em, 'Okay, you guys, listen up. I'm going to pass the soccer ball and when you hold it you have to say one thing about how you're handling the game. Everybody gets a turn, everybody listens.' I even remembered that we're supposed to have something in the center," he added. "So I put myself in the middle and started off the ball." He was proud of this attempt, and the boys accepted his leadership. These are hopeful signs.

I am currently working with a fledgling community organization called Sustainable South Whidbey, an informal gathering of local people looking for ways to keep this island livable for the children now in grade school. In a subgroup studying local issues of justice and public safety I am looking for ways to offer the circle for conflict resolution.

At meeting number one, I suggested everyone put something from their pockets in the center of the rug in one member's living room. That's all the PeerSpirit structure that it seemed appropriate to introduce. Here I need to be a peer, to not impose circle unless there is a readiness to try something new. So, like many others who carry the circle, I hold the tension between what I know helps coalesce a group and the different styles that emerge as we come together. Even calling in this barest thread of containment and centering allowed us to express emotions. Our eyes were moist as we spoke of our commitment to this community.

I had recently been reading about "sentencing circles," an experiment in cooperative justice between the judicial system in Canada (and now in the United States) and tribal councils. When tribal members, especially juveniles, are in repeated trouble with the law—for drinking, disorderly conduct, assault, or domestic violence—district courts work with native elders to refer the offenders back into the community for restitution and rehabilitation. The sentencing circle is open to all members of the tribe and is designated sacred space. Passing an eagle feather talking piece, the tribal council first mourns the loss of its members to drugs and early death, grieves in front of the young ones who are losing their way, and invites them to realign with traditional values, to get straight with their spirits, their lives, their community. The entire tribe takes responsibility for helping them make amends and new choices and live by them. "We know who you are," they remind a young man or woman. "We know your parents and your grandparents. We are watching you. You cannot avoid us. . . . Come home. Come back within the sacred hoop of your people."

Talking in the living room at a neighbor's house along the cliff, I say to the study group, "I want this kind of accountability in our community. I want to know that we could provide such help, and receive it, and I don't know if this is possible. The island population is growing fast. I myself am a newcomer here. But I miss the campfire. I miss the presence of somebody among us who can listen to stories of pain and confusion and offer some suggestion besides calling the cops or threatening a lawsuit, or defensively going ahead and making decisions that have drastic consequences because it's their property, or their right, or their frustration. How can we break this cycle?"

At meeting number two, one of the men brought a candle. Again, everyone put out jewelry or something from their pockets. We did three rounds of the talking piece. A local fireman sitting next to me turned and said, "Thank you for slowing us down."

We are seeking to identify the spiritual drive that underlies our commitment. The spring I was finishing this book, we met weekly, learning to be in dialogue, trying to discover the process that would help us hold broad intention. Once a week—coping with everyone's schedule, prior commitments, travel, family emergencies—we resisted the pressure to abandon our search and held to the process.

There are a dozen study circles addressing areas such as land use, food resources, wellness, alternative economics, community celebrations. The south end of the island is a spread-out rural community of over twelve thousand people—new-consciousness types and middle-aged hippies, commuters to the Boeing plant and other city jobs, small-town Democrats and many small-town Republicans, mainline church people, fundamentalist Christians, Buddhists, a tiny Jewish prayer group, radical and conservative retirees, military personnel, bored teenagers just looking for a place to skateboard. There are loggers and environmentalists, farmers and developers, and much tension about what direction the island's growth will take. Those of us in the study circles have as our loose philosophy the goal to embody three harmonies: harmony within, harmony with each other, harmony with nature. Each group is developing in its own ways. It may take years for the impact of our work to be felt in the ever-changing, expanding dynamics of the community.

On the night of the large community gathering that started these efforts, a citizen who didn't come grabbed the fireman's sleeve and told him, "If I could spring the Oklahoma City bomber from jail, I'd send him to the union hall to get rid of you tree-huggers all at once." He was not joking. The polarities of the world are here.

The Calling

I hosted our fifth study group at my house. We sat in the living room, a low glass coffee table between us. I offered tea and cookies, a Koosh ball talking piece, and a tier of candles. We kept resisting the impulse to jump on a project—though several had been suggested—and do something just to be able to report action. We kept asking ourselves why we had joined this particular study group.

The evening sunlight was shooting almost horizontally from the mountain ridge across the water and into my living room. The branches of five Douglas firs that ring the house cast patterns of shifting light against the walls. More deeply than I had in a long time, I felt the backing of these tall green beings, the web of life that held us. I felt reminded of how dependent these trees are on the decisions being made in our conversation and the ways we will choose to live.

We admitted to each other that to be present in the moment when people have shifted from hate and distrust into reconciliation is, for each of us, the deepest experience of the Sacred. When the breach has been healed, we are humbled by the presence of holiness. We want to be there, we said; we want to know how to help create such moments in our community. The room went very still. We listened to the silence as long as we dared—a retired psychiatrist, a fireman, an artist, a mediator, and me. We have not yet actually called this a circle. We have not yet laid out the kinds of structures outlined in this book. But now the longing has been spoken and the covenant made, so we will create whatever container is needed to hold us.

We are going somewhere, this group. I see it out of the corner of my eye, a council of witnessing and reconciliation. I turn to look and it disappears; I see only the trees. We haven't yet grown into the vision, but we are on our way.

We are going somewhere that none of us has been. This circle or the next one, willing to catch the nimbus. We are seeking to discover the circle's transformational powers as well as its practical applications and healing properties. This is the edge of the edge—to practice all that has been suggested here and then be willing to be carried by the circle into what we do not yet know we are capable of.

In Phoenix, Arizona, where our friend Kit Wilson calls the Grandmothers' Circles, there is a weeping acacia tree she planted in her backyard when she bought the house in 1991. It was a little sapling, expected to grow in desert conditions to about eight or ten feet. Within five years, the tree is twenty feet high, and spreads another twenty feet in long feathery branches. This growth is a phenomenon Kit credits to the women in her circles. Much healing work goes on in the glass-walled living room that faces into the acacia tree's courtyard. "When we're full of energy, feeling our power," Kit says, "and we need a way to send it back, individually or in whole groups, the women and I have gone out in the yard to pray over that tree. We ask the tree to take the healing. . . . I don't know, but maybe it's magic." And maybe that magic is what the circle has to offer us next.

Along the south side of my house, Ann and I have planted a small Douglas fir. In the spring of 1997, it is a bright green baby, eight and a half inches tall. The tiny sapling is our experiment to see what circle energy might do, to see how changing our minds about what is possible can be manifested in the world around us. At the end of my morning prayers, I send a blessing to this newcomer among the trees that circle my house.

I look at the deforested hillsides in the distance. If this little sapling starts heading for its spot in the canopy, I'm calling all the grandmothers and grandfathers, all the mothers and fathers, all the sisters and brothers, all the children and babies and heading for the hills with fir cones and prayers. Maybe—maybe—if we believed in the world, it wouldn't take forty years for the trees to return. Maybe—maybe—if we believed in each other, it would be possible to live in harmony with natural order.

When we are given a big idea to carry forward, I believe we are also given the help we need to carry it. Our major learning is how to perceive help when it comes in so many unanticipated guises, at unacknowledged moments, in different forms than we were expecting, while we are looking the other way. It is our irregularity of perception that causes the heart to contract in fear and the mind to freeze in hesitation. Over and over again we have to find the faith to look around and open ourselves to the act of noticing—just at the moment we are sure all is lost.

None of us can travel any further by ourselves. Alone, our hearts become stony and guarded. Alone, we become frightened. But in gatherings of neighbors, sitting with a candle in the middle and an attitude of openness to the possibilities, we may become students of the circle.

So come on into the circle. . . . We're sitting in my living room, looking for the way to call in healing. We're down in the meadow, dancing and drumming. We're in the conference room, passing a talking piece and making plans. We're in the church basement, figuring out how many people could sleep here and what kind of community might be called in off the streets. We're out in the wilderness, reacquainting ourselves with the earth. We're over at the country club, negotiating between the retirees and the caddies. We're at the dining table, passing a salt shaker and hearing how everybody's day went. We're having coffee at the senior center, deciding how to take care of each other as we age. We're out in the backyard, sitting silently among the plants and animals who cohabit this little patch of ground. We're playing with a ball of light, tossing it hand to hand, amazed at what we do.

And something is called forth within us by these circles. We find strength and renewal. We can be life's faithful pilgrims again, able to touch source, to touch stone, to be grounded in Spirit. We have come to this point in history to fulfill a purpose that we may not fully understand. We have come to this place in time to receive a gift, and to know how to offer that gift back to the world. We prepare the place inside us which will receive, which will give. We go inside and make center, make altared space. Make ready. Clean the cobwebs, light the oil lamps, set the sacred objects into their niches. Hold the place so that the circle may come. And not be afraid to act. And not be ashamed to hope.

THE PEOPLE
        Formed a circle round the Fire,
                each showing an attentive face
                        to every other person.

AND THEY SPOKE
        each waiting quietly
                till the other had finished,
                        as they had learned to do,
                a circle of silent listening
                        framing the wisdom each contained
                until the wisdom of all was spoken,
                        contained at last
                                by the Circle of the People.

. . .
Thinking now
        of the quiet circle of listening hearts,
                they were filled with understanding
                        of the value of their way.

AND A FIRM RESOLVE SWEPT THROUGH THEM.
. . .
THEY DECIDED
        To be a People
                who would perpetuate and refine
                        this manner of ordered council
                                which they had achieved.

                                PAULA UNDERWOOD,
                                The Walking People

RESOURCES AND ENDPIECES

Generic Use and Respect for Intellectual Property

Circling is a growing revival, and many similarities exist in how people are bringing the circle back into the culture. "Calling the circle" is both a book title and a generic phrase describing the action of convening. It will be a wonderful success for the circle if the phrase "calling the circle" comes into common usage and understanding. Please feel free to use this phrase. If you combine the phrase "calling the circle" with the idea that the circle is "the first and future culture," please reference this book as the source of connection.

Within the generic language we use to reintroduce the circle, we consider PeerSpirit circling to offer specific contributions which we hope, as a matter of courtesy, will be referenced and credited. These contributions include:

- the three principles of circling
- the word *PeerSpirit* as it refers to the context and conduct of the circle functioning under the three principles
- the agreements of circling

In the circle, we work toward a more humane and interpersonal culture. We ask only simple acknowledgment that in calling this or that circle you are calling upon information presented in this book. Written or verbal acknowledgment and reference should be: "These concepts first appeared in the book *Calling the Circle: The First and Future Culture,* by Christina Baldwin, published by Bantam Books, 1998."

The word *PeerSpirit* itself was conceptualized by Christina Baldwin. We offer the concept of PeerSpirit as a gift to the culture, with hopes that it will come to represent a standard of conduct inside which people may trust that certain guidelines and principles are understood and applied within the circle. It is our hope that the word *PeerSpirit* will take on an understanding similar to that of the phrase "Twelve Step Group." There are many varieties of Twelve Step groups, but anywhere in the world a person seeking a certain kind of circle may walk into a Twelve Step meeting and find a familiar structure at work. May PeerSpirit become that common and used that widely.

People calling a circle they refer to as "a PeerSpirit circle" are strongly urged to abide by PeerSpirit structure, while adapting these structures to fit the needs of their circle.

People responding to a call to join "a PeerSpirit circle" are strongly urged to pay attention to the structure of the group and ascertain that the group is abiding by the agreements and principles presented in this book.

The word *PeerSpirit* in combination with the tag line "in service to the circle" is a registered trademark and the business name for seminars presented by Christina Baldwin, Ann Linnea, and their associates.

GUIDE TO PEERSPIRIT CIRCLING

This guide serves as an easy-to-use reference to the PeerSpirit structure. Please refer to the relevant chapters for full explanations and applications of these PeerSpirit principles and agreements.

The Three Principles

PeerSpirit circling is based on three principles:

1. *Rotating leadership.* Each person helps the circle function by assuming small increments of leadership. In PeerSpirit circling, leadership shifts moment by moment and task by task. Rotating leadership trusts that the resources to accomplish the circle's purpose exist within the group.
2. *Sharing responsibility.* Each person pays attention to what needs doing or saying next and does his/her share. In PeerSpirit circling, responsibility also shifts moment by moment and task by task. Shared responsibility is based on the trust that someone will come forward to provide whatever the circle needs: helping each other take action, calling for silence, or offering the next meeting space.
3. *Relying on spirit.* Each person places ultimate reliance in the center and takes his/her place at the rim. Through simple ritual and consistent refocusing, the center, literally and symbolically, becomes sacred space—a place where everyone's willingness to listen dwells.

There are stages of preparation that are very helpful before the first actual gathering of people.

1. *Set intention.* Intention provides the basic foundation for calling a circle. Setting intention means getting clear about what you want to create, what you want to change or accomplish, what seems to be missing that you are trying to find, what you are trying to fulfill for yourself. To clarify the intention for this circle, use whatever focusing skills are most helpful to you.

   Write a simple statement of intent. The simpler the statement, the easier it will be for people to decide whether or not this circle fits their needs, directions, goals, and aspirations. It may take you a long time to make this statement succinct and clear.

   You may also find it useful to begin a background book—a three-ring notebook that allows you to create divided sections for inserting newspaper and magazine articles, notes from telephone and personal conversations, copied pages from other sources, and blank pages for writing, sorting, and editing ideas. The background book serves as a collection point for all the pieces of information, ideas, questions, and suggestions that relate to your quest for clarity.

2. *Gather feedback.* Share your thoughts. Talking about an idea is good practice and helps clarify intention.

   When people listen to a story, they raise questions that help you sort through your assumptions. In the background book, keep track of their questions and use them like homework assignments—to research and clarify your intention.

3. *Envision the group.* The more you refine your intent, talk with others, and respond to questioning, the clearer your vision of the circle becomes. Imagine being in a circle that is carrying out the intention you have defined.

   The next question is: While you have been setting intention, talking to people, and creating your vision, who has come to mind as a potential member for this circle? Who has expressed interest? Think about the attributes you hope they will bring. Make a list of these people.

4. *Invite people to come to the first circle meeting by writing out your intention in one or two paragraphs.* What does a person need to know in order to decide if s/he is interested in joining? Keep editing this statement until it reflects your intention. Even if you are going to invite people verbally,

by talking on the phone or meeting with them, a short written paragraph is a good way to clarify your statement. People may want to see something written so they can consider the invitation. Begin contacting people to find out if they are interested in joining the circle.

The First Gathering of a New Circle

1. *Prepare the space.* It is essential to literally arrange the seating in the form of a circle. When people find their place at the rim of a circle, half the work of explanation is already done. Sitting in a circle allows time to notice who's there, to greet each other, say names, get comfortable, and settle in.

   Make a sacred center. Have something tangible in the center of the circle to focus the group's energy. The center is collective energy, and belongs to the group, like open space, like a village square. Collective energy, highest intention or spirit, is always present, but may not always be acknowledged in usual meetings.

   The definition of spirit, and what goes in the center, needs to be appropriate to each group. As caller of the circle, you are the translator—the one who introduces the circle in a way that fosters acceptance and recognition. Before the group gathers, set out whatever center respects your group. In business, you might use a small candle and placards with the company values printed on them; in a spirituality group the center might consist of a scarf and candles and natural objects. There is much room for creativity, and simplicity works well.

2. *Open the circle.* Use some form of ritual to begin the circle. Silence, lighting a candle, reading a quote, or singing a song are simple rituals that call forth the reflective attention of the group.

3. *Tell the story of the idea.* How did this idea come to you and why have you asked this particular group to gather? Your willingness to talk first gives other people time to get comfortable and models what kinds of things you might want them to say in a few minutes.

   Be organized in your thoughts; it's okay to have written notes. If you tend to be long-winded, follow your outline and then be quiet. If you have been sitting at the center of the circle while talking about the center, it is important now to move back to the rim, to be part of the group in an egalitarian way.

4. *Introduce the talking piece.* A talking piece is any object designated to grant the person holding it the right to speak. Using a talking piece

guarantees that people are heard or have the opportunity to be heard. When one person has the piece, others listen without interruption or commentary. The use of a talking piece controls the impulse to pick up on what people are saying, to interrupt with jokes or sympathetic remarks, or to ask diverting questions.

The practice of using a symbol of power that passes from hand to hand has been used in councils from earliest times. The talking piece is a great equalizer among those who differ in age, race, gender, or status. The piece assures that everyone at the rim has an equal voice.

Most often, the talking piece is passed from hand to hand around the circle so that everyone knows when his/her turn is coming. If someone is not ready to talk when the piece comes by, it is perfectly acceptable to pass the piece on. After a complete round, the piece may be passed again or placed in the center for people to retrieve if they have something to add. In smaller circles or among long-standing groups, the piece may simply reside in the center and people reach for it when they are ready to contribute. Encourage people to trust the process. Don't carry on when you have nothing to say, and don't be afraid to take your turn when you have a contribution to make.

Not every conversation needs to be held with the talking piece, but it is an excellent way to heighten attention and slow down interactions so that circle members really listen to each other.

5. *Set clear circle agreements.* Agreements provide the interpersonal safety net of circling. They define the parameters of mutual understanding inside which the circle agrees to self-govern.

   In a circle, where you will spend significant time and energy, and where you are practicing new ways of being with others, these agreements need to be articulated so that everyone in the group has similar expectations and understandings of what is appropriate. See Appendix A for suggested PeerSpirit Circle agreements.

6. *Check in the first time around the rim.* This is a chance for everyone to introduce themselves, react to what has been said about intention, discuss the agreements, and share their own stories about what brings them to the circle. The use of the talking piece greatly helps this process.

7. *Keep track of commitments.* You already have a background book—a notebook full of your intention building and preparation—and this, or another notebook, can now become the circle logbook.

   The circle logbook contains the circle's agreements, group and individual commitments, task statements, practicalities of meeting arrangements, and accountability (even accounting, if necessary). In the logbook, members maintain a record of what is actually going on in the circle and use it to revive memory and review who agreed to do what. The logbook holds the circle's history. You may include formal sections to track the ongoing work of the circle and informal sections to keep track of the fun—photographs, anecdotes, and so on.

Keeping the logbook is part of sharing leadership. The convener for the next meeting will probably carry the logbook and bring it to the next session. Some circles make a ceremonial box or basket to hold the center objects, the logbook, and other paraphernalia that symbolize their particular circle. Whoever has the basket calls the next meeting of the circle. The convener takes responsibility for offering or setting up space, arranging time, bringing circle materials, and making sure everyone knows the arrangements. The convener usually changes meeting by meeting so that this duty is shared among circle members.

Congratulations! You have called the circle.

8. *Close the circle with respect.* It is important to close with a ritual signaling that the circle meeting is over. Blowing out the candle, holding hands, and offering a quote, song, or silence are all simple gestures of closing the circle.

Attention is required to hold the rim while circling. One purpose of opening and closing the circle with ritual is to signal when this level of attention is required and when it is okay to relax. A circle that has met for only a few hours usually requires only a simple, short acknowledgment. At the end of a long seminar or ongoing group, when sharing has been deep, the closing needs to reflect the intimacy that has developed.

Sustaining the PeerSpirit Circle

Circling has structure, orderliness, balance, commitment, and natural cycles. To sustain a circle for more than a few meetings, the group needs to adapt and follow certain structures. Sustaining the circle requires that the three principles be lived, moment by moment. The most reliable way to ensure that the principles function is to call them into the circle often. Recite them so they are fresh in everyone's mind.

1. *Build continuity.* One of the first collective duties of the circle is to design its continuity by choosing the framing devices that will be used

to organize circle activities. In most circles, continuity building consists of the following elements:

- *Design opening rituals.* Ringing a bell, lighting a candle, laying a circle of ribbon out on the floor or tabletop, reciting an invocation, meditating in silence, and shared movement are all opening rituals.
- *Establish a pattern for meeting.* In informal settings, check-in is often followed by meditation, council, journal writing, celebrations, and so on. In formal settings, check-in is followed by establishing an agenda, following the agenda, deciding on tasks and actions, volunteering to do tasks between meetings, and setting structure in place for the next meeting.
- *Preserve group history.* Read from and add to the logbook, arrange things in the center, in some settings tape conversations that set the course of action, and take photographs of major events, accomplishments, and rites of passage.
- *Close with ritual.* Silence, singing, and blowing out the candle are respectful ways to release the center.

2. *Set time and commitment.* Time limits are essential. People need to know how long a commitment they are making. They need to know that if the circle evolves in a direction that doesn't fit their needs or interests, there will be a graceful way for them to exit.

    The circle's intention and tasks determine much of this overall timing. It's also necessary to know how much time the circle will require for the actual meetings, the amount of commitment required between meetings, and the length of time the circle is contracting to exist.

3. *Choose a form of council.* There are basically three forms of council: conversation, talking piece, and silence.

- *Conversation* is the most common informal manner of meeting together. In conversation, people pick up on what another is saying, react, interact, brainstorm, disagree, persuade, and interject new ideas, thoughts, opinions. The energy of open discussion stimulates the free flow of ideas. Conversation can also overwhelm those who aren't comfortable leaping into the verbal fray. There are times when conversation is essential to group process, and times when process will work better if it's slowed down a bit, allowed a calmer pacing and more contemplation. This is when a talking piece is called for.
- *Talking piece council* invites a more structured dialogue. One person speaks; the group listens attentively. Talking piece council is a good

form for gathering story and information from the whole group, to garner insight and collective wisdom, and to create consensus.

- *Silence* usually has not been considered a form of meeting, but in a circle, where ultimate reliance is spiritual, it is an essential element of each meeting, and also at times important as the main form of gathering. To explain silence, use whatever language communicates best to your group: meditation, prayer, supplication, silence, centering inward, holding the rim. Silence allows us to acknowledge spiritual presence without dogma. Imagine the impact of a fifteen-minute silent council used as a time of centering before a longer talking piece council.

Some form of calling on center and maintaining centeredness belongs in every gathering of PeerSpirit circling. Perhaps you begin circle with a few minutes of silence. Perhaps you begin with song, by reading a poem, by striking a chime or bell, by blowing on the shofar or conch shell. How you choose to settle inward will be a creative expression of your particular circle. The form of meditative summons doesn't matter: What matters is that individually within this circle, you and every other member practice calling on your best intentions, invoking the High Self, acknowledging the Sacred, and being open to mystery so that wisdom may find its way through you.

4. *Attend to group process.* Most of the time, group process will hardly be noticed because it is functioning well. Group process gets noticed when it is falling apart. Social discomfort and occasional confusion are unavoidable and natural. One way to help group process is by using a circle guardian.

5. *Name a guardian of the circle.* The single most important aid to group process and reminder of spiritual center is the use of a guardian, who volunteers to watch and safeguard group energy. While serving as guardian, a person does his or her best to be extraordinarily aware of how the energy is flowing and group process functioning. To employ this simple method of guardianship, the circle needs to supply itself with a small bell, chime, rattle, or rain stick—any object that makes a pleasant and loud enough sound to be heard during conversation. Then, usually rotating on a meeting-by-meeting basis, one person volunteers to serve in the guardian role. The guardian has the group's permission to interrupt and intercede in group process for the purpose of calling the circle back to center, to task, to respectful practices.

Discussion may have become heated; the facilitator may be struggling to respond to questions; someone holding the talking piece may not be aware that s/he has rambled on and lost group attention; or someone may share something the group needs to sit with respectfully before another person speaks. At these moments, the guardian calls for silence using the agreed-upon signal, holds that silence for anywhere from fifteen seconds to several minutes, and, when the group is ready, releases the silence so that the pattern of meeting may resume.

6. *Rotate leadership.* A commitment to hold the rim is a commitment to claim individual leadership. A PeerSpirit circle is an all-leader group; the leadership passes like a baton among group members. Group facilitation does not disappear, but facilitation shifts from a model of permanent leadership to a model of changing and inclusive leadership.

7. *Restate intention.* Working to understand, articulate, and clarify intention is the step most commonly ignored in circles. In the honeymoon phase of a new circle, common intention is often assumed. In the disruption phase, lack of common intention is exposed. Reworking intention can save a circle that's floundering, or help a group understand why things just keep not working.

   Intention stating is a process of self-examination for the individual and for the group. Holding intention in PeerSpirit is a marriage between personal drive and collective vision.

8. *Observe the practices of council.* In attending to the verbal skills of circle, there are three practices that govern what we offer the group from our position on the rim:

   a. *Intentional speaking* means contributing what has relevance, heart, and meaning to the topic of the moment.

   b. *Attentive listening* means focusing clearly on what is being said by someone else.

   c. *Conscious self-monitoring* means considering the impact of our words and actions before, during, and after we interact.

   These are the interpersonal skills we offer the circle. These skills allow us to maintain the three principles. They are complex skills. No one will do them perfectly.

9. *Respond creatively to difficulties.* The ability to create peer community is based on communication and compromise. PeerSpirit requires a different kind of energy, a different kind of patience. There is no leader to fix your circle when it's not working. Trust that everyone in the circle is willing to work in order to preserve the integrity of what has been created.

   If you are disturbed by what's happening in circle, hold council with yourself: write in a journal for an hour discharging your thoughts. What are your assumptions? Is your fear or anger disproportionate to the actual occurrence? Are your present emotions related to past events? Ask yourself twenty questions or list twenty assumptions you're making.

Issues will arise: Conflict and misunderstanding and different ways of treating each other are unavoidable realities when people gather in groups. Real trust comes from going through the bumpy, scary, risky, and vulnerable aspects of circling.

Remember to apply the protocol for reconciliation in Appendix C.

10. *Use consensus and voting to stay clear.* Consensus is a process in which all participants have to come to agreement before a decision goes forward or action is taken. Consensus is applied when a group wants or needs to take collective responsibility for actions. In a peer circle, there needs to be a sense that everyone supports what the circle is about to do. It doesn't require that everyone have the same degree of enthusiasm for each action or decision. Consensus provides a stable, unifying base. Once consensus is reached, the circle has the authority to speak as "we."

In the middle of a circle meeting, voting may be done by instituting a thumb signal. Thumbs-up—"I'm for it, ready to support and do it." Thumbs-down—"I'm against it. I don't think this is the right way for us to go." Thumbs-sideways—"I have a question that needs addressing or a comment I need to add before I can decide."

Body Practices in Circle

It is respectful to walk into a circle and observe boundaries. The body needs a level of trust as much as the mind does. There are several practices of touch that help sustain the circle. You need to consider how and in what ways you are comfortable participating. Men and women have different understandings about touch as manipulation or domination. This is an area where healthy hesitation helps establish trust.

1. *Eye contact and sound:* At the beginning of the circle, be silent, look at each other, listen. Listen to your own inner self. Listen to the center. Touch down. Center down. Come into your body with some stretching exercises or deep breathing. Breathe, hum, sing, chant.
2. *Heart drumming:* The drum is a universal instrument that has always been in the circle and comes to us from First Culture. You don't actually need a drum to try drumming. The body is covered with skin, like a drumhead, and makes a pleasant resonating thump when played.

Thighs and calves are satisfying to slap gently. *Lub-dub-dub* or *1-2-3-4* are basic rhythms.

Drumming is a good way to literally establish harmony after time away. Playing off one another's rhythms, following first one person and then another, coming into shared beat, losing it, laughing, refocusing—all these bring the circle together in a profound way.

3. *Touching:* Hands are powerful instruments in a circle. With or without actually touching palm to palm, you can pass energy in a ring, ground energy beneath you, extend hands into the center, or reach out and pull energy in. You can pull energy down from the sky or send it spiraling upward.

   While you are learning your personal and collective levels of comfort, ask before touching someone with your hands. Tell people how and if you like to be touched. In every circle, always assume there is a wide range of comfort regarding touch.

4. *Backing:* One way of being touched that can feel literally and symbolically supportive is backing. You have probably used the phrase "Would you back me up on this?" or "I could use your backing."

   In the circle, backing has several variations. The idea is to literally stand or sit behind someone and cover their back. *Upon direct request,* you may put your palm flat against a person's spine, resting the heel of the palm between the shoulder blades and extending the fingers upward. This is a subtle way to provide meaningful touch in a public setting or business environment. Simply standing right behind someone, not touching, provides a strong sense of support.

Four Stages of a Circle's Life

A circle has a natural life span—four stages that occur as the circle moves through time and in the course of every meeting. How the four stages occur in the microcosm of a single meeting indicates how the four stages are progressing in the macrocosm of the circle's life span.

1. *Building trust.* Trust is developed by creating a structure that every member may count on and by experiencing a history of respectful interaction. Everything discussed so far in sustaining the PeerSpirit circle builds trust.

   Circles may meet weekly or once a year. Between meetings people have experiences that impact their willingness and ability to be present to the group. People mature, change their minds, meet individually, and find resolutions to issues outside council. At each meeting, people need to greet each other again and check out the level of trust. The group needs to know what is being brought back to the circle by each member.

When the circle regathers, trust is reestablished as people restate their relationship to each other and to the group's intent and purpose. The check-in fosters the reestablishment of trust by including words, eye contact, body language, and, if appropriate, touch. As you reenter the circle, practice being aware of your reactions and interactions with others on all these levels.

Trust is also built by a track record of doing tasks well, treating each other respectfully, solving problems, holding focus, and moving forward to carry out intent. People are energized by accomplishing what they have agreed to do.

2. *Carrying out intent.* Intent needs to be reestablished and acknowledged on a meeting-by-meeting basis. Deviation from intent needs to be discussed and negotiated. Carrying out intent is an exhilarating phase of the circle's life. Accomplishing intent brings with it stress, excitement, celebration, and group cohesion. This is the circle at its greatest triumph: working together, building a sense of comradeship in the accomplishment.

3. *Reconfiguration.* As goals are accomplished or a level of maturity is stabilized over time, a void in direction occurs: Now what?

Some people may want to leave the circle: Their direction or priorities have taken them elsewhere, they need to move on, commitments have changed, personality clashes have developed, or someone wants to start another circle. This is a time when others may want to define a new purpose and pursue the next accomplishment. It's helpful if each member can be clear and not unduly influenced by others or by his or her own nostalgic attachments to this circle.

However the circle proceeds—toward the next meeting or toward the next cycle of commitment—new goals need to be set in place to provide the foundation for continued action. Reconfiguration draws the circle back into council to reshape, redirect, and restate its collective energy. This is a time when people need to step forward again, take on responsibilities, or shift their role and relationship to the group. It is a time for careful, openhearted listening.

4. *Letting go.* No matter how dynamic and successful a circle is at continuing to find purpose, and no matter how committed its members, there will come a time to acknowledge the closing of the cycle. There are circles that meet for a week, such as seminars and annual gatherings.

Others meet for a few months, such as task forces and planning groups. Some circles meet for years: book clubs, social action or environmental groups, consciousness-raising or spirituality circles.

Letting go is a time of grief and celebration. A dynamic circle is a significant presence in your life. Prepare for grief, expect it, talk about it in council, have the courage to say good-bye in whatever ways fit you and the circle. In ordinary settings, or during times of celebration, people may forget that grief will also be present. Monitor sudden impulses toward irritation or withdrawal and ask yourself if grief is perhaps the real emotion.

Letting go, whether of one meeting or a long-term experience, is a time when ritual helps. Ritual provides a container for handling your emotions. Through ritual's symbolism, ordinary actions are infused with spiritual presence and we remember to honor the mystery of the circle. Some form of ritual will develop in how your circle gathers, conducts itself, and parts. Leave-taking needs simply to be acknowledged so that everyone knows when the meeting is over or when the circle is complete.

Wherever you may be in the life span of your circle, may your circle open and disperse, and its heartspace remain unbroken.

APPENDIX A:
PeerSpirit Circle Agreements

Circle agreements provide the interpersonal safety net of circling. They define the parameters of mutual understanding inside which the circle agrees to self-govern.

1. *What is said in the circle belongs in the circle.* Confidentiality allows people to speak their minds knowing that they will not be gossiped about. Confidentiality allows people to take verbal risks, to experiment with ideas, to keep changing their minds as their understanding grows.
2. *The circle is a practice in discernment, not judgment.* Discernment is the ability to listen, sort, and speak without having to be "right" or in total agreement before other people's opinions and views can matter. Someone else's view doesn't have to be right or wrong; it may simply be different.
3. *Each person takes responsibility for asking the circle for the support s/he wants and needs.* Asking for what you need next allows you to stay at the rim and avoid power struggles and personal drama as ways of getting attention. There are times when your request may not be responded to in the manner you expected; this is not failure, it is learning. Generally, if a request fits the task and orientation of the group, someone in the circle

This material originates in the work *Calling the Circle: The First and Future Culture,* by Christina Baldwin (New York: Bantam, 1998). This page may be used in PeerSpirit circles. When in circle, please credit the lineage of this material and send blessings to all those who hold this form.

will have both the willingness and resources to respond. If a request doesn't fit task and orientation, there will be a lack of interest. Circle members will learn to negotiate what they can and cannot do, and hold intention for the direction of group energy.

4. *Each person takes responsibility for agreeing or not agreeing to participate in specific requests.* This is the corresponding half of the above agreement. Circle requires a fine degree of attention to how time and energy are used in group process. If members are practicing these two agreements, the circle will continuously self-correct its course. Often circles show consensus or take a vote by using a thumbs-up, thumbs-sideways, or thumbs-down signal on decisions and actions that require approval. Thumbs-up signals agreement. Thumbs-sideways indicates that someone has further questions to raise; it encourages ongoing discussion that can impact the wisdom of the decision that emerges. Thumbs-down is used to indicate disapproval, but may not necessarily block an action. A person can put a thumb down to state, "I don't support this action, but the group may proceed if it chooses."

5. *Anyone in the circle may call for silence, time-out, or ritual to reestablish focus, to recenter, or to remember the need for spiritual guidance.* When employing a group guardian, each person agrees to drop into silence when the guardian rings a bell, shakes a rattle, or makes some other agreed-upon sound that calls for silence. During silence, each person returns to breath and focuses on the center and his/her highest intent. When the guardian rings the bell the second time, s/he will briefly explain why s/he called for silence. The reason could be simply calling for a stretch break or reminding people of the need to follow a particular agreement. The presence of a guardian of the process, who ideally is not the same person as the rotating leader, is crucial to reminding everyone to rely on spirit when the next step is unclear.

6. *Agreements are adaptable. If something is not working, revise the agreements and maintain the process.* Agreements define how the intent of the circle is carried out. If trouble develops, the group can work together to search for an agreement that will better support group process and group intention.

This material originates in the work *Calling the Circle: The First and Future Culture,* by Christina Baldwin (New York: Bantam, 1998). This page may be used in PeerSpirit circles. When in circle, please credit the lineage of this material and send blessings to all those who hold this form.

Other agreements that have developed as PeerSpirit has been introduced in a wide variety of settings include:

7. *Ask before touching.* Circle settings vary widely, and what is appropriate in a professional setting is very different from what is appropriate in a personal circle. The purpose for a circle will influence the level of personal sharing and will affect the camaraderie and casualness of a group. Remember that people come from different personal histories regarding touch and may have painful experiences regarding intrusion.
8. *Refrain from violence, threats of violence, or violent language.* When a circle is called to solve a thorny problem or address ongoing conflict, this can be an important agreement. The practice of circle is the practice of respect for each other.
9. *Practice listening without interrupting.* This can be an important reinforcement of the talking piece idea even when the form of council currently in use is open discussion.

There may be additional specific agreements that apply to your group, either now or in later sessions. Be prepared to write this list and additions, to have copies available for the group, and to bring agreements up for review after the circle has met for a while and people know more about how they want the process to work.

This material originates in the work *Calling the Circle: The First and Future Culture*, by Christina Baldwin (New York: Bantam, 1998). This page may be used in PeerSpirit circles. When in circle, please credit the lineage of this material and send blessings to all those who hold this form.

APPENDIX B:
CHECKLIST FOR PEERSPIRIT
CIRCLE AGENDA

Date:_____

Time opened:_____

Time closed:_____

Facilitator (if used):_____

Guardian:_____

Sponsors by agenda items:

Name:_____

Item:_____

Negotiated discussion time:_____

Work needing to be done/by whom:_____

_____

_____

_____

Date of next report/outcome or completion:_____

_____

This material originates in the work *Calling the Circle: The First and Future Culture*, by Christina Baldwin (New York: Bantam, 1998). This page may be used in PeerSpirit circles. When in circle, please credit the lineage of this material and send blessings to all those who hold this form.

Name:_____

Item:_____

Negotiated discussion time:_____

Work needing to be done/by whom:_____

_____

_____

_____

Date of next report/outcome or completion:_____

Name:_____

Item:_____

Negotiated discussion time:_____

Work needing to be done/by whom:_____

_____

_____

_____

Date of next report/outcome or completion:_____

Name:_____

Item:_____

Negotiated discussion time:_____

Work needing to be done/by whom:_____

_____

_____

_____

Date of next report/outcome or completion:_____

Reminders for next meeting:

_____

_____

_____

_____

_____

_____

_____

_____

APPENDIX C:
PROTOCOL FOR RECONCILIATION IN PEERSPIRIT CIRCLES

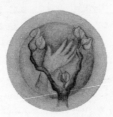

What makes challenges resolvable is the willingness of the people involved to solve the problem.

This protocol is generic. It should be creatively tailored to fit the components of any circle. The need to follow a complete protocol should be congruent with the depth of charge released into the group.

STEP 1: *The guardian (or, if the guardian is immobilized at the moment, anyone who wishes to assume that role) acknowledges that charged energy has entered the circle.*

Maybe someone takes a rattle from the center (since the circle is being "rattled"), shakes it, and says, "I see trouble has entered the field," or "Opposition rises," or "I feel a break in the rim," or, simply, "Ouch." This is said without drama.

STEP 2: *Everybody in the circle comes to full attention.*

Their contribution is to energetically snap into full presence: to hold the container and get centered. The Three Breaths are useful here. Attentiveness acknowledges that what occurred impacts everyone in the circle, not one or two people.

This material originates in the work *Calling the Circle: The First and Future Culture*, by Christina Baldwin (New York: Bantam, 1998). This page may be used in PeerSpirit circles. When in circle, please credit the lineage of this material and send blessings to all those who hold this form.

STEP 3: *With the rim held, the circle decides whether it—as a holistic body—needs to deal with the rupture immediately, or can assign it to a later time.*

This negotiation is usually facilitated by the guardian or the leader of the moment.

 a. The guardian asks the two who exchanged tension: "Are you present? Shall we address what just happened?"

 b. The guardian asks: "Is everybody else present?"

If people can remain present and want to continue with following the agenda, setting aside another time to respond to the disruption is fine. That time needs to be negotiated, but should not be so much later that it becomes avoidance.

STEP 4. *The circle enters into a protocol of listening and witnessing. Each member contributes his or her attention, and energy is sent to and drawn from the center.*

 a. Everyone in the rim takes Three Breaths and asks *him/herself*:

 • "How are my feelings/reactions being acted out by the two who exchanged tension?"

 • "Where did I jump to for safety? affinity? taking sides?"

 • "How can I help? Am I clear enough to listen impartially?"

 b. The two who exchanged tension are offered physical backing: to have an ally/witness who sits beside them, or stands behind them, so they are not alone in holding the energetic charge of what has occurred.

 c. The entire group takes time out to be in silence. In a small altercation, the Three Breaths is usually enough to center everybody. In a more dramatic break, five minutes of writing in the third person, using the phrase "I see a circle where . . . ," will help people articulate in a nonjudgmental way what's happening. If the circle takes time to write, the guardian may pass the talking piece, asking everyone to read his/her perception without comment or editing.

 d. Each party may also ask for a recorder, who writes down the essence of what s/he says, so there is a reference point. This also slows down the impulse to overexplain.

 e. Witnessed dialogue begins.

  Y: "I got mad when you suggested . . ."

This material originates in the work *Calling the Circle: The First and Future Culture*, by Christina Baldwin (New York: Bantam, 1998). This page may be used in PeerSpirit circles. When in circle, please credit the lineage of this material and send blessings to all those who hold this form.

X: "Do you mean . . ."

Y: "Yes." (Or "No," and then restatement occurs.)

X: "What I meant was . . ."

The recorder may read what was just said back to the circle. The purpose is for each person to feel heard, to have the differences honored, to let the two who exchanged tension hear what each has said to the other. *Agreement may arise, or may not arise.* The circle can hold our differences as long as we are holding them consciously.

    f. Guardian: "Now that you understand what your intentions were, does each of you feel clear and present?"

Assuming X and Y say that they are present, the guardian may check on the rest of the circle, and call for a stretch break before the meeting continues.

STEP 5: *The circle expresses gratitude for safe passage and learning.*

After tension has lifted or conflict has been resolved, the trust level of the group may need to be rewoven. Some acknowledgment of gratitude is very grounding. The guardian—or anyone so moved—may say, "I want to acknowledge the courage of those who went through this learning on behalf of the whole circle. Thank you."

This material originates in the work *Calling the Circle: The First and Future Culture*, by Christina Baldwin (New York: Bantam, 1998). This page may be used in PeerSpirit circles. When in circle, please credit the lineage of this material and send blessings to all those who hold this form.

BIBLIOGRAPHY AND
CIRCLE RESOURCES

This bibliography represents some of the cultural context inside which the circle is reawakening. It is drastically incomplete, but offers a partial map for putting your own journey into circle into context. The joy in each of these books is that many of them also contain a bibliography, so we may explore the information, stories, histories, and possibilities that led many writers and thinkers in considering the foundations for Third Culture. These listings are the most current citations.

Ceremonies and Rituals

Cahill, Sedona, and Joshua Halpern. *The Ceremonial Circle* (San Francisco: Harper San Francisco, 1992). A practical and inspirational guide for creating ceremony and ritual for "all those who dance in the circle." The book also includes interviews with well-known ceremonialists such as Starhawk, Vicki Noble, and others.

Eclipse. *The Moon in Hand* (Portland, ME: Astarte Shell Press, 1991). A lovely book of rituals and meditations that has as its focus the wheel of the Four Directions—the magic circle of life.

Foster, Steven, and Meredith Little. *The Roaring of the Sacred River* (New York: Prentice-Hall, 1989). A wonderful resource, particularly for those interested in the Native American vision quest and wilderness rites.

Paladin, Lynda S. *Ceremonies for Change* (Walpole, NH: Stillpoint Publishing, 1991). When Paladin's husband died, she created a special ceremony to scatter his cremains. This experience opened a door for her into the use of symbol and ceremony to celebrate and note life changes. In this book, she teaches others how to create ceremonies—an act she calls her "giveaway."

Starhawk. *Spiral Dance* (New York: HarperCollins, 1989). An exploration of the Goddess religion and a wealth of information on ritual and ceremony.

———. *Truth or Dare* (San Francisco: Harper San Francisco, 1989). Through ritual, myth, story, and symbolism, Starhawk examines the nature of power. In her beautifully poetic but informative style, she shows how to exercise "power-with" instead of "power-over." Her examples of ritual and ceremony will be particularly useful for circle work.

Cultural Perspectives

We are a global people, global seekers, trying to find our way to renewed culture and spirituality. People raised in one tradition may feel drawn to other traditions in this search. We need to respect that in spite of the ravages of the last 5,000 years, indigenous peoples have held the remaining wisdom of First Culture for us all, and approach their wisdom with humbleness.

Arrien, Angeles. *The Four-Fold Way* (San Francisco: Harper San Francisco, 1993). A sensitive, cross-cultural approach to studying shamanic teachings of indigenous people and how this wisdom can lead us to wholeness.

Bancroft, Anne. *Origins of the Sacred* (London and New York: Arkana, 1987). The subtitle of this book is *The Spiritual Journey in Western Tradition*. A fine look at the European indigenous roots of spirituality among the Celtic, Nordic, Greco-Roman roots that predate Christianity.

Lawlor, Robert. *Voices of the First Day: Awakening in the Aboriginal Dreamtime* (Rochester, VT: Inner Traditions, 1991). This is a personal and comprehensive study of the indigenous people of Australia, as close to understanding as an outsider can achieve. An important sociological and spiritual document.

Macy, Joanna. *World as Lover, World as Self* (Berkeley: Parallax Press, 1991). A beautiful collection of talks and essays that apply Buddhist philosophy to everyday living as active citizens in a shared world.

Underwood, Paula. *The Walking People: A Native American Oral History* (San Anselmo: A Tribe of Two Press, Institute of Noetic Sciences, 1993). I believe this is one of the most important spiritual documents printed in modern times. Paula Underwood carried this tradition for her family lineage, her tribal lineage. The ancient ones who are given voice again through her tale teach us the philosophical and spiritual foundation of First Culture and provide a map for where we need to go.

Workplace and Everyday Life

Fox, Matthew. *The Reinvention of Work: A New Vision of Livelihood for Our Time* (San Francisco: Harper San Francisco, 1994). This book reframes how we might live in Second Culture and bring spiritual considerations into the heart of our work lives.

Hawley, Jack. *Reawakening the Spirit in Work: The Power of Dharmic Management* (San Francisco: Berrett-Koehler Publishers, 1993). Hawley provides a much-needed and direct response to the call for spirit in the workplace, showing us models of successful managers motivated by spirit who are bringing out the best in people. Hawley believes *all* leadership is spiritual.

Mander, Jerry. *In the Absence of the Sacred: The Failure of Technology and the Survival of the Indian Nations* (San Francisco: Sierra Club Books, 1992). An absolute cornerstone book for thinking about the impact of megatechnology. Mander's words give us a place to stand and consider our personal and spiritual values.

Montuori, Alfonso, and Isabella Conti. *From Power to Partnership* (San Francisco: Harper San Francisco, 1993). Using Eisler's *The Chalice and the Blade* as a guide, the authors explore other ways to work and learn cooperatively.

Senge, Peter M. *The Fifth Discipline: The Art and Practice of the Learning Organization* (New York: Doubleday/Currency, 1990). The chapter on team learning is an excellent way to address the spiritual elements of communication in the business environment.

Sinetar, Marsha. *Ordinary People as Monks and Mystics* (New York: Paulist Press, 1986). In this classic study, Sinetar explores the ways people are striving to make sense of their lives.

Strauss, William, and Neil Howe. *The Fourth Turning: An American Prophecy* (New York: Broadway Books, 1997). A startling and scholarly prophecy by the authors of *Generations* about a new American era that will begin just after the millennium.

The Spiritual Context

Baldwin, Christina. *Life's Companion: Journal Writing as a Spiritual Quest* (New York: Bantam Books, 1991).

Eisler, Riane. *The Chalice and the Blade: Our History, Our Future* (San Francisco: Harper San Francisco, 1988). An intense look at 40,000 years of human history. This book is the basis for much understanding of original culture, hierarchical culture, and a model for coming into a partnership culture.

Eisler, Riane, and David Loye. *The Partnership Way* (San Francisco: Harper San

Francisco, 1990). This is the practical workbook for understanding how to move into a partnership way of viewing the world. It is designed for group study and provides a good way for a circle to gather, educate itself, and decide what further functions it would like to have.

Fox, Matthew. *The Coming of the Cosmic Christ: The Healing of Mother Earth and the Birth of a Global Renaissance* (San Francisco: Harper San Francisco, 1988). Fox, like so many who meet in circles all over the world, calls for a *metanoia:* a change of mind. "When a civilization is without a cosmology it is not only cosmically violent, but cosmically lonely and depressed," writes Fox. It is time, he says, to move from the historical Jesus to the quest for the "Cosmic Christ," an inclusive sacred wisdom.

LaChapelle, Dolores. *Sacred Land, Sacred Sex—Rapture of the Deep* (Durango, CO: Kivaki Press, 1992). This book is as broad a look at how we live on the planet and with each other as the title implies.

Osborn, Diane K., editor. *A Joseph Campbell Companion* (New York: HarperCollins, 1995). This is a beautiful and useful little book of Campbell wisdom that intertwines his own words with the words of those he studied and respected.

Women's Spiritual Perspective

Bolen, Jean Shinoda. *Crossing to Avalon* (San Francisco: Harper San Francisco, 1994). A revealing and personal story with elements of universal and women's spirituality.

Gadon, Elinor. *The Once and Future Goddess* (San Francisco: Harper San Francisco, 1989). This book can single-handedly educate the reader in the history and hope of the goddess tradition. Gadon has done tremendous historical research and relates it to modern imagery and emerging art and spirituality. Her selected bibliography will keep you going to the library and the bookstore for the next five years.

Murdock, Maureen. *The Heroine's Journey* (Boston: Shambhala, 1990). This book traces the heroine's journey and serves as a guide for those who are on a path to discover their complete spiritual selves.

Noble, Vicki. *Shakti Woman* (San Francisco: Harper San Francisco, 1991). Riane Eisler describes this book aptly as "a passionate call for women to reconnect with our goddess heritage and reclaim our ancient powers of healing before it is too late for ourselves and our Mother Earth."

———, editor. *Uncoiling the Snake* (San Francisco: Harper San Francisco, 1993). "Uncoiling the Snake," writes Vicki Noble, "refers to the deep, hidden structure behind things and the sacred patterns to which shamans in all cultures attune themselves." This is an anthology of stories, poems, pictures, and essays that inform and celebrate women's power to heal.

Spretnak, Charlene, editor. *The Politics of Women's Spirituality* (New York: Double-day/Anchor, 1982). This is an important and eclectic collection of essays on the rise of spiritual power within the feminist movement.

Men's Spiritual Perspective

Hudson, Frederic. *The Adult Years: Mastering the Art of Self-Renewal* (San Francisco: Jossey-Bass, 1991).

Liebman, Wayne. *Tending the Fire: The Ritual Men's Group* (St. Paul: Ally Press, 1991). Guidance for men wishing to understand and reform in council.

Connecting with the Earth

Gore, Al. *Earth in the Balance: Ecology and the Human Spirit* (New York: Dutton, 1993). A comprehensive discussion of global environmental issues. Gore expertly explores the connection between spirituality and environmental activism.

Halifax, Joan. *The Fruitful Darkness* (San Francisco: Harper San Francisco, 1993). This is a personal account of Halifax's spiritual journey and reconnection to the earth.

Hunt-Badiner, Allan, editor. *Dharma Gaia* (Berkeley: Parallax Press, 1990). Essays on Buddhism and ecological consciousness. Inspires and encourages readers to connect and work together to save the earth and ourselves.

Hynes, Patricia H. *Earth Right* (Rocklin, CA: Prima Publishing and Communications, 1990). A hands-on resource book and guide for how to reclaim our earth. After explaining environmental problems in a nontechnical way, Hynes offers creative ideas for action and resources for further information.

Linnea, Ann. *Deep Water Passage: A Spiritual Journey at Midlife* (New York: Pocket Books, 1998). Ann's reflection's on the literal and metaphoric journey help both women and men look at the heroic aspects of all life passages.

Seed, John, Joanna Macy, et al. *Thinking Like a Mountain* (Santa Cruz, CA: New Society Publishers, 1988). A collection of essays, meditations, and writings to help people connect with the earth and establish a council of all beings.

Circling with Children

Milord, Susan. *Hands Around the World* (Charlotte, VT: Williamson Publishing, 1992). 365 ways for children to learn about other cultures and connect with other children around the world. Her ideas are empowering, creative, and fun.

Schimpf, Ann [Ann Linnea], et al. *Teaching Kids to Love the Earth* (Duluth: Pfeifer-

Hamilton, 1991). 186 activities, leading children through Sense of Wonder Workshops consisting of curiosity, exploration, discovery, sharing, and passion. A nationally award-winning educational tool for teachers, parents, and others working with children.

Circle Skills, Shadows, and Conflict Resolution

Andrews, Cecile. *The Circle of Simplicity: Return to the Good Life* (New York: HarperCollins, 1997). A solid teaching on simplifying one's life-style and coming into learning communities.

Johnson, Robert A. *Owning Your Own Shadow* (San Francisco: Harper San Francisco, 1991). "The fire of transformation and the flower of rebirth are one and the same," writes Johnson. Owning one's shadow is a necessary step in reclaiming ourselves—putting ourselves back together again so we might, in turn, heal our fractured world.

Luhrs, Janet, editor. *Simple Living: The Journal of Voluntary Simplicity* (Simple Living Press, 2319 N. 45th St., Box 149, Seattle, WA 98103). Quarterly journal with tips and articles on living simply and how it works.

MacGregor, Alexandra, et al. *Transformation and Tribal Learning: How to Organize, Facilitate, and Participate in a Learning Circle* (Burnaby, BC: Open Learning Agency, 1993). A booklet published by the Open Learning Agency to teach both facilitators and participants how to use Learning Circles to stimulate insight, creativity, learning, and growth. For communities, workplaces, families, and individuals.

Sheeran, Michael J. *Beyond Majority Rule* (Philadelphia: Religious Society of Friends, 1993). Quakers have been meeting in circles and governing by consensus since the 1600s. Sheeran traces the Friends' tradition of religious decision making and its applicability in contemporary society.

Starhawk. *Dreaming the Dark* (Boston: Beacon Press, 1989; 15th edition 1997). This is groundbreaking work on the structure, dynamics, and spirituality of the circle. It is the philosophical basis for her novel *The Fifth Sacred Thing* (see listing under fiction).

Zimmerman, Jack, and Virginia Coyle. *The Way of Council* (Las Vegas: Bramble Books, 1996). This book provides a method for training both professionals and nonprofessionals in basic communication skills using the council model. It's an excellent contribution to the field.

Fiction and Stories that Point the Way

LeGuin, Ursula. *Always Coming Home* (New York: HarperCollins, 1985). In this "archeology of the future," LeGuin creates a whole culture for us to consider: maps, songs, mythology, history that has yet to come to pass.

Starhawk. *The Fifth Sacred Thing* (New York: Bantam, 1994). Set in the early years of the twenty-first century, the circle is used as the governance of a Third Culture enclave in the Bay Area. Much good teaching woven into a gripping story.

————. *Walking to Mercury* (New York: Bantam, 1997). A prequel to the above novel.

People Doing Circle Work in the World

This resource list represents a sampling of people I knew of personally in spring 1997. Please add your own names to this list and the names of others you discover as this movement grows.

Angeles Arrien: Her work with the Fourfold Way is widely known and mentioned in this book's text. She offers seminars and training and many teachers have respectfully incorporated her work into their understanding of the container of council. For more information contact: P.O. Box 2077, Sausalito, CA 94966.

Barbara Borden, Heartbeat Culture: An extraordinary drummer, percussionist, and performer, Borden combines drumming and circle, bringing the drum to the center of council. She draws groups together for ceremony, rites of passage, and weekend councils in which PeerSpirit provides the structure for honoring the wisdom of Heartbeat Culture. Contact her through: P.O. Box 1424, Mill Valley, CA 94942; phone and fax: 415-388-5340. For recordings, especially her CD: *Beauty in the Beat*, contact: cloud9@well.com or www.well.com/user/cloud9

Cheryl Conklin: She is a ceremonialist offering a course and manual "Into the Fullness of Being: Pathways of Spiritual Empowerment" designed to bring people into an understanding of their spiritual life and provide them the tools for living from spirit-centeredness. She is available for workshops and conferences. Contact her via e-mail: CallCheryl@AOL.com

The Council Circle Foundation, Dennie LaTourelle, c/o The Center for the Study of Sacred Psychology: Providing experiences in council, and council teacher training, Dennie works extensively to create a circle-based community that can impact the spiritual environment in her city. Contact: 823 Summit Rd., Santa Barbara, CA 93108. Tel.: (805) 969-5324.

The Council of All Beings: A deep ecology experiential process, organized through John Seed and offered by a number of facilitators throughout the world. A newsletter and facilitator list is available. Contact: John Seed and Eshana c/o Rainforest Information Centre, Box 368, Lismore NSW 2480 Australia. Tel.: (61)(0)66218505. E-mail: jseed@peg.apc.org

The Council Process: Jack Zimmerman, in collaboration with Virginia Coyle at the Ojai Foundation, offers introductory training for prospective council leaders, plus intermediate training and a semiannual "Gathering of Council Leaders." Contact: 9739 Ojai-Santa Paula Rd., Ojai, CA 93023.

Earth Drum Council: This was founded in 1990 by Morwen and Jimi Two Feathers to provide opportunities to drum and dance in community. They offer an annual gathering in western Massachusetts and one day gatherings in Cambridge, bringing Third Culture to Harvard Square. Contact: P.O. Box 1284, Concord, MA 01742. E-mail: earthdrum@earthdrum.com or www.earthdrum.com

EHAMA Institute: Self-Knowledge and Earth Wisdom Teachings, meti teachers, RainbowHawk, WindEagle, and "a traveling medicine band" of colleagues apply native traditional teaching and perspective to modern issues. They travel and teach in North and Central America and Europe. Contact: 31440 Loma Prieta Way, Los Gatos, CA 95030. Tel.: (408) 282-4537. Fax: (408) 454-9129. E-mail: FireHawk@Ehama.org

The Grandmothers' Circle: Based on the work of Mary Diamond and unifying under the prophetic phrase "When the grandmothers speak the earth will heal," Kit Wilson and Jo Norris help older women call themselves into circle to experience the spirituality and empowerment of aging. Kit and Jo offer initial facilitation to create Grandmother Circles in many locations. Contact: The Grandmothers' Circle, P.O. Box 23/38th St. Mail, 3728 East Indian School Rd., Phoenix, AZ 85018. Newsletter: $10.00 per year. SASE for information.

The LearningWay: Paula Underwood is the director and developer of The LearningWay Company, a nationwide council-based program used in education, corporate training, and health services. She has trained and certified a network of people who apply her Native American methodology to modern problem solving. Note her book, *The Walking People*, referenced earlier. Contact: P.O. Box 216, San Anselmo, CA 94979, or web-site at: http://members.aol.com/ToTPress/ for seminars, training, and newsletter based on Paula's life-long learning.

Living Systems: Marlow Hotchkiss, Colleen Kelley, and Robert Ott are codesigners of The Box, a self-guiding course in deep ecology and personal mastery. They take years of experience in group and social process and council training and work in major corporate settings. Contact: P.O. Box 5495, Santa Fe, NM 87502. Tel.: (505) 474-5448.

Rogers-McKay: Named after their mothers, this non-profit educational organization was founded in 1996 by Meredith Jordan and Eleanor Mercer. These women introduce shared leadership models focusing on the growth of the circle in churches, schools, mental and health-care settings, and community service organizations. They are originators of group retreats and are planning a New England-wide conference of women and girls in 1999. Contact: P.O. Box 1725, Saco, ME 04072. Tel.: (207) 284-1034. E-mail: rogersmckay @lamere.net

Tenfold™ PeerSpirit Circles for Women: Tenfold is a facilitated weekend that leads to ongoing peer circles using PeerSpirit structure. Note the examples in this book. Harriet Peterson and Sarah MacDougal were in the first Tenfold conducted by Christina Baldwin and Ann Linnea in March 1993, and have become primary facilitators of this seminar. Contact: Tenfold, P.O. Box 83, Taylors Falls, MN 55084. Tel.: (612) 465-4902. Fax: (612) 465-3104. E-mail: tenfold@gte.net

Tribes: A New Way of Learning Together: Since 1987 when Jeanne Gibbs originated this process for social development and cooperative learning, tribal circles have been flourishing in classrooms. Her books and curriculum training apply the circle in school settings. Contact: Interactive Learning Systems, 1505 Bridgeway, Suite 121, Sausalito, CA 94965.

Please keep adding your own resources.

ACKNOWLEDGMENTS

THE GRATITUDES:

- Thank you to David Kyle for believing in this book first and seeing that it came into its first life in the world.
- Thank you to Pam Meyer and Brian Crissey for joining David in the support and publication of the first edition.
- Thank you to Susan Seddon Boulet for the original cover art. May she be dancing with the angels.
- Thank you to the pioneers who came into circle and called me into circle, and whose seeking inspired a colearning/coteaching process that is truly peer spirited.
- Thank you to Bonnie Marsh, a true leader, and the folks of the Strategic Development Unit aka "the circle" at Fairview Health Services, for taking this work to heart.
- Thank you to Joe Durepos for taking up the cause of this book and finding it a new home, and for carrying his spirit into the center of the circus.
- Thank you to Debbie Orenstein for being wise counsel in the Second Culture matters of contracts and "intellectual property."
- Thank you to Toni Burbank for her longtime support of my writing, and for letting the circle call to her, bringing forth this new edition. Through Bantam, she created the opportunity for this writing to be presented in fullness.
- Thank you to Robin Michaelson for standing at Toni's threshold, helping in all the ways she does to keep a project moving between the worlds.
- Thank you to Colleen Kelley for the cover art on this edition and for the deeply circled spirit she is. She has been a walks-her-talk sister in my life since the Women's Camp in 1992.

THE BEATITUDES:

- Blessings to Ann Linnea, cocarrier of PeerSpirit circling, peer-spirited and free-spirited teacher in a thousand ways, beloved wild woman who speaks for trees and has "come inside" so that those beings who live outside may have a chance.
- Blessings to Colleen, Carl, and Erin Baldwin and to Bill and Donna Humphreys for their familial support during much transition.
- Blessings to Barbara Borden for helping us hold the beat.
- Blessings to the fine people who became amalgamated and transformed into the central "characters" in this book—the school and neighborhood group, the project team, Demetria's women's circle.
- Blessings to the colleagues who stepped in close to help us think about how to carry this work forward. The collaboration circle of 1997–98 included: Janel Beeman, Kathleen Bjorkman-Wilson, Cheryl Conklin, Leah Green, Edna Groves, Christine Irving, Meredith Jordan, Jim Kellar, Sarah MacDougall, Harriet Peterson, Dana Reynolds, Pamela Sampel, Linda Secord, Marina Telfer, Jean Ure, and Kit Wilson. There is so much good heart in the world: it's important to remember this, and to count on each other.
- Blessings to the chapter sisters, Meredith Jordan, Edna Groves, Kit Wilson, and Leah Green, for holding the rim on Chapters Eight and Nine.
- Blessings to Sarah MacDougall and Harriet Peterson for "adopting" Tenfold and seeing that this contribution to circle work has a chance to thrive.
- Blessings to Jessica Waters, pattern-keeper of the PeerSpirit office, fast typist, decipherer of my handwriting, and mistress of the *delete* for esoteric phrases.
- Blessings to my friends, just 'cuz you keep holding with me—you are the list my heart recites every morning, asking for our shelter in the day.
- Blessings to Willow, official greeter at Will O'Heaven cottage, and to the mountains, water, sky, and trees that hold this hearth.

PERMISSIONS

CHAPTER 7
Reprinted from *Human Robots and Holy Mechanics*, by David T. Kyle, published by Swan Raven & Co.

CHAPTER 8
This poem was written in circle by Helen Douglas, a writer and bookseller in Vancouver, British Columbia.

CHAPTER 9
Reprinted from *The Marriages Between Zones Three, Four and Five*, by Doris Lessing, published by Vintage Books.

CHAPTER 10
Reprinted from the poem "A Great Wagon," in *The Essential Rumi*, translated by Coleman Barks, published by HarperCollins. Copyright © 1995 by Coleman Barks.

ABOUT THE AUTHOR

Christina Baldwin has taught journal writing seminars internationally for over twenty years, and has contributed two classic books to this field: *One to One: Self-Understanding Through Journal Writing* (M. Evans, 1977; revised edition, 1991) and *Life's Companion: Journal Writing as a Spiritual Quest* (Bantam, 1991).

Christina has always conducted her teaching in circles. In the early 1990s, she began exploring how to help people bridge from personal consciousness to social action using the circle as the primary source of support. Her explorations led to this book, *Calling the Circle*.

In setting after setting, when the principles and practices of PeerSpirit Circling have been applied, she has seen the circle flourish among people, leading to empowerment, accomplishment, and community. She firmly believes that the circle will contribute to societal transformation.

Christina holds a bachelor's degree from Macalester College and a master's degree from Columbia Pacific University. In Washington state, she and her partner, author/educator Ann Linnea, have founded a small company, *PeerSpirit™ . . . In Service to the Circle*, through which they conduct seminars, lectures, training, and consultation.

PeerSpirit services range from corporate consulting to outdoor adventure trips, with a primary focus on Circle Practicums, which train individuals to facilitate and participate in PeerSpirit circles in a variety of settings, from couples and family councils, to business teams, and community action groups. For general information, please send a self-addressed, stamped envelope to: Peer-Spirit, Box 550, Langley, WA 98260, or leave a message on voicemail: (360) 331-3580. You can also visit us on the web at: www.peerspirit.com.

ABOUT THE ARTIST

Colleen Kelley is an artist, author, and teacher, who lives in New Mexico. She received her Master of Arts degree in fine art from San Francisco State University. Her artistic work, including book and magazine covers, has appeared in numerous publications, and she has exhibited in many one-person and group shows over the past 25 years.

For the cover painting, Colleen chose the symbol of the Tree of Life. She has been influenced by the visionary Lakota medicine man Black Elk, whose visions revealed a time of harmony and balance when people of all backgrounds would come together in a sacred circle with the Tree of Life at the center. The hands that intermingle within the leaves of the Tree represent the interconnectedness of all peoples. The dancing figures, below the roots of the Tree, are motifs from rock art of the Ghost Dance found in Nevada. The book's interior art also draws upon themes of renewal and interconnectedness.